LAURENCE KING

Published in 2005 by Laurence King Publishing
71 Great Russell Street, London WC1B 3BP
T: +44 20 7430 8850 F: +44 20 7430 8880
E: enquiries@laurenceking.co.uk
www.laurenceking.co.uk

Copyright © 2005 Central Saint Martins College
of Art and Design, University of the Arts, London.
First published in Great Britain in 2002. Second
edition published 2005 by Laurence King
Publishing in association with Central Saint
Martins College of Art and Design.

This book has been produced by Central Saint
Martins Book Creation, Southampton Row,
London, WC1B 4AP, UK.

A catalogue record for this book is available
from the British Library.

ISBN-13: 978-1-85669-436-0
ISBN-10: 1-85669-436-4

Design: Christopher Wilson

Printed in China

Cover: garment design by team for
Coco de Mer project: Mark Fast, Holly Albright,
Leila Heinel, Delia Covezzi, Siad Mohamoud,
Myung Cha, Bettina McCabe, Laura McCraig
Model: Bettina McCabe
Photography: Esther Johnson

Frontispiece: garment design by team:
Jennifer Carrol, Mischa Notcutt, Isaac Raine,
Fanny Karst, Georgia Beavis, Angeline Lam,
Laura Bradley, Teresa Buck
Model: Jennifer Carrol
Photography: Esther Johnson

Introduction

Womenswear. Design by Louisa Parris, winner of the L'Oréal Professional Student Award 2004.

Fashion is a subject of vital interest; in the urban centres of the world fashion matters enormously, especially to the young. Apparel and leisure shopping have become social, cultural and financial phenomena as fascinating and acceptable a study as literature, theatre and the fine arts.

Fashion is an international language and a global business. Fashion designers and models are now as celebrated and profiled as politicians, athletes and movie stars. To the ingenue, the world of fashion seems to be populated with a firmament of celebrities and to promise a glamorous and carefree lifestyle, when, in fact, only a small proportion of fashion professionals – the most talented and the luckiest – live like this. Most will have worked tremendously hard to achieve their apparent 'overnight' success.

At the point of choosing careers, discovering modes of self-expression and confirming their identities, many young people are drawn to the world of fashion. Yet fashion is a mysterious chimera. Elegance, beauty and expense are no longer reliable guides to what is 'cool'. Outfits applauded on the runway often never make it to the stores. Dress codes for work and leisure are evaporating or changing. Just as we get used to one 'look', its counterpart comes into vogue. Why do we need or wish to constantly re-define and adorn ourselves? Who makes the rules and who breaks them? Fashion seems responsible for the mayhem, but it is also the creative source of an exciting and enormously profitable industry. So how do you become a fashion professional? Is it luck, talent, personality or education? What are the choices?

Fashion is a popular career option; it is one of the most oversubscribed fields in higher education. While it is true that some of the great designers of the twentieth century had little or no formal training, very few can now succeed in this field without preparation. A degree is still the best weapon in a jobseeker's armoury. It is difficult to enter the industry without the minimum of a Bachelor of Arts degree qualification. Surveys have shown that graduates earn on average twenty-five to thirty per cent more than those without formal training.* Employers, unable to finance training schemes, are increasingly looking for graduates to fill vacancies. Higher education courses aim to teach and nurture the skills required in the marketplace. While they cannot guarantee success, they offer thorough and compatible training. Moreover, their links with the industry make them highly useful for a student's future career. Becoming a fashion professional, whether in retail, management, design or promotion, is not a soft option, and the demands are considerable – creatively, personally, intellectually, technically and even physically.

> 'Designers have to play many parts – artist, scientist, psychologist, politician, mathematician, economist, salesman – combined with the stamina of the long-distance runner.' Designer, Helen Storey

The majority of fashion industry employees are never famous or rich, but work happily enough behind the scenes in satisfying jobs for more or less ordinary wages. Yet it can be a joy to find that you are paid for doing what you love best.

Who this book is for

This book will be of use primarily to the aspiring student, but it will also be of interest to the fashion enthusiast. It attempts to give a balanced insider view of fashion and fashion education, and to explain the talents, skills, techniques and vocations that

* Peter Elias and Kate Purcell, 'Seven Years On: Graduate Careers in a Changing Labour Market' (London: Higher Education Careers Services Unit, 2004).

qualify a student to work in the apparel industry. The majority of fashion books are biographies of individual designers, technical manuals or cultural histories; they do little to explain the training, the modern industry or the process of turning the creative impulse into a marketable product. This book shows how the designer and merchandiser can become skilled at reading the prevailing aesthetic, altering it and applying the imaginative result to the human body in a desirable and marketable way. Since the 1980s, much of the manufacturing of European and American clothing has moved offshore to the East. In the West, fashion is now a service industry where creativity takes place against a backdrop of different tastes, lifestyles and market sectors, global trading and growing technological complexity. This book explores the differences between markets and manufacturing styles, traditional methodology and newfangled computer-aided processes and systems. There may be only a handful of apprenticeships in tailoring and design jobs in haute couture but new technology and a thriving market indicate that unprecedented job opportunities are becoming available. It is predicted[†] that there will be more small companies within the industry and that they will need innovators, expert management and products of high quality to satisfy the growing demand for distinguished and individualized products.

While *Fashion Design* touches on many aspects of its subject, it can only provide an overview; the more technical and advanced facets of pattern-drafting, dressmaking and tailoring or marketing practice are not included. Many of these techniques require hands-on practice and cannot be learnt from a book. There are no projects for the reader but many suggestions for consideration, further reading and investigation. This book does not give advice on how to dress well or forecast the future of fashion, but for anyone who is committed to a career in the fashion industry it will give an insight into how others have achieved their goals. It aims to inform, inspire and guide, often by using the testimonies of those who have already travelled the route, walked the walk and talked the talk.

Menswear

How to use this book

Fashion Design is both a manual and a career guide. Although some of the information may be stated as fact, there is no right or wrong way to become a fashion professional or reach an effective fashion solution. Fashion people are often rebels who know that the rules are made to be broken. It is my experience that every student and student group is unique, both in terms of personality and response to the world they encounter. The same project can yield entirely different results in different hands at different times. One of the great pleasures of being a student, and indeed a teacher, is the experience of sharing and learning from the surprises, triumphs and mistakes. The examples of project works, teaching and learning styles, and pathway information or syllabus are not offered prescriptively. I am grateful for the suggestions, observations and contributions to this work from students, colleagues and professionals.

In this second edition of *Fashion Design* I have attempted to incorporate previous omissions and address the rapidly widening gulf between time-honoured fashion practices as they are conventionally taught and the fast-moving ground of twenty-first-century manufacturing, marketing and promotion. Fashion does not stand still and graduates must hit the ground running. Diagrams and practical and technical data have been improved upon, and there are comprehensive lists of resources, texts and industry

† The Textiles and Clothing Strategy Group, 'Making it Happen: – A National Strategy for the UK Clothing and Textile Industry' (London: Department of Trade and Industry, 2002).

bodies for consultation. Fresh examples of sketches, artwork and photography have been included to capture the atmosphere and excitement of college and professional environments. In acknowledgement of a wide readership and the increasingly global trade, the historical, geographical and cultural perspective has been extended in this edition. Expanded descriptions of job opportunities, working conditions and requirements for careers in the fashion industry can be found in the final chapter and will be useful as a guide to selecting the right path for a foundation study or degree course.

The fashion degree **syllabus** typically sets out to familiarize students with increasingly complex practical and intellectual demands, and simulates many of the tasks and sequences that the real-life designer or creative needs to master. In this book, the range of information and concepts that a student is likely to encounter is set out across seven chapters, which can be dipped into and consulted in any order. Like any other industry, fashion and education have their own jargon, and a mastery of it will go some way to opening up apparent mysteries. Throughout this book the use of bold type indicates that an explanation of the words and terms can be found in the glossary (pages 216–18) or the list of pattern-drafting and sewing terms (pages 227–31). Pages edged in brown indicate tables, diagrams or illustrations that can be photocopied as study aids. Lists, detailed information and taxonomies are shown in boxed subsections to the text. At the end of each chapter there is a list of useful resources relevant to the subject. And at the end of the book you will find sources and address lists for suppliers, fashion and educational organizations, and places of research for further inspiration.

Have you got what it takes?

Before launching yourself on what may be a long and arduous path to a career in the fashion industry, it pays to try and find out whether you have the right qualities and have a realistic idea of your own strengths and weaknesses. Opposite is an alphabetical checklist of the desirable personal qualities and skills you will need to demonstrate in order to enter the field. Evaluating yourself on a scale of one to five will help you to gauge your aptitudes. Discuss your score with a friend or teacher to see where your talents and shortcomings lie.

Above all, you need talent. A talent for fashion design is not necessarily the same as a talent for drawing, nor is it the ability to sew, although it does include both of these. Fashion design goes far beyond this, and what will be expected of you is the ability to research, absorb and synthesize ideas and skills. Fashion creativity is the ability to produce new variants and solutions to the age-old problem of clothing the body and developing a refreshing and exciting awareness of it in a contemporary context.

'The trick is to give people what they never knew they wanted.'
Diana Vreeland, editor of American *Vogue* from 1963 to 1971

Design by Alexander McQueen, nominated British Designer of the Year 1996, 1997, 2001, 2003, International Designer of the Year 2003 and awarded the CBE by Her Majesty the Queen in 2003.

Checklist of personal qualities and skills

Ambition	Strong will to achieve practically, conceptually and financially
Artistic 2D skills	Ability to visualize, draw and paint in two dimensions
Artistic 3D skills	Ability to visualize and create articles using a variety of materials
Assertiveness	States point of view clearly, stands by beliefs
Business acumen	Numerate, able to spot opportunities, aware of costs/benefits. Logical
Charm	Gets on well with others and communicates. Co-operation
Colour sense	Important for range-building, print, childrenswear and knitwear
Commitment	Works hard, open to learning, prepared to go the extra mile
Communication skills	Delegates, explains, listens and negotiates. Speaks to groups
Competitiveness	Uses abilities to give the edge without malice
Confidence	In own ideas and skills, and in others. Poise, balance of ego and humility
Conscientiousness	Thorough, diligent, ethical, takes the rough with the smooth
Creativity	Naturally original; generates new ideas and enjoys making things
Curiosity	About society, people, design, function and form, etc. Well informed
Decisiveness	Quick to make decisions and take responsibility or command others
Efficiency	Time planning and organization of information and materials. Thrifty
Energy	Physical stamina and health, sticks to the job. Works long hours
Flair	Makes hard work seem effortless. Good grooming, chic
Flexibility	Adaptable and sees others' criticisms as useful. Accepts change
Health	Stamina, reliable, no drug, weight or alcohol problems
Humility	The ability to ask for help, admit weakness, know limitations
Humour	Sees the funny side, not bitchy, creates a good atmosphere
Imagination	Abstract ideas and inspiration well-tuned to what a task requires
Independence	Of thought – not behaviour. Ability to work unsupervised or freelance
Initiative	Get up and go, starts things and solves problems by doing – not thinking
Languages	Fluent in other languages, willing to travel
Leadership	Authority or status as spokesperson or adviser
Literacy	Articulate, both written and spoken word. Good phone manner
Organizational skills	Planning, timetabling, co-ordinating, meeting deadlines. Finishes jobs
Passion for fashion	Involvement, inspiring others with clothing and ideas
Patience	Sees things through, tolerant of repetitive tasks. Suffers fools
Perception	A quick eye, graphic skills, troubleshooting and intellectual skills
Practical skills	Wide ranging, can be learnt, but should be appropriate for the task
Punctuality	Good timekeeping is valued
Resourcefulness	Ingenuity, lateral thinking, problem solving. Making do
Risk-taking	Daring, 'chutzpah', foresight, forecasting and entrepreneurial skills
Talent	Unusual level of ability, especially sketching or styling. Salesmanship
Team player	Shares, enjoys group activities, recognizes role in the bigger picture
Temperament	Friendly, even-tempered, calm
Versatility	Ability to turn hand to different tasks, unfazed by challenges
Writing skills	Ability to write letters, reports, reviews. Analytical skills

The first steps

If this list has not left you daunted, and you still believe that a career in fashion is for you – go for it! Start by collecting college prospectuses and brochures to help you choose where you would like to study and what academic qualifications are needed. Colleges put on exhibitions of their graduating students' work at the end of the final term. For fashion courses there is usually a catwalk show and also an exhibition of portfolio work, sometimes held independently of each other. Contact the college office to enquire. Don't be daunted by the standard of final-year work; this is what you should aspire to, not what would be expected of you in your first year. By visiting the degree shows you will get some idea of the range of pathways open to you, and the quality of the course and its range of resources. It's worth asking the students, too, about their own experiences of the course.

Which college?

The aim of all fashion courses is to make the training as relevant as possible to finding work in the industry. However, colleges vary quite considerably in their focus and approach and in their facilities. Some are better equipped with machinery and technology; others have inspiring and skilled staff. A good balance of all these factors is desirable but not inevitable.

Nowadays, colleges often offer both full-time and part-time courses. Sandwich courses require students to spend a period in a work-experience programme or industrial placement. There are also internationally recognized credit schemes that allow students to pursue a period of study at another institute or university or in another country. Some courses are biased towards technology, while others emphasize practical skills. Some will be combination degrees that include business or cultural studies. The time allotted to studio practice and self-directed learning or attendance will vary enormously, as will the length of time required to take the qualification itself.

Colleges are keen to show prospective students their facilities and exhibit their strengths. Open days for this purpose are usually held well before the application forms need to be sent in. It is important not to rely solely on the prospectus or word of mouth when choosing a college. Location, atmosphere and infrastructure will all become much clearer during a visit, and visitors are likely to be given access to parts of the campus that are normally out of bounds at other times. Moreover, college tutors will not be impressed if a candidate turns up for an interview without having visited previously – unless, of course, you live overseas.

Which course?

College prospectuses list a bewildering range of courses. Unless you have grown up with a burning desire to be a hosiery designer or milliner, it is very hard to pick your way through the minefield of possibilities. Don't worry: colleges assume that you may make a mistake and will want to change options later, although it does help if you can narrow the field beforehand. Before applying for any course, you should investigate the level of qualification, syllabus, curriculum, methods of study and the subject pathways or options available. Many colleges will expect you to define your chosen pathway on the application form. Others will run a diagnostic programme that will help you to find your areas of aptitude during your first, or freshman, year.

Fabric design

The most popular path for students is womenswear design. Many courses focus almost exclusively on this area, and currently this field attracts seven times more applications than any other. Womenswear, however, has long had a reputation for being the most fickle sector of the clothing industry, with the greatest and fastest turnover of jobs. It may be useful to visit a large department store and work your way around from floor to floor, assessing the merchandise. Go from the 'madame' department to the trendy concessions and ask yourself not what *you* like to buy or wear, but which sector of the market interests you from the designing, fabrication and customer points of view. Perhaps it is streetwear, extreme sportswear or accessories. All are valid areas in the study of fashion.

Broadly the subjects on offer are womenswear design; menswear design; fashion marketing; fashion textile design; knitwear design; and fashion communication and promotion. Fashion with business studies or with merchandising are also commonly available. A few colleges also have childrenswear, lingerie, sportswear or shoes and accessories as options. You may be able to choose only one path or you may be able to mix and match a number of disciplines.

Call colleges or check their websites for brochures, and make sure you have the correct forms and dates for submission of applications. Carefully review the cost of fees and any additional requirements.

Application procedures

The procedures required when applying to a college vary considerably. In addition to listing academic qualifications and experience, the application form normally requires you to write a brief essay about yourself, your interests and achievements, and your reasons for wishing to join the course. Try to write as succinctly as possible and avoid clichés; check spellings carefully – especially the names of designers who have inspired you – and have someone read over your effort and give an opinion before you commit it to the form. Keep a copy and refer to it before your interview, as you will probably be asked questions based on what you have written. You may be asked to supply a confidential reference from a teacher or employer.

Most art college courses will require you to show a portfolio for assessment, usually at an interview. Interviewing differs from college to college, especially in the time given to each candidate. In a few cases you may not actually be seen, but your portfolio will be reviewed by an expert team of staff. It is therefore very important that you have an idea of the amount and kinds of work you should submit (see below). Most college applicants build up a strong portfolio on a foundation or other pre-college programme. Some colleges offer short courses or summer school programmes on portfolio presentation; tutors on these programmes will help you define and refine your area of interest and show you how to edit your portfolio.

The interview portfolio

At an interview for a college place at foundation or first-degree level, your examiners will be looking for a wide range of artistic abilities rather than a very narrowly focused interest in fashion alone. You will be expected to have made some life studies from actual observation, showing an awareness of the body as a three-dimensional form, as well as rapid line drawings that suggest its fluidity and movement. Colour studies (but not college exercises) and paintings and drawings that show your confidence and control over a wide range of media will also be helpful.

Knitwear

College interviewers will expect to see lively sketchbooks or notebooks as well as finished artwork.

Sketchbooks showing your visual research and ideas and experiments in progress will stand you in good stead. Demonstrate a feeling for fabric by keeping clippings and ideas for their use in a sketchbook. Fashion drawings are expected but not essential. Never copy from published photographs, illustrations or other sources; use your own drawing skills, even if they are undeveloped, and try to show a good sense of line and proportion. If you have done three-dimensional work or sculptures, show photographs of them rather than bringing them with you. Similarly, if you have made garments there is unlikely to be time to show or model them. At this point, teaching staff will not be interested primarily in your technical expertise but in your ideas.

Organize the work so that it is easy to go through, as a series of projects or in order of impact rather than chronology. You don't have to mount, frame or finish work; this can make it look too precious or heavy. Put charcoal and pastel drawings in plastic sleeves or paper to prevent smearing. Know your way around your portfolio; you will probably be asked to point out a favourite piece of work or explain some aspect of a project. Be prepared to talk about your own design processes and show how you arrived at a solution.

The interviewer will possibly challenge you to see how open you are to criticism or how you cope with some pressure. You are likely to be asked which designers you admire and why, and how you envision your future. Your own style and grooming will be noted but do not 'dress to impress'. Aim to come across as relaxed, yet committed.

In Chapter VII there is a section on how to put together a professional portfolio which you might find helpful. However, be aware that at this early stage in your career the interviewers are looking for your raw potential and not a slick, 'know-it-all' presentation.

The college syllabus

The content of a syllabus will vary according to the programme of study and the particular needs and interests of the students. Time given to different subjects will vary, too, and tutors will bring their individual expertise to bear on the course.

A comprehensive fashion-design syllabus aims to deliver the following:

- Awareness of contemporary fashion and visual culture
- Basic principles of pattern-cutting and draping fabric
- Computer-aided design (CAD)
- Design development
- Drawing and illustration
- Fabric awareness: type, performance and sourcing
- Fashion basics: silhouette, proportion, colour, detailing and fabric manipulation
- Garment construction and technology
- Independent study
- Marketing and business awareness
- Presentation (portfolio) and communication techniques
- Range-building
- Research techniques and methods
- Technical specification and costing
- Written work, as in report-writing and cultural studies

Ask for an example of the timetable and how the course is structured. Typically, fashion degrees last three years (although courses of two, four and five years also exist), each year being divided into three terms or two semesters.

The first year

During the first year, projects are often short and diverse so as to give students a broad, basic grounding in the various fashion-related areas. The greatest attention is given to stretching students' abilities to assimilate information and tackle research – which can later be turned into original design work. Some time is devoted to practical assignments to improve skills, confidence and speed. The results of the project work are put together in a portfolio, which over the years builds into a professional representation of a student's ability and style.

The second year

By the second year, students are likely to have a greater sense of direction and will have gained confidence in their abilities. Usually they will have learned the basic skills and how to work co-operatively with staff and fellow students. This is a year for consolidating abilities, with the focus on getting the balance right between teamwork and the evolution of an individual style. Projects will usually be of four to six weeks' duration and will help refine students' interests and talents within their chosen course of study.

Second-year students often make more ambitious garments and enter competitions and sponsored projects. At this stage students often work in teams or pairs in order to hone their co-operative and interpersonal skills. They are less closely supervised in the hope that they will reach the level of maturity and self-discipline required to progress to the next stage of the course.

'If you wanted to, you could do nothing – but why?' Second-year student

Work experience: the internship

At some point – usually between the second and third years – some fashion courses offer an industrial placement or work-experience period of varied or negotiable length. This is an opportunity to work in the industry: in design studios, production or promotion, at home or possibly overseas. At this juncture the student should have enough practical skills and commitment to be useful as a junior employee, as well as enough maturity to use the opportunity to evaluate his or her own qualities and ambitions within a real working environment.

If a student works for a company long enough, he or she may experience the full cycle of a collection, from initial idea to public reception. This can be an enjoyable and salutary lesson. The student may be exposed to aspects of fashion and production that are new and inspiring or that uncover previously untapped talents.

The internship is a period of study, not time out, and students are usually asked to produce a written report on their placements, including a critical analysis of the organization for which they worked. The internship is often an assessable component of your degree or may gain you a separate qualification award. It is worth remembering that the fashion industry is very keen to take on graduates who have prior experience of the workplace, and that a placement can lead to a lasting association – or can at least be a source of useful contacts.

Casualwear

'*I went to India. I met lots of craftsmen and was able to realize the potential of working with embroidery.*' Designer Matthew Williamson

Final year

'*When I was at college I did a lot of designing on paper and not much making. You don't get time to make things properly in the first and second year. I found it very frustrating just working with illustration. In the final year it all comes together and you can see the results of what you have been learning. I really liked that.*' Designer Suzanne Clements

During the final year the projects are more intensive, giving students time to explore the ideas in depth and to perfect their techniques. The year ends with the most important and exciting project brief of all: the final collection (see page *183*). This is the students' opportunity to refine their interests and allow their self-expression, style and proficiency to blossom. Each student is asked to design a range of between six and ten outfits appropriate to their specialist study. The final collection should prove that he or she can maintain a sustained involvement in the management and resolution of their work and is able to design independently and to a professional standard.

At the end of this process, students have the opportunity to show their outfits to the examination board, to staff, fellow students and an invited audience (including industry professionals) at a catwalk show. Their portfolios may also be exhibited to the public – press, sponsors and many interested manufacturers attend degree shows in order to find employees. A student should now be ready to leave the nest as a fully fledged fashion designer.

Studying abroad

There are many initiatives for studying abroad, either as part of your university course or in the form of internships in the industry that are supported by educational establishments, government departments and non-profit-making organizations. Research the courses, universities and what opportunities are offered, and confirmed, before making further arrangements. You will need to find out what qualifications, documentation and visas are needed to satisfy legal requirements. The processing of applications and documentation can take between three weeks and six months so the decision to go abroad is not to be taken lightly. It is usually essential to have proficiency to a specified standard in both the written and spoken language of the country you'll be studying in. This level will vary with the course or job chosen. Universities will have international offices and staff who can help you find accommodation and settle in. However, this is not necessarily the case with commercial companies. You are usually expected to be able to finance your fare and accommodation, either through personal funds or through payment from an employer; universities and colleges may demand fees paid in advance.

Many universities require that students do internships abroad to gain practical experience and training related to their course of study, and doing so can play an important role in personal development when the experience is in an international setting. There are a number of regulations and safeguards to be observed, and your internship company will be expected not only to remunerate you, but also to write a report reviewing your tenure with them.

Whatever your origin, in college you will find yourself among others who share the same interest in fashion, and quickly make alliances.

The larger fashion brands have formalized procedures for student placements and welcome enquiries well in advance of the work period. If you apply directly to a fashion company you will need a well-crafted **curriculum vitae (CV)** or résumé that lists your qualifications, achievements and interests. You may be invited to an interview, either at home or abroad, or asked to send examples of your work. If you attend in person always take a portfolio or prepare a CD of your work. If you have friends or relations in the country where you wish to study this can boost your application and also be a source of personal support. The British Council has an extensive programme of opportunities for overseas applicants to study in the United Kingdom and vice versa. The Council on International Educational Exchanges facilitates and administers internships in the United States that provide up to eighteen months' practical training for full-time students or students who have completed their studies.

Further reading and additional resources

Noel Chapman and Carol Chester. *Careers in Fashion*, London: Kogan Page, 1999
Elaine Stone. *The Dynamics of Fashion*, New York: Fairchild, 1999
Peter Vogt. *Career Opportunities in the Fashion Industry*, New York: Checkmark, 2002

Schools and student information

Education UK www.educationuk.org
The British Council's list of universities and colleges in the United Kingdom

University and Colleges Admission Services www.ucas.co.uk
Database of undergraduate courses and foundation degrees. UCAS is the UK's central organization
    through which applications are processed for entry to full-time undergraduate courses

www.arts.ac.uk/studyabroad
Studio-based study-abroad programmes for students of art, design
    or communications in the heart of London

The National Union of Students www.nus.org.uk
The NUS site features a useful Student Help section with links to educational bodies,
    funding bodies, career services and more

European Work Experience Program www.ewep.com
EWEP provides the opportunity for students from Europe to gain work experience in London,
    and to explore the British way of life

www.unofficial-guides.com
Run by students for students, this site offers useful information on social life, facilities,
    accommodation and so on at UK universities

www.fashion-school-finder.com
Directory of fashion courses in the United States

www.fashionschools.com
American fashion-school finder

www.academix.de
Advice for those who want to study outside Germany

The Council on International Educational Exchanges
www.councilexchanges.org

London
52 Poland Street
London W1V 4JQ
UK
Tel 020 7478 2000
Email infoUK@ciee.org

New York
205 East 42nd Street
New York, NY 10017-5706
USA
Tel 212 822 2660
Email intUSA@ciee.org

Paris
1 place de l'Odéon
75006 Paris
France
Tel 33 144 42 74 74
Email infoFrance@ciee.org

Context

Context

It would hardly be possible to become an effective designer or stylist without contextual knowledge of the historical, geographical, economic and social realms within which you plan your creative career. Colleges and universities offer a wide range of liberal arts, cultural studies, and business **modules** and **electives** to degree students. Attending **seminars** and writing essays may be a compulsory and assessable component of a fashion course and should not be regarded as time better spent in the studio. Lessons learned and insights gained from past analyses and theories, and from the practice of group discussion, intellectual enquiry and academic writing, will prove inspiring and invaluable throughout school, and essential later in your career. Socio-economic conditions and the marketplace are in a constant state of flux and the context and motivations for clothing purchases can change many times in your professional life. Fashion designers cannot rely on intuition. Astute research and the ability to read the signs of change is the starting point for all design and good business, and will put you ahead of the game.

Above Fashion students in 1897 investigate clothing engravings in the Bibliothèque Nationale, Paris.

Right John Galliano playfully mixes historical, sartorial and literary references in his designs. Here, Marie Antoinette meets Anna Karenina.

Historical context

Not all fashion courses offer fashion history as a subject. It is well worth the effort to acquaint yourself not only with garment names, silhouettes, materials and the roster of legendary designers, but also with the underlying social, environmental and technological conditions that led to changes in dress taking place. The fashion world is frequently inspired by the past; designers, display professionals and stylists need to understand how to allude subtly to the silhouette or styling of a particular era or mix the palette of ideas in a new, and sometimes ironic, way. It is beyond the scope of this book to cover such a vast subject, but the time line on the following pages highlights significant costume changes and links them with their originators and contemporary events. It will help you to find research material and to recognize context and period when you observe clothes in paintings and films, and at the theatre. Some universities and colleges have costume and fabric archives, and many have image banks. Fashion-school libraries often have bound copies of magazines covering many decades, as well as current journals.

The majority of museums offer reduced rates to students or free admission on certain days. Costume galleries are happy for them to come in and sketch quietly, but some have restrictions on photographing the garments on display. You can learn a great deal from drawing garments; being forced to look closely at proportion and line, and historical manufacturing methods, can be inspiring. Many museums and collections, such as the Victoria and Albert in London and the Costume Institute at the Metropolitan Museum of Art in New York, have excellent websites which show garments that are too fragile to be put on display. Historical and contemporary fashion-research archives are available on the Internet and images or background text can often be downloaded. A number of prestigious museums work closely with design colleges and will show small groups around archived collections if the tour is booked in advance.

Ethnic and folk costumes are also rich sources of inspiration. National and local galleries have extensive collections of these and it is still possible to find shops that sell both original and contemporary examples. Vintage-clothing shops frequently have superb twentieth-century clothes. It is inspiring to wear and admire the craftsmanship of the past and worthwhile being able to spot valuable gems and labels among the dross – even a pair of rare Levi's can stand out in a pile of lifeless clothes, and could fetch a fortune at auction. You may discover fabric, trimmings and accessories to recycle for use in your own work. Charity and thrift shops can be treasure troves of information on the construction of garments; it costs next to nothing to buy an old dress and then deconstruct it to make a pattern.

Film, theatre and television are great sources of inspiration as they not only demonstrate the clothes of an era or location, but also the hair, make-up and styling, and the deportment and manners, that complement them. Sometimes it is the 'mood' rather than the garment that can set the context for designs. From time to time fashion designers such as Jean-Paul Gaultier, Armani and Donna Karan have been asked to design for film, stage or television. Your ability to research and either authentically replicate or subtly update the looks of the past will be an invaluable asset. There is a list of leading international costume museums and collections at the end of this chapter.

Top By browsing in antique textile and costume shops you can discover the fascinating techniques used for making clothes in different eras.

Above Coco Chanel (1883–1971), developed her business from a small hat shop to a great couture house. Among the pioneering styles she introduced were the acceptable use of jersey and knitwear for social occasions, the ensemble suit, the little black dress, the pea jacket, bell-bottom pants and bold costume jewellery.

Fashion time line

Date and key events

Late 18th century

1775–99 American Declaration of Independence; French Revolution; Industrial Revolution

19th century

1804–30 Napoleonic Empire; Battle of Waterloo

1830–65 Photography, and sewing and knitting machines. Britain is the centre of industry and world trade; France is the centre of art and culture

1870–90 Invention of light bulb and telephone; 1889 *Vogue* magazine launched; department stores open in cities

20th century

Russian Revolution; women given the right to vote. Public transport and air travel; increased communications result in a culture of holiday travel

1914–18 World War I; cinema popularizes fashions. End of silent movies. Zipper trademarked

Designers and influences

Rose Bertin, dressmaker to Marie Antoinette; tailor Andre Scheling. Sumptuary clothing laws and wealth dictate appropriate dress until the rise of the bourgeoisie

Hippolyte Leroy, tailor to the Empress Josephine. Romantic eclecticism influenced by Beau Brummel

Charles Frederick Worth dresses Empress Eugénie and Queen Victoria

Redfern, Paquin, Doucet, Lucile. Creed and Henry Poole tailor menswear

Jeanne Lanvin, Callot Soeurs, Fortuny, Paul Poiret. Rise of female designers; training schemes for dressmakers

Delaunay, Bakst, Lelong. Influence of modern art: Fauves, Cubists, Vorticists

Silhouette and style

Luxurious brocades, wide-hipped panniers, corsets and wigs give way to shepherdess styles, and plain unadorned fabrics in patriotic colours for men and women

High-waisted chemises, narrow Empire line dresses. Indian cashmeres and American cottons. Bonnets and millinery. Regency high collars, breeches, frock coats, frills and flamboyance

Puff sleeves, low necklines, bell shapes; the crinoline and corsetry at its most extreme during the reign of Queen Victoria (1837–1901). Less flamboyant menswear; white shirts, waistcoats, frock coats, trousers, boots

Broad breast and bustles, draped skirts, bloomers for sports. Working women wear practical 'Gibson girl' separates. Introduction of the brassiere. Men wear suits with long trousers

Disappearance of corsets; S-shaped silhouette gives way to chemise. Hobble skirts are followed by looser styles due to motor cars and mobility. Lampshade tunics, drapery. No waist. Use of new fibre – rayon. First rayon spectator sportswear introduced, and bloomers and knickers worn by women

Emancipation and revolutionary styles; square cuts. Increasing sobriety in menswear. Suits and practical dress

1775   1785   1800   1820   1850   1885   1910

1920s Weimar Republic in Germany; Prohibition in the USA; invention of television

1926 General Strike in Britain
1929 Black Friday stock market crash

1930s
1936–39 Spanish Civil War
1937 Edward VIII abdicates

1940s
1939–45 World War II; atomic bomb. Clothing coupons and rationing; DuPont develops nylon
1947 Synthetic dyes introduced for new acrylic and polyester fibres

1950s
Elizabeth II; availability of domestic washing machines; television becomes leading medium
1955 Civil Rights movement in USA
1957 Sputnik space satellite launched by the Soviet Union

Vionnet, Gres, Ricci, Jean Patou and Coco Chanel develop simpler and more practical styles for the current lifestyle. Shortage resulting from the depression; Jazz and nightclub dance crazes, the charleston and tango, bring in short backless dresses

Mainbocher, Schiaparelli, Adrian, Balenciaga, Molyneux, Hartnell

Creed, Hardy Amies. The rise of American designers: Blass, Cashin, McCardell, James, Norell

Intellectuals, artists and musicians displaced and dispersed by the war create new communities of influence

Dior's 'New Look'. Couture houses Chanel, Givenchy, Balmain and Fath reopen. Italian industry revives and American styles are more widely seen

Belville Sassoon, Hardy Amies. Italian designers: Pucci, Ferragamo, Cerruti. American designers: Adrian, Claire McCardell, Oleg Cassin. Elvis Presley, James Dean and Marlon Brando become teen idols and influence menswear styles

---

Boyish look: flat-chested, low waists, bias cuts; women have short hair. Fake jewellery, beading, fringes and fur wraps. Baggy men's suits. Men wear casual knitwear

Depression; longer body lines, figure-skimming silhouette, 'tea dresses'. New fibres. Influence of Hollywood stars

Precision grooming. Detailed suits. Extremes of wealth and poverty. Princess line; belts and waists, sensible shoes, suits

Practical, quasi-military styles, womens' trousers, 'make do and mend' approach, platform shoes. Women had worn practical clothes for war work, and many women continued in supporting roles in the workplace. Men wear single-breasted suits

Sophistication; concave posture. Hourglass silhouettes, fuller, longer skirts, nylon stockings, accessorized ensembles. Lightweight, easy-care synthetic fabrics

New 'youth market'; girlish looks (Audrey Hepburn and Juliette Greco), full skirts, sweaters, flat shoes. Unisex styles. Rock and roll, denim and gingham. Jeans become accepted casualwear

1914   1920   1926   1930   1942   1947   1952

Date and key events

1960s
John F. Kennedy elected president of USA
1963 President Kennedy assassinated; transatlantic telephone cable
1965 Vietnam War; space race; Cold War; Civil Rights Act gives all US citizens the right to vote

1967 The Summer of Love
1968 Paris riots
1969 Moon landing

1970s
1974 Nixon and Watergate scandal, USA
1979 Shah of Iran ousted by fundamentalists; Margaret Thatcher becomes first female Prime Minister of the UK

1980s
1981 Marriage of Diana Spencer and Prince Charles
1982 Falklands War; videos and MTV popularize youth styles

Designers and influences

Yves Saint-Laurent, Cardin, Courrèges, Rabanne. First generation of art-school trained designers: Thea Porter, Jean Muir, Foale and Tuffin. USA designers: Anne Klein, Halston, Beane

'Swinging' London boutiques: Mary Quant, Biba, Bus Stop, Mr Freedom. YSL's Rive Gauche. Jacqueline Kennedy, wife of US president, is influential role model – repopurarizes Chanel suit, pillbox hats and the short, bob haircut

Influence of Paris couture wanes. Bill Gibb, Ossie Clarke, Zandra Rhodes, Anthony Price

Halston, Perry Ellis, Ralph Lauren, Norma Kamali, Betsey Johnston, Calvin Klein, Diane von Furstenburg. Growth of Women's Movement; bra-burning and casualwear, dungarees and protest T-shirts. Clothing licences proliferate

Vivienne Westwood, Body Map, John Galliano

'New Romantic' music movement and Studio 54 New York nightclub scene. High fashion becomes increasingly international: Adolfo Dominguez, Calvin Klein, Donna Karan, Armani, Missoni, Versace, Alaïa, Lagerfeld, Lacroix, Gaultier, Gigli, Valentino, Jil Sander, Kenzo. TV soaps *Dallas* and *Dynasty* watched by millions worldwide and influence upwardly mobile fashion choices. DuPont's Lycra stretch fabrics

Silhouette and style

The sack shape, knee-length skirts, Chanel suits. Sharply tailored Italian suits for men and trouser suits for women. Bikinis and bra-less tops. Kinky boots for women and Chelsea boots for men

Miniskirts, PVC and paper dresses, colourful geometric prints, tights; influence of Pop Art on fashion. Cult of the fashion photographer and 'dolly bird' models: Twiggy and Shrimpton. Rebels, Beatniks and the Beatles

Hippie movement, Eastern styles: 'maxi' skirts, long hair, florals, embroidery, beads, suede, cheesecloth. Colour and flamboyance return to menswear. Layered looks, jersey and knitwear popular

Glamour versus feminism – disco fashion, sexy and glittery versus flat chests, Doc Martens flat shoes, dungarees, designer jeans. Power dressing, Chanel suits and shoulder pads, big hair towards end of decade

Fashion makes an alliance with youth music. Punk, anti-fashion, bondage and fetish clothing, street fashions. Unisex dressing. Power shoulders

Street versus high style epitomized by icons Madonna and Princess Diana. Cult of the healthy body, sportswear, stretch jersey. Travel and work favour 'easy dressing' as women take up more executive roles in the workplace

1958

1967

1972

1974

1978

1980

1985 Live Aid
Late 1980s AIDS; Tiananmen Square
massacre
1987 US stock market crash
1989 Fall of the Berlin Wall

1990s
International trade agreements GATT and NAFTA
1991 Gulf War; apartheid ends;
collapse of Soviet Union
1992 Bill Clinton elected US president
1993 Personal computers widely available
1995 OJ Simpson trial
1997 China reclaims Hong Kong; death of
Princess Diana

21st century
2000 President Bush takes US presidency
2001 Destruction of World Trade Center in New
York by terrorists
2002 Introduction of the euro curency in Europe
2003 Iraq War
2004 President Bush re-elected

Japanese designers: Issey Miyake, Yohji
Yamamoto, Rei Kawakubo. Belgian designers:
Dries Van Noten, Ann Demeulemeester.
Independent designers struggle to survive
economic downturn

Rise of international high street labels: Esprit,
Benetton, Gap, H&M, DKNY, Tommy Hilfiger

Humour in fashion: Dolce & Gabbana, Moschino

Growth of designer labels owned by fashion
conglomerates. Brand awareness. Rebirth of
labels: Prada, Hermès, Gucci, Fendi. Diversity of
styles widely available. Donatella Versace takes
on Versace after Gianni, her brother's,
assassination

Post- Modern designers: Martin Margiela,
Helmut Lang, Hussein Chalayan, Jil Sander. US
designers Todd Oldham, Tom Ford, Anna Sui,
Richard Tyler

British and American designers work in Paris
couture: John Galliano, Alexander McQueen,
Marc Jacobs, Julien Macdonald, Stella McCartney,
Tom Ford and Michael Kors

Moulin Rouge: return to corsetry and dance
styles. Accessories become important as style
necessities; Manolo Blahnik, Jimmy Choo, Fendi,
Gucci, Prada. Growth of Internet shopping;
growing cult of the celebrity as fashion icon

Countercultural, anti-excess clothing expressing
intellectual and artistic aesthetic. Loose,
architectural cuts, black, worn with flat shoes.
Men wear more sportswear and there are 'dress
down Fridays' in the workplace

Cult of supermodels and celebrities. Casual
sportswear and jeans. Trainers. Natural
silhouettes and baggy jeans

Trade recession, grunge and deconstructed
styles; ecologically friendly fibres, recycling, anti-
fur. Oversized silhouettes, androgyny. Revivals of
1960s and 1970s fashions. Glamour versus
conceptual fashion and hip-hop youth styles. The
baseball cap and pashmina scarf are key
accessories

East opens gates for international
manufacturing. Trade barriers dissolve. Internet
speeds communication. High-tech production.
Return of the bias dress and high heels, feminine
styles

Eclecticism, individualism, fashion as a spectacle.
Dismantling of the glamorous myth. Backlash
against mass-market labels; revival of craft
techniques and vintage clothing

1985

1997

2000

The uses of clothing

Fashion is a specialized form of body adornment. Explorers and travellers were among the first to document and comment on the body adornment and dress styles that they encountered around the world. Some returned from their travels with drawings and examples of clothing, sparking off a desire not only for the artefacts themselves but also for an understanding of them. Eventually the study of clothing came to be an accepted part of anthropology – the scientific study of human beings.

Fashion frequently looks to the shapes and materials of the past as an inspiration for new styles. Vintage clothing is admired not only for the workmanship and detail that it is rarely possible to achieve today, but also triggers a nostalgia for bygone lifestyles. This 'emotional' aspect of clothing is an important element of design. Nevertheless, however much one might want to reintroduce the look of the corset or crinoline, it is wise to consider the social and political conditions and needs that made such items effective in their time and to apply similar analysis to contemporary styles. Anthropologists and ethnographers no longer have heated debates about the meaning of the rise and fall of hemlines in wartime, but they continue to throw light on the role that fashion plays in individual and group identity. The politics of identity are closely associated with the clothing we choose to wear. The focus is now on the uses of clothing in rites of passage and as manifestations of social preoccupations and cultural shifts. Today we have much greater freedom of choice than our predecessors had, and very few sumptuary laws that forbid or enforce the wearing of particular garments.

Cultural theorists and clothing analysts have focused primarily on four practical functions of dress: utility, modesty, immodesty (that is, sexual attraction) and adornment. In his book *Consumer Behaviour Towards Dress* (1979), George Sproles suggested four additional functions: symbolic differentiation, social affiliation, psychological self-enhancement and modernism. Each of these eight functions is discussed briefly below.

Utility

Clothing has evolved to meet many practical and protective purposes. The environment is hazardous, and the body needs to be kept at a mean temperature to ensure blood circulation and comfort. The bushman needs to keep cool, the fisherman to stay dry; the firemen needs protection from flames and the miner from harmful gases. Dress reformers have typically put utility above other aesthetic considerations. For example, in the 1850s the American publisher and suffrage pioneer Amelia Jenks Bloomer took issue with the impracticality of the crinoline and advocated the wearing of women's trousers, called 'pantalettes' or 'bloomers'. The notion of utility should never be underestimated; consumers often choose clothes with concerns such as comfort, durability or ease of care in mind. In recent years, fitness clothing and sportswear – themselves originally utility items – have dominated the leisure-clothing market and become fashionable as indicators of health and youthful stamina.

Modesty

We need clothing to cover our nakedness. Society demands propriety and has often passed sumptuary (clothing) laws to curb extravagance and uphold decorum. Most people feel some insecurity about revealing their physical imperfections, especially as they grow older; clothing disguises and conceals our defects, whether real or imagined. Modesty is socially defined and varies among individuals, groups and societies, as well as over time.

Above Utility: as well as wearing heavy protective equipment, this coal-mine rescue worker is also carrying a caged linnet that will warn him if harmful gases are present.

In many Middle Eastern countries a debate still rages between liberals and fundamentalists as to how covered a women should be, and in many contemporary societies women still wear long skirts as a matter of course. Europeans are generally less inhibited than Americans, but the trend for 'casual Fridays' and dressing down for the office has been imported from the United States. Club and beachwear reveals more of the body than at any previous time in history, and images of naked bodies are ubiquitous in advertising and the media.

Immodesty (sexual attraction)

Clothing can be used to accentuate the sexual attractiveness and availability of the wearer. The traditional role of women as passive sexual objects has contributed to the greater eroticization of female clothing. Eveningwear and lingerie are made from fabrics that set off or simulate the texture of skin. Accessories and cosmetics also enhance allure. Many fashion commentators and theorists have used a psychoanalytic approach,

Modesty and Immodesty

Top In parts of the Middle East, strict laws still forbid women to reveal any part of their bodies.

Above left In Western society this type of beachwear is considered absurd and antiquated.

Above The shifting erogenous zone: in the 1920s the legs and the back were the focus of attention, enhanced by dance crazes such as the charleston and the tango.

based on the writings of Sigmund Freud and Carl Jung, to explain the unconscious processes underlying changes in fashion.

The concept of the 'shifting erogenous zone' (developed by JC Flugel, a disciple of Freud, in about 1930) proposes that fashion continuously stimulates sexual interest by cycling and focusing the attention on different parts of the body for seductive purposes, and that a great many articles of clothing are sexually symbolic of the male or female genitals. From time to time overtly sexualized clothing, such as the codpiece or the brassiere, come into vogue.

Adornment

Adornment allows us to enrich our physical attractions, assert our creativity and individuality, or signal membership or rank within a group or culture. Adornment can go against the needs for comfort, movement and health, as in foot-binding, the wearing of

Adornment

Above A girl from Yemen is decorated with flowers and ornaments on her wedding day.

Right The tattoo is a permanent corporal adornment.

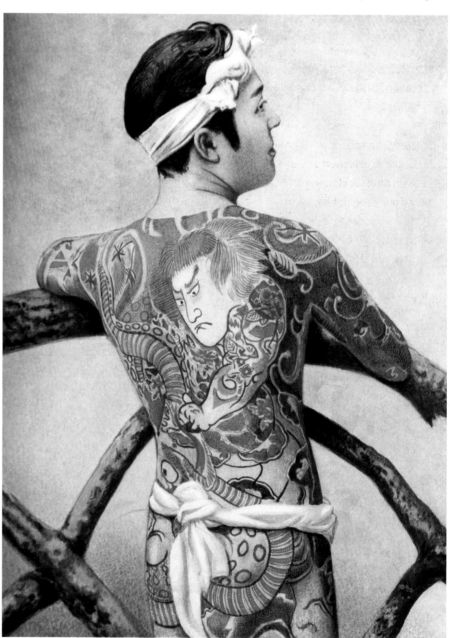

corsets or piercing and tattooing. Adornments can be permanent or temporary, additions to or reductions of the human body. Cosmetics and body paint, jewellery, hairstyling and shaving, false nails, wigs and hair extensions, suntans, high heels and plastic surgery are all body adornments. People generally, and young women in particular, attempt to conform to the prevailing ideal of beauty. Bodily contortions and reshaping through foundation garments, padding and binding have altered the fashionable silhouette throughout the ages.

Symbolic differentiation

People use clothing to differentiate and recognize profession, religious affiliation, social standing or lifestyle. Occupational dress is an expression of authority and helps the wearer stand out in a crowd. The modest attire of a nun announces her beliefs. In some countries, lawyers and barristers cover their everyday clothes with the garb of silk and periwig in order to convey the solemnity of the law. The wearing of designer labels or insignia, and expensive materials and jewellery, may start as items of social distinction, but often trickle down through the social strata until they lose their potency as symbols of differentiation.

Social affiliation

People dress alike in order to belong to a group. Those who do not conform to the accepted styles are assumed to have divergent ideas and are ultimately mistrusted and excluded. Conversely, the fashion victim, who conforms without sensitivity to the rules of current style, is perceived as being desperate to belong and lacking in personality and taste. In some cases clothing is a statement of rebellion against society or fashion itself. Although punks do not have a uniform, they can be recognized by a range of identifiers: torn clothes, bondage items, safety pins, dramatic hairstyles and so on. This dress code was developed by the British fashion designer Vivienne Westwood as an anarchic jibe against the conventional, well-groomed fashions of the mid-1970s.

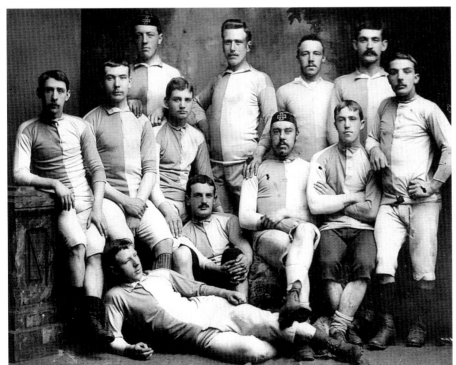

Symbolic differentiation
Top The coronation gowns of George V and Queen Mary denote authority and status through their weight and the expense of the materials used.

Above At the other end of the social scale, a Pearly Queen marks her position in the community by emulating the regal robes and embroideries with buttons.

Social affiliation
Left Soccer teams and their supporters dress alike in order to demonstrate allegiance and conformity.

Psychological self-enhancement

Although there is social pressure to be affiliated to a group, and many identical garments and fashions are manufactured and sold through vast chain stores, we rarely encounter two people dressed identically from head to toe. While many young people shop with friends for help and advice, they do not buy the same outfits. Whatever the situation, individuals will strive to assert their own personal identity through the use of make-up, hairstyling and accessories.

Modernism

In parts of the world where fashionable clothes are widely available, dress can be used to express modernity. In the media-rich environment of capital cities, being seen to be ahead or abreast of new styles and aware of current events can give us the edge in an increasingly competitive employment marketplace. The right clothing can grant us access to the right places and the right people. Our acceptance of modernity, whether as designers, early adopters or consumers, serves as an indicator of our creativity, adjustment and preparedness for the future.

> 'All fashion is clothing, although clearly not all clothing is fashion ...
> We need fashion, rather than clothes, not to clothe our nakedness but to clothe our self-esteem.' Colin McDowell (1995)

Psychological self-enhancement
Below Dress codes exist at all levels of society. Doc Marten boots and frayed jeans were ubiquitous rebel youthwear throughout the 1970s and 1980s.

Practical criteria

New clothes can help people to feel confident; expensive or familiar brands serve as status symbols and create tribal allegiances. Whether we find this state of affairs appealing or distasteful, it is necessary for even the most avant-garde or dissident designer to be aware of the primary practical considerations used by consumers to select choices to fit their lifestyles. Listed below are some crucially important criteria for designers to keep in mind. They are rarely mentioned in fashion reports or magazines and are seldom seen to be at the forefront of the creative design process, yet they inform our impulse to buy and satisfy our real, and subliminal, needs.

Price

For the majority of consumers price is the most important purchase consideration. However much they may desire an item, they must balance its perceived value with its cost and their own budget. The value to an individual is not only the amount of wear a garment will provide. At the top end of the market, designer fashions are made in limited quantities and with more expensive fabrics and trimmings: the basic costs are higher than in the middle and mass markets where economies of scale can be obtained. All consumers like to feel they are getting value for their money. Different brands may charge wildly different prices for garments that are very similar. It is up to the **retailer** to make adept choices of merchandise and **mark up** prices that entice the consumer. There are a number of ways of **costing** a fashion item and creating market price points, and these are explained in more detail in the next chapter.

Quality

Quality of fabric and manufacture is a decisive factor in buying clothing, and is closely linked to price and the consumer's pre-purchase evaluation of durability through care and cleaning. The gradual upturn in working hours means that there is less time to look after clothes, and the inconvenience and cost of dry-cleaning, and environmental concerns, have tipped the balance in favour of easy-care and drip-dry fabrics for middle-market garments. There are differences in the quality of stitching, seam finishing and lining at different price points. Classic clothing and high fashion are expected to endure. Knitwear, for example, is often cut and sewn at the lower end of the market but 'fully fashioned' at high price points, and the cost of luxury yarns such as silk and cashmere cannot be imitated. On the other hand, with summer vacation clothing and partywear there is almost an expectation of disposability after use, so these garments can be highly fashionable but more crudely made.

Fit

The fit of a garment is an essential component of its saleability and is the responsibility of a good designer. Statistics indicate that a very large proportion of the population finds it difficult to find fashions that fit. Good fit is a critical performance factor in sportswear and lingerie. Fit is difficult to quantify, beyond measuring the body, because individuals have variable preferences for ease. It also mutates with fashion. Baggy jeans can be in vogue at the same time as tight tops. In some styles the fit is the most important fashion element and may not be apparent until the garment is tried on. Some designers, such as Perry Ellis, Rei Kawakubo and Azzedine Alaïa (the 'King of Cling') have innovative approaches to fit and make it a selling point of their collections. Many brands evolve dimensions that are specific to their target market, sometimes based on customer feedback but more often on an imaginary or wishful demographic. There is no international standard for garment sizing but in recent years a number of studies have been made in the United States, UK, Europe and China to determine average and typical sizes and the grading between them. This is leading to more realistic and accurate measurements. Now that fashion brands are becoming increasingly global, it is required that clothing is labelled with the equivalent size protocols for different nations. It is in the interests of the fashion designer to be aware of natural and average proportions for the target market, and to design with a true **fit model** rather than an idealized body in mind, or the clothing will remain on the rails.

Comfort

There are times when fashionable clothing demands sacrifices of comfort and fit (e.g., stiletto heels, bondage pants or PVC miniskirts) but the general momentum is towards increasing well-being. Improvements in home heating and the effects of global warming on temperate climates have leavened out all but the most acute differences between seasonal wear. Innovations in fabric technology have led to lighter fabrics, stretch materials, seam-free manufacturing and multifunctional materials; finishes such as anti-creasing properties result in clothes that travel well and require less time and care (see chapter IV). There are new developments in microfibres that can deliver vitamins and aromas, and protect against harmful environmental conditions such as radiation. Consumers now also demand the emotional comfort of knowing that the suppliers of their clothing follow ethical and sustainable methods of production and disposal of waste. Reports such as Naomi Klein's *No Logo*, an exposé of the exploitation of workers and resources in Third World manufacturing, has prompted a conscientious movement towards fashion companies with transparent and accountable employment practices. Attitudes and beliefs are themselves fashionable and create trends.

Relevance

Fashion and clothing need to be appropriate for the lifestyle, work and leisure occasions of consumers. In the suburbs the styles required will be significantly different to those appropriate to the business climate of the city, although not necessarily any less fashionable. Trends that are significant for one age group or social clique may not be suitable for another. The idea of fashion being 'dictated' by designers is now outmoded. The increase in **quick response (QR)** manufacturing has ushered in a more rapid reaction to seasonal and social requirements and to what customers want. Many retailers work closely, and on a daily basis, with manufacturers to ensure that they are providing the type of stock their customers ask for. Based on electronic point-of-sale (EPOS) analysis, chain stores can deliver quite different merchandise in different parts of the country. Retail space is limited and very costly, and wholesale buyers assess the attraction, visual impact and sales potential of collections rather than individual items. It is the responsibility of retailers to read local social and economic conditions, to spot market niches and to supply appropriate merchandise. In the following chapter, there is an explanation of how market sectors are segmented and trends forecast in order to help the professional designer to create relevant fashion.

Brand

Brands usually build up their reputation and loyal following over many years of satisfying consumer expectations of consistency, and by advertising their unique qualities. By supporting brands many consumers hope to take on and affiliate themselves with such qualities. For example, Burberry and Pringle are quintessentially

Political, social and ethical beliefs can have a strong impact on fashion trends. Here an activist for PETA (People for the Ethical Treatment of Animals) is arrested during a protest outside *Vogue* magazine in New York, 2003. The use of fur in fashion diminished during the late twentieth century because of similar campaigns and their endorsement by models and celebrities, but is now on the rise.

classic British brands that imply quality and conformity while Versace is a label that exudes glamour, sex and extravagance. Branding is a key issue in fashion promotion and marketing, and is further complicated by traditional retailers commissioning 'private label' merchandise and creating their own brands. Celebrities and the brands they endorse are a powerful motivation for some consumers, and there is a growing trend towards celebrity 'private label' collections that are designed and produced by contracted manufacturers. Chain stores and independent retailers also have brand profiles or 'mission statements' and expect the designers they promote to comply with quality standards and terms and conditions that will justify the confidence of their customers.

Convenience and service

Consumers have increasingly less time and patience for shopping and trying on the stock; nor do they want to wait in line at checkouts. Shoppers must find what they are looking for quickly and easily, and they expect high standards of assistance and an in-depth selection of size and colour ranges. Many store buyers avoid garments that lack 'hanger appeal' – clothing that is difficult to imagine on the body – because so many people dislike changing. Shopping from home through the Internet and catalogues is convenient and has increased dramatically in recent years, which has created an escalating culture of buying, trying and returning unsuitable items. Stores try to counteract such practices by making shopping as pleasant, entertaining and fulfilling an experience as possible, and many offer loyalty discounts and special offers. In turn, middle-market design labels and manufacturers are careful to place their merchandise in locations that best reflect their own marketing concepts. For many brands it is important to be offered in the same context as rivals. This makes it all the more important that styling, quality and price points are finely tuned. Some brands have a selective distribution policy in order to maintain **exclusivity** and retailers compete for the honour of carrying the collection. New developments in computer-aided manufacturing are resulting in a return to offers of individually personalized designs and made-to-measure items. Stores that offer such services often gain the advantage.

Economic context

Consumer spending depends on income levels. After taxes and necessary items such as food, housing and fees are paid, a 'discretionary income' is left. Expenses for students are unlikely to be exorbitant, but independent adults, families and the elderly use their disposable income on insurance, school fees, investments, health, furniture and entertainment, which makes less available or prioritized for fashion. This is one of the reasons why fashion is usually targeted on those with available disposable incomes.

Unstable economic periods and periods of inflation lead to conservative buying and clothing that gives the best value for money. Fashion really does change in varied economic climates as differences in the amount of fabric used, the cost of trimmings and what is available and acceptable take effect. In prosperous times, people are more willing to pay dearly for fashion and show it off. In a recession, the amount of money circulating falls and production is cut, fewer styles are available and bright and unusual colours tend to disappear. Lay-offs and hiring freezes, further reduce spending, especially on small luxuries and fashion. Cheap labour sources in the Far East, Mexico, the Caribbean, eastern Europe and North Africa are threats to domestic manufacturing, yet most consumers believe that there should be free trade, availability of choice and low prices.

Foreign exchange markets have a formidable influence on the value of national currencies. Global economic conditions can have a see-saw effect on the price of imports and exports. When a currency is strong and goods are therefore expensive at home, it is tempting for retailers to import cheaper foreign merchandise. When a currency is weak it is easier for manufacturers and design companies to export clothing. Fashion buyers are given budgets and their money may buy more in one country than another. The euro was introduced to eliminate exchange-rate fluctuations and paperwork complications when trading across European borders, and to make it easier to compete in world markets.

An excellent product line or the ability to supply it exclusively is a considerable export bonus. The availability or shortage of products from various suppliers may be due to international conditions of trade rather than demand. Raw materials and merchandise are traded like currency on the commodities markets of the world. Wool is traded in Australia, silk and cashmere in China, and cotton is the staple fibre of the United States. From time to time, climatic, economic or political conditions can cause shortages of materials. A failure in 1999 of the indigo crop, the natural product with which denim is dyed, created a crisis in the jeans industry, a substantial loss of jobs and the demand for alternative dyes. The research into synthetic fibres and dyestuffs has been partially motivated by the need to find alternative sources of supply. Sometimes economic conditions are created artificially. For example, China has often restricted the export of silk in order to raise its market price; and in 2001, the Chinese fashion industry bought enormous quantities of wool from the Australian market, creating a world shortage and effectively raising prices globally. Not only do governments and customs and excise departments make rules for, and impose restrictions on, trade between countries, but there are a number of international watchdog groups that regulate and referee these conditions.

The Multi-Fibre Arrangement

The World Trade Organization (WTO), in Geneva, Switzerland, and the United Nations negotiate and set rules governing trade behaviour, labour standards and intellectual copyright between member states. The repercussions of trade agreements and legislation on the fashion industry are a key, but invisible, factor determining the types, quality, price and availability of high- and low-cost fashion in the marketplace. The Multi-Fibre Arrangement was a temporary trade agreement established under the General Agreement on Tariffs and Trade (GATT) by the WTO in 1974. Approximately thirty countries agreed to establish quotas to limit and combat unfair trade practices, such as flooding markets with cheap imports from countries with low labour costs. The trade agreement has been gradually phased out since 1995, and 1 January 2005 hailed the beginning of a new free market – but not necessarily a fair market. Global competition in manufacturing and costing is intensifying and causing declines in manufacturing in the United Kingdom and Europe, and a worsening balance-of-trade deficit as more goods are imported and fewer exported. The United States has stringent customs and excise regulations, and 'rules of origin' that make it difficult to import fabrics and garments manufactured in the European Union that have a number of origins (e.g., suits made from fabric woven in Turkey, embroidered in Germany, designed in the UK and made into garments in Portugal). There is also the North American Free Trade Area (NAFTA) agreement established between the US, Canada and Mexico which allows preferential terms for garments produced in Mexico, the Caribbean and some South American countries. Tariffs, taxes and duties are used to protect the home market from competition. In countries where it is difficult to achieve competitive pricing there will be a greater emphasis on marketing design, **quick response**, new technologies and ethical business practices as selling points.

The importance of price as a motivator or as a deterrent to buying fashion is indisputable, but many people today are unaware of the proportion of disposable income and time clothing involved in previous eras; no matter which social class someone belonged to, it was necessary to spend time planning or creating a cost-effective wardrobe for the coming season. The rich had a multiplicity of social occasions for which there were protocols of appropriate dress and necessary visits to tailors. The poor would have to spend time making and mending. Women were almost entirely dependent on men economically until the latter half of the twentieth century when they took on significant roles in the workplace. This required a sensible uniformity of dress. Expensive items such as coats and suits would be expected to last a number of years and would be less likely to support strong fashion detailing. Sweaters would be hand-knitted and started months before they were needed. Trimmings and cheap accessories such as scarves were used to update and freshen outfits. Post-war prosperity and the invention of mechanized processes, and cheap fabrics and chemical dyes, saw the first wave of inexpensive, accessible (and even 'disposable') fashions for all ages and economic groups. In comparison to the pro-rata value of clothing a hundred years ago the cost today is a relatively low proportion of the average income, and shopping is seen as a leisure activity. The mean cost of clothing in Europe is lower than it was twenty years ago. Buying something to 'be fashionable' is now a forceful and acceptable motivation in its own right. In the developed world people can afford to buy new clothes very frequently and closer to the time at which they need them.

The language of fashion

A study of fashion history and of the costumes and customs of different countries will reveal that all societies, from the most primitive to the most sophisticated, use clothing and adornments to communicate social and personal information. Just as we attempt to read the facial expressions of those around us, we also read the signals given by their clothing and draw inferences, sometimes mistakenly, about the kind of people they are. This non-verbal communication – the language of fashion – can be learnt like any other language (see opposite).

Throughout history many items and styles of clothing have taken on symbolic meaning, so facilitating the identification of strangers. In his book, *The Fashion System* (1967), the French critic Roland Barthes wrote on the symbolic language of clothes and the way that they inform our socio-political orientation. The study of the signs and symbols that communicate information is called semiotics.

We buy clothes and wear them in combinations that are deliberately or subconsciously contrived to convey either true or false impressions of ourselves to others. Some of the personal characteristics that we wish to reveal or hide include our age, sexual orientation, size, shape, economic or marital status, occupation, religious affiliation, self-esteem, attitudes and importance. In theatre and film, costume designers actively manipulate the symbolic meaning of clothing by loading the characters with items that we recognize as typical of various occupations and attitudes. A wide range of stereotypes has evolved in this way.

It is the job of fashion designers to experiment with identity and appearances through dress. They must offer clothing that allows people the opportunity to project their own fantasies, be it pop star or princess. In recent years designers have also been challenging the traditional messages communicated by clothing. The diversity of ethnic and subcultural styles has led to distortions of the codes: for example, cardigans worn with saris or tweed jackets worn with jeans. Fashion designers have borrowed from the semiotics of clothes and pushed the boundaries by intentionally destroying principles and harmonies of clothing through oversizing, using clashing colours, designing without reference to body contours, creating sexual ambiguity, using juxtapositions of unusual fabrics and deliberately poor or exposed finishes. For the fashion historian, journalist and anthropologist, learning, interpreting and adding to this creative lexicon is of vital interest.

Left Leather, tattoos and chains are stereotypical garb for the rebel or rocker.

Messages traditionally communicated by twentieth-century Western clothing	
Masculinity	Trousers, ties, broad shoulders, rough or heavy fabrics, outdoor clothing
Femininity	Skirts, low necklines, defined waists, delicate fabrics
Sexual maturity	Tight clothing, transparent or shiny fabrics, high heels
Immaturity	Shapeless, loose clothes, dungarees, childish prints or patterns, bright colours, flat shoes
Dominance	Uniforms, uncomfortable fabrics, oversized shoulders, dark colours, leather, metal buttons, large hats and accessories
Submissiveness	Impractical fabrics and frills, pale colours, decorative shoes
Intelligence	Reading glasses, blue or dark stockings, sombre colours, briefcase
Conformity	Dull, chain-store clothing, pressed creases, low-key colours
Rebellion	Extreme clothing and hairstyles, tattoos, piercing, unusual shoes or no shoes at all
Occupation	Uniforms, suits, wearing of tools and trade accessories
Origin	Indicated by town or country clothes or regional dress
Wealth	Gold jewellery and gems, clean or new clothes, perfect fit, identifiable fashion labels, dramatic colour, fur, perfume
Health	Casual or sporty clothing and logos, body-revealing cut, slim figure, trainers (sneakers)
Age	Adherence to past styles

Global context

The economic context of fashion is no longer a local or national issue. Fashion is a global enterprise and an international language that crosses ethnic and class boundaries. International apparel conglomerates have the financial clout to buy raw materials and ship them to be manufactured at the lowest cost and risk. Manufacturers no longer have massive centralized production lines; manufacturing is now spread out over many locations where labour, skills and warehousing costs are cheap and abundant, and regulations less stringent than at home. The fashion conglomerates buy up labels and businesses from across the globe that fit their 'portfolio'. National costumes and customs continue to erode, Western clothing is ubiquitous and there are few untapped markets left. The labels and logos of the large transnational companies are icons of style recognized from London to Lisbon, San Francisco to Singapore. While it was once highly unusual for an Englishman such as Charles Frederick Worth (see Paris, overleaf) to work abroad, we now see French, Spanish and American chains such as Kookai, Zara and Gap in the global high street. It is no longer possible to deduce from a name or label where a design or its maker originated. Some see this rampant globalization and the need for public companies to make profits for their shareholders as the beginning of the demise of the unique qualities that differentiated the product or manufacture of one country from another. Financial and fashion commentator Teri Agins of the *Wall Street Journal* argues in her book, *The End of Fashion*:

> 'When a company goes public, it's the end of fashion. It means the end of too tight pants and fashion for fashion's sake. It means commodity merchandise – polo shirts, jeans, sweaters and blazers – that sell year in year out. Such consistency keeps the earnings up and stock price rising.'

A Charles Frederick Worth gown from 1875.

Governing bodies
FRANCE
La Fédération Française de la Couture du Prêt-à-Porter des Couturiers et des Créateurs de la Mode
Operates three Chambres Syndicales: Chambre Syndicale de la Couture Parisienne; Chambre Syndicale du Prêt-à-Porter, des Couturiers et des Créateurs de la Mode; Chambre Syndicale de la Mode Masculine
UNITED KINGDOM
The British Fashion Council
Runs the London Designer Collections and London Fashion Week in conjunction with industry sponsors
UNITED STATES
The Council of Fashion Designers of America (CFDA)
ITALY
Camera Nazionale della Moda Italiana
Fiera di Milano

Complex and incestuous business relationships give rise to fashion designers working simultaneously on freelance contracts for different labels, at different price points and in a number of locations, by modern means. A fashion designer, buyer and merchandiser must be prepared to travel frequently. Like rock stars and their entourage, designers take their shows and their shops across the world to the most receptive markets. The relative cost of air travel and freight has plummeted, shopping tourism is on the increase. Niche markets are becoming harder to identify, and must be acted upon quickly. It is essential to visit cities, and international trade fairs, to promote lines widely and to check out trends and manufacturing capacity in far-flung places. An understanding of the differences of approach and competition in the top fashion cities is of vital importance, not only to style decisions but also to business. Observation of buying patterns, customs and procedures can help you to prevent costly mistakes, optimize the value of designs and forecast future global trends.

Fashion cities

The Internet may make shopping easier and manufacturing may be moving offshore, but fashion design originates in cities, where eighty to eighty-five per cent of designers work. Each city has its own 'design identity', or characteristics. Not only are cities a source of inspiration by night and day, buyers and salespeople prefer them for convenience and distribution. All suitably sized companies have showrooms in the major cities, and within each city there are one or two specific fashion and garment districts.

Paris

Although the fashion world is constantly growing and dispersing, the French capital, Paris, still retains its traditional dominance. Many designers feel that making it in Paris is the standard to strive for. The reason for this goes back to the nineteenth century when, in 1858, the Englishman Charles Frederick Worth, who is generally considered to be the first couturier, founded a design house in Paris – at that time the cultural and artistic capital of Europe, if not of the world. Because of the popularity of his gowns, which were worn by such illustrious women as Queen Victoria and the Empress Eugénie, Worth's creations fell prey to counterfeiters. To protect his designs he founded the Federation of Parisian Tailors in 1868. The body was responsible for the marketing and manufacturing of fashion and in time grew into the organization now called La Fédération Française de la Couture du Prêt-à-Porter des Couturiers et des Créateurs de la Mode.

There are stringent rules for qualification and acceptance of membership of the Créateurs de la Mode; a business must have an atelier (design studio) or salon (showroom) in Paris, employ at least twenty full-time staff and stage two collection showings of at least seventy-five outfits twice a year, during the spring and autumn.

The traditional Paris garment district is in the Sentier, although design ateliers and studios are now widely dispersed throughout the city. The upmarket, haute couture area is in the rue Faubourg Saint-Honoré and along the avenue Montaigne. The French clothing and textile industry is the second largest market in the European Union with an estimated 3,000 companies and 80,000 employees and a turnover worth €26.6 billion. Italy and Germany sell more clothing than France but the French excel in high quality and luxury products. The lingerie market alone is worth about €2.5 billion. In recent years the French clothing market has seen a dramatic seventeen per cent of market share going to large sportswear retailers such as Decathlon, Go Sport and Intersport.

Couturier Jacques Fath adjusting one of his evening gown creations, worn by his wife, before his Paris show in 1946; a floor polisher works laboriously in the background.

The fabric-manufacturing areas in France are the Midi-Pyrenées for the production of carded wool, and the environs of Lyons which, since the invention of the jacquard loom, has produced some of the most beautiful and expensive silk and *nouveauté* materials in the world. Textile manufacturing is generally in decline, except for new technological fabrics and fibres. The production of clothing in France has declined dramatically in the last ten years, especially men's suits and women's tailored clothing (down by eighty-five per cent), most of which are now produced in Tunisia, Morocco and Indo-China – countries that have traditional and historic links with France. Much higher-end French ready-to-wear and knitwear is made in Italy and China as the manufacturing quality is better than in France. The retail market is dominated by specialist fashion chain stores, and the number of independent boutiques has declined by almost nineteen per cent in twelve years. On the other hand, mail order and e-commerce represent a growing sector at eight per cent of the apparel market. Foreign chain stores such as Zara and H&M account for approximately twelve per cent of retailers in France. The French were slow to market their ready-to-wear and high-street ranges abroad, but have recently sent junior labels such as Morgan and Kookai into foreign markets.

A private showing for couture clients at the House of Balmain, Paris (1953).

French style

French design is characterized by clarity of silhouette but complexity of cut; a fit that is close to the body contours, with a certain roundness. Traditional tailoring methods using inner structure and linings are still preferred. Good detailing in the finish and highly skilled handiwork mean that details like bound buttonholes and scalloped edges are more likely to be seen in French designs. Designers tend to use lighter weight suitings and fabrics that give a crisp, pressed finish. Embroidery, lace and beadwork have long been a feature of haute couture collections.

The government in France has always been very supportive of the needle trades, and French design firms and supporting industries are mutually co-operative and willing to experiment. Television is government-owned and gives French fashion free exposure to help generate home and export sales. The government also offers subsidies to couturiers who use more than ninety per cent French fabrics in their collections. Because it is comparatively easy for designers to achieve their creative ambitions in Paris, the city has become internationally central to the industry. Many British, Japanese and European designers now show their ranges there and have moved their main fashion offices and salons to Paris. In 1989 the French government provided seven million francs to build a salon for showing collections at the Louvre, encompassing four halls and seating for 4,000 people.

Haute couture

Haute couture is the top end of the market and commands the highest prices. It is built on the prestige and success of made-to-measure, hand-stitched, one-off outfits sold to the affluent and socially mobile. Notable couture houses active today are Valentino, Versace, Chanel, Dior, Lacroix, Givenchy, Balmain, Balenciaga, Lanvin and Yves Saint-Laurent.

Originally, couture design was by its very nature a slowly evolving, customer-centred form of fashion. However, after the revolutionary 'New Look' created by Christian Dior in 1947, collections were increasingly made without regard to individuals' wishes, instead following the vision of the designer. Later, during the 1960s, designers such as Pierre Cardin, André Courrèges and Paco Rabanne pioneered the idea of haute couture as experimental, artistic fashion. Because of the very high prices it commanded, this kind of haute couture gradually lost ground to boutique fashion designers such as Mary Quant, and American designers like Rudi Gernreich and Ralph Lauren.

Today, haute couture is no longer appropriate to most lifestyles, and creating it is not as lucrative as it was. Prices are prohibitive and the core clientele is estimated to consist of just 2,000 women, the majority of whom are wealthy, elderly Americans. Many couture houses form part of the stable of powerful conglomerates such as LVMH (Louis Vuitton, Moët Hennessy). Ownership of these luxury labels changes hands for vast sums of money, often without the knowledge of the general public, but in recent years there have been frequent, ugly takeover battles and lawsuits. The collections are used as glamorous advertisements for other products owned by the conglomerates, including cosmetics, perfumes and accessories, **diffusion ranges** and **licenses**. There is a continuing debate about the viability of haute couture: in 1991 Pierre Bergé, chief executive officer of Yves Saint-Laurent, declared that couture would be dead in ten years.

> *'Couture is busy disappearing up its own arse. Modern European high fashion becomes more and more like modern art: inward-looking, elitest and, most damaging of all, laughable.'* Colin McDowell (1994)

Haute couture seems to be flagging, but in recent years large fashion houses have employed young designers with 'attitude' to revamp their image. The development of demi-couture and boutique lines, such as Versus (Versace), Miu Miu (Prada) and YSL Rive Gauche, which provide a better return on investment, has also stimulated their fortunes.

The haute couture collections are shown in Paris after the prêt-à-porter for the same season. Tickets are strictly by invitation only. Because the clothing is made for fewer clients, it does not require the same time frame and delivery seasons that prêt-à-porter or mass manufacturing demands. The clothing is almost always made in-house, at the atelier, partly due to the need for fittings and partly for secrecy.

Prêt-à-porter – ready-to-wear

Prêt-à-porter fashion represents a wide range of clothing made for the wholesale department store and boutique market at different price points, and has become the model organization for fashion trade fairs. Today there are 1,200 exhibitors and approximately 43,000 buyers at Prêt-à-porter Paris® (registered as a trademark to prevent copycat events). The collections are shown in Paris twice yearly, in February and September, at the Porte de Versailles.

Pierre Cardin was the first couturier to show a prêt-à-porter collection in 1959, and Yves Saint-Laurent was the first to open a prêt-à-porter shop, Rive Gauche, in Saint-Germain on the left bank of the Seine – the birth of the independent boutique, this effectively began a revolution in shopping. In the 1980s and 1990s high-end collection designers made an impact with ready-to-wear collections: Thierry Mugler, Claude Montana, Azzedine Alaïa, Sonia Rykiel and Martine Sitbon. Marithé and François Girbaud

The French couturier Yves Saint-Laurent with Betty Catroux (right) and Loulou de la Falaise outside his new ready-to-wear shop in New Bond Street, London in 1969. Saint-Laurent had created a sensation in Paris with the opening of a 'boutique' in an unfashionable district, the Rive Gauche, and brought the phenomenon across the Channel.

pioneered the use of new technology, such as chemical washing and laser-cut finishes in jeans and casual daywear. Jean-Paul Gaultier has been a force in innovation and youthful design for twenty years, and has recently shown that he is equally capable in the realm of couture. Since the 1980s, when an influx of Japanese designers began to show in Paris, there has been a steady infiltration of international labels into the fashion fairs. Young and upcoming French and Paris-based designers such as Jerome L'Huillier, Olivier Theyskens, Gaspard Yurkievich, Lucien Pellat-Finet, Lutz and Jerome Dreyfuss show at the Prêt-à-porter under the umbrella of 'Atmosphere', organized by the Chambre Syndicale. During Paris fashion week (now twelve days), some store buyers and journalists see up to ten shows a day, and are bused from one venue to the next from dawn until midnight. There are dozens of after-show parties to attend and a vigilant press keeps a watch on the pecking order and seating positions of favoured celebrities and buyers. Although there is an official schedule and official venues for fashion shows, designers, especially the avant-garde and up-and-coming ones, often choose to show

off-schedule in unusual locations in order to preserve their 'outsider' image. This frequently throws the timings of the shows into chaos, but adds to the theatricality of the event.

In Paris the standard is very high, and many ranges are diffusion lines of couture houses or designed by top names. However, unlike the haute couture collections, prêt-à-porter has competition from ready-to-wear shows in other fashion cities – London, Milan and New York – at approximately the same times. In addition, lower-priced ranges and accessories are shown in an exhibition hall at the Porte de Versailles. Today many designers work for couture houses and also have their own ready-to-wear labels.

London

The garment-design industry in London is centred north of Oxford Street in Great Portland and Great Titchfield streets. However, it is increasingly dispersed and many younger designers have studios and workshops in the old manufacturing areas of Shoreditch and Hoxton in the East End. The reputation of British textile mills for cotton, woollen and worsted suitings has stood British designers in good stead. Cut-price production costs, and efficiency, in central Europe and the Far East mean the British fabric industry remains under threat. The better-equipped factories are set up for mass manufacturing clothing for chain stores, and are reluctant to produce the smaller quantities of garments that designers need. Unlike in France and Italy, there is no network of craftspeople or small provincial units willing to make them. During the recession of the late 1980s the designer-fashion trade collapsed. After an injection of government funds it is regaining its reputation for exporting well-made clothing on time, and is worth £600 million today.

British style

On the traditional side, there is a highly regarded export clothing market for British styles of knitwear, raincoats and outdoor clothing, such as Jaeger, Aquascutum and Burberry. Liberty prints are world-renowned, and Londoners and international visitors alike still visit London's Savile Row for specially tailored suits.

During the 1980s Princess Diana promoted the top dressmakers and couturiers and brought to prominence names such as Bellville Sassoon, Bruce Oldfield, Catherine Walker and the Emanuels, who made her wedding dress. Jasper Conran, Margaret Howell and Scott Henshall are upholding the classic themes.

Britain also has a reputation for anarchic and eccentric fashion. From Mary Quant and Biba in the 1960s to Vivienne Westwood and Alexander McQueen today, British designers have been particularly successful at leading the youth market and at changing fashion directions. The rest of the world looks to London for ideas. Anarchic young designers made London the 'swinging' fashion capital and swiped the idea of boutiques from the French in the 1960s. In the 1970s street fashions such as Vivienne Westwood's punk, and 'Buffalo Girls', and Body Map's lively designs, created around a vibrant music scene, continued the buzz. John Galliano and Alexander McQueen, Britain's *enfants terribles*, have crossed the Channel and transformed themselves from rebellious youth designers into couture-house masters. They have demonstrated to young British designers how to mature and put their talents to work. Stella McCartney has also made her mark in Paris. Today there is a generation of more conceptual rebels: Hussein Chalayan, Shelley Fox, Jessica Ogden, Tristan Webber and Robert Carey-Williams.

City study visits

If the fashion world is homogenizing thanks to global trading, how do you identify the unique qualities of French, British and American styles? What is different about Belgian or Japanese cutting? Where in the world should you choose to work? While you are at college you are likely to have the opportunity to make cultural and educational visits to at least one of the fashion capitals. Fashion-show weeks are held in rotation by the major cities. There is continuous controversy about who should show first in the season, and ongoing fragmentation of the organizing bodies and groups, venues and schedule of events. The Internet is probably the most reliable source for events and dates which are in constant flux.

The fashion capitals are fascinating and inspiring places, and visits during fashion weeks are especially fruitful. The galleries and stores, well aware of the influential coterie in town, pull out all the stops to mount relevant displays and after-show nightlife is a buzz. If you are on a study visit you need to keep focused on the purpose of the trip, and use the occasion for research and to practise your evaluative skills when in the stores or at shows. Colleges are occasionally able to arrange visits to factories and studios as well as to the collections, exhibitions and events. At times your student ID card will gain you entry to places that exclude the public, sometimes at reduced rates. At other times you may need to masquerade as a professional. A few organizations hold public ticket days at the end of the trading week. There is no guarantee of entry to shows, but with energy, ingenuity and waiting in line you can usually manage to see a few. Younger designers often welcome a receptive audience, and placement and internship schemes mean that you may even find a role helping behind the scenes. Have some simple business cards printed to give to any contacts you may make. Take a sketchbook, a camera, a phrase book, an address or notebook and a good map. You will need some smart, fashionable clothes and flat shoes for all the walking and waiting you will do. Do not take photographs inside shows or stores unless permission is granted. Remember that although the shows and exhibitions may have the glamour and appearance of an entertainment, they are serious professional business events and you are expected to show respect for the business being conducted and behave in an appropriate manner. If you are lucky you may even be asked to the after-show party.

Ready-to-wear designers of international standing include: Nicole Farhi, Rifat Ozbek, Jasper Conran, Betty Jackson and Clements Ribeiro. In menswear Paul Smith is internationally successful with twelve shops in the UK and 200 in Japan. Joe Casely-Hayford, Oswald Boateng and Charlie Allen have all given new life to the classic suit. High-street chain stores such as Whistles, Jigsaw, Oasis and Warehouse lead the pack for excellent quality and design at reasonable prices. The high street market has been dominated for a century by mass retailers Marks and Spencer who, at one time, could claim a quarter of all clothing revenues in the UK. Today, large groups such as Arcadia, who own Top Shop, Burtons Menswear, Dorothy Perkins and Miss Selfridge, are challenging that supremacy.

London Fashion Week, which is organized by the British Fashion Council, runs the fashion-show schedule, exhibitions and British Fashion Awards. In association with major corporate sponsors it also supports less-established designers with shows and competitions, to find and promote new talent. Created in 1983 as a non-profit-making company it seeks to help British designers to develop their businesses. The BFC has close links with the UK's top fashion design colleges through its Colleges Forum, which acts as an interface between industry and colleges.

British designers are much appreciated abroad but often fail to be prophets in their own land. Top creative positions in fashion, advertising, photography, magazines and design are held by British people all over the world, yet in Britain corporate industry tends to dismiss creativity as irrelevant rather than the fuel that drives the sales. In recent years the government has attempted to redress this imbalance but France, Italy and America have much stronger government-supported fashion infrastructures and there is a considerable 'brain drain' of UK-educated designers to European and American fashion houses. There are a number of initiatives and fashion-competition opportunities for start-up businesses – Fashion Fringe is an example – which aim to keep the talent at home.

New York

The apparel industry is the leading industry in the state and city of New York, and the fourth-largest in the United States, with almost $200 billion in sales at the millennium. It is a multi-billion dollar industry, with over 7,000 clothing manufacturing firms – making it the largest employer in the state – and can offer a dazzling variety of products at every price range because of the size of its domestic market and distribution network. However, it is in decline, as it is in western Europe, with work contracted to offshore suppliers. Initially it grew up around the skilled immigrant working-class areas of the Lower East Side of Manhattan in the late nineteenth century. The inventions of the sewing machine and paper pattern soon turned the art of the neighbourhood dressmakers into an industry.

Until World War II, when the United States was effectively isolated from Europe, the fashion industry was in thrall to French fashion. American executives, magazine journalists and illustrators, as well as wealthy, fashionable women, would travel across the Atlantic and stay in Paris for the haute couture shows. Because of the prohibitive costs of shipping and transporting clothes, Americans were allowed to attend shows for a fee – a 'caution' – or buy sample garments and the patterns and rights to reproduce them 'line for line' at home. For this reason, the US has suffered from the perception that its fashion trade lacks originality.

Opposite The trouser suit was popularized by Mary Quant in 1960s London. A demand for cheap and fashionable clothes led to a proliferation of boutiques and independent shops.

American style

During the 1930s, and up until the 1950s, interest in New York fashions derived from Paris originals was strong, and led to a healthy mail-order, paper pattern and magazine market. On the West Coast, Hollywood helped to promote an all-American style and a prevailing, and continuing preference for a certain type of tall, lean beauty and elegance. The movies and awards ceremonies remain an important source of information on fashion trends.

During World War II, the lack of contact with Paris meant the fashion industry needed a new strategy – it came to rely on its own creativity. Some talented European designers, tailors and manufacturers fled to the United States for safety, where they were employed at the higher end of the market in fashion-starved New York and Hollywood. It was in the broader market, and especially in women's workwear, that the greatest innovations were made. The home-grown cotton industry and the emphasis on work and sportswear dovetailed to bring about a casual and honed-down style of dress that proved to be the US's strongest contribution to the garment industry. American machinery, fibre and fabric developers and low-cost mass-production techniques all ensured leadership in the new arena of casualwear and sportswear. This fresh style of fashion was truly indigenous and in tune with the spirit of the times.

When the war ended and international contacts resumed, American women were reluctant to be dictated to by Monsieur Dior in Paris, with his 'New Look' and its full skirts and corseted waists. They were ready for change and American designers such as Claire McCardell and Bonnie Cashin provided an authentic home-grown, easy-to-wear designer response to the new era. In the 1960s the US gained an ideal ambassador for modern American style in Jacqueline Kennedy, wife of President John F Kennedy. She promoted the designs of Mainbocher and Norman Norell whose pioneering spirits have been followed by Halston, Ralph Lauren, Calvin Klein, Perry Ellis, Liz Claiborne and Donna Karan. The menswear market was equally buoyant and the smart casual look, typified by Ralph Lauren's Polo line, was much in demand in Europe.

It could be said that, despite the thriving American market, fashion was seen to be almost entirely Eurocentric until the 1980s. In the realm of eveningwear and special-occasion dressing, the industry lacked the confidence to challenge its European counterparts. Until the new millennium, Paris ignored the threat of American fashion designers such as Oscar de la Renta, Geoffrey Beene and Halston. However, the collections and diffusion lines shown by designers Donna Karan and Calvin Klein have not only been endorsed by the most well-known of celebrities, but have achieved massive sales figures and are the clear choices for urban socialites in the new millennium; and Marc Jacobs and Richard Tyler continue to grow in stature. American designers, such as Tom Ford and Michael Kors, have been courted by European couture and ready-to-wear companies, while Europeans Helmut Lang, Max Azria and Catharine Malandrino have opened stores in the United States and are finding receptive markets. American sportswear and denim continue to have worldwide appeal, and stores such as Gap, Esprit and Tommy Hilfiger successfully penetrated the European casualwear and streetwear high-street cartel in the 1990s. Brands like Nike and Timberland have become essential footwear for the urban warrior. Less well known in Europe are the designers who have orientated themselves towards a youthful, trendy or rock-and-roll style, such as Patricia Field, Norma Kamali, Betsy Johnson, Anna Sui, Zac Posen and Jeremy Scott.

Avant-garde American labels are beginning to appear on the runways: Imitation of Christ, AsFour and Carlos Miele. Malls and shopping centres are dominated by Target, the Limited, J. Crew, Gap and its spin-offs – Old Navy and Banana Republic. Wal-Mart, TJMaxx and Daffy's are the leaders in value and discount stores.

The fashion industry in New York is still very much centred around one small area. Manufacturers occupy the showrooms and offices on Broadway and Seventh Avenue to Ninth Avenues between 27th and 42nd Streets. Seventh Avenue is even nicknamed 'Fashion Avenue'. Many of the most prestigious names and companies can be found in a single building – 550 Seventh Avenue – and share the same lift. One designer told me she had occupied the same office on three different occasions under the auspices of different companies. Such close proximity favours camaraderie and gossip. Today, the high price of real estate means much less mass manufacturing, and more specialized small orders, are done in New York. There are also large production areas in Los Angeles, Chicago and the southern and south-central states where space and costs are at less of a premium. The United States jobs out the bulk of clothes production to Mexico, South America, the Caribbean, Korea, Taiwan, India, Indonesia and China.

The governing body for the New York collections is the Council of Fashion Designers of America (CFDA), a non-profit trade association of over 250 high-profile fashion and accessory designers. It was founded in 1962 by a panel of fashion luminaries that included Bill Blass, Norman Norell, Rudi Gernreich and Arnold Scaasi. Membership is by invitation only and is limited to noteworthy fashion companies with a minimum of three years' trading from a primary business base in the US. The CFDA runs the prestigious annual CFDA fashion gala awards for womenswear, menswear, accessories, publishing, retailing, photography and entertainment, and the Perry Ellis award for emerging talents. It supports educational initiatives and the transitional stages between college and start-up businesses by operating the CFDA/*Vogue* fashion fund for new business development, scholarships and professional development programmes of seminars.

New York holds five 'market weeks' for different sectors of the market, rather than two fashion weeks. The main trade shows are: the International Boutique Show, Premier Collections, Styleworks, Intermezzo and Seventh on Sixth. For menswear there are: the Exclusive, Eurostyle and Mode Coast. Although designers like to stage fashion shows, and are fond of an excuse for a celebrity event, the real business of sales is done weeks beforehand in the showrooms on Seventh Avenue or in 'trunk shows'. At the high end of fashion, the latter method of marketing, using a travelling salesperson with sample garments, is almost unique to the American market.

Milan

Italy was devastated (more so than France) by World War II and its after-effects, and the country took a relatively long time, even with financial aid from the United States, to recover. However, it has since grown to a position of tremendous strength in the fashion industry through excellent craftsmanship. Fashion is Italy's second-largest industry after food products, and the country is the largest exporter of textiles and clothing in the world. It dominates in the areas of footwear, leather and knitwear, and is especially good at producing men's ready-to-wear (*moda pronta*) suits. Although manufacturing is dispersed throughout Italy, Milan is its nerve centre, close to the silk-printing industry in the lakeside town of Como and the wool processors of Piedmont. The Italian fabric industry is an exciting and innovative business receptive to the demands of designers worldwide. Knitwear is produced around Florence, Prato and Bologna. Milan is also one of the nerve centres for fashion-magazine publishing, and many modelling agencies have their headquarters there. Italians are prepared to spend a high proportion of their disposable income on clothing, and they expect quality. Italy has fewer mid-range clothing lines than most other countries.

Italian style

Italian fashion is known for having a greater subtlety of colouring and texture than French fashion, and for using softer and heavier wools. Eveningwear designers love jersey draping and fabrics that have a supple handle. The designer Giorgio Armani has been responsible for the development of the unstructured suit, both for men and women, which provides comfort as well as relaxed elegance. The look is particularly popular with Americans, and the lower-priced Armani diffusion lines also sell well in the US. Luxury Italian design companies of note include: Armani, Versace, Byblos, Gianfranco Ferre, Fendi, Dolce & Gabbana and Missoni. Labels with a historical tradition and a record of high quality such as Pucci, Gucci, Prada and Salvatore Ferragamo have been rejuvenated recently and are now leading the world in innovative accessories and fashion. Designer sportswear such as Stone Island, Blumarine, Sisley, Emporio Armani and MaxMara offers exceptional quality and classics are always updated with new trimmings and details. High street companies such as Benetton provide colour and a wide choice at low cost.

The Milan fashion fair, the 'Milanovedemoda', is held at the enormous Fiera di Milano fairground on the outskirts of the city. The Camera Nationale della Moda, Italian fashion's governing body, is building an alternative fashion centre in the Garibaldi area called Città della Moda e del Design – Fashion City – in which they are investing in excess of €400 million. It will house an exhibition and show centre, a fashion museum to archive the designers who have contributed since the 1950s to the 'Made in Italy' revolution, and a university where fashion will be taught. Fashion is a serious business in Milan; there are fewer avant-garde or street-style labels than in the other fashion capitals, but Italians are highly appreciative of British and Japanese creativity and employ large stables of young designers in their workshops.

Tokyo

In the 1980s Japanese fashion designers appeared suddenly on the international catwalks. Their effect was revolutionary. They espoused an entirely different aesthetic from that commonly seen. It was demanding, uncompromising and avant-garde: loose, long and sculptural shapes that bore little relation to the body, dark colours, raw edges, sometimes all-black collections, rips and holes that were reminiscent of the distressed punk style and unusual but highly technical and innovative fabrics. Some commentators saw the creations of Issey Miyake, Rei Kawakubo of Comme des Garçons and Yohji Yamamoto as an ugly, 'bag-lady' look. Some adored them as wearable art and welcomed the intellectual and conceptual aura that wearing them conveyed. While the look has failed to sell well to the American market, it has a loyal and enduring following and has been of enormous influence to a generation of design followers, particularly the Belgian school. Japanese design liberated fashion from the Western style of cutting and the need to finish everything 'just so'. Over time the designers, while not quite compromising their visionary approach, have met the European design markets halfway with collections in softer colours and **fabrications** or diffusion ranges, such as Miyake's 'Pleats Please' label, which are more flattering to the body. The highly regarded Japanese designers now choose to show in Paris at the prêt-à-porter collections. They maintain large workforces, showrooms and shops in the city (the fashion pack is reluctant to fly as far as Tokyo and back every season). However, the Japanese have put Tokyo on the map as the fifth capital city for fashion. The fashion market in Japan has been under financial pressure due to the recent instability of the yen. Rather than import Western fashions, many large Japanese corporations continue to finance avant-garde and developing fashion and lifestyle lines, and negotiate worldwide licensing agreements for branded products.

Other fashion cities

A large number of European and American cities hold fashion weeks but, like Tokyo, they are not part of the usual core schedule for the press and department-store buyers. In the last decade Belgian designers such as Ann Demeulemeester, Martin Margiela, Dries Van Noten, Walter Van Beirendonck and Dirk Bikkembergs have consistently produced forward-looking and uncompromisingly Modernist fashion. First showing in London, where they felt they would have a sympathetic audience, and later, in Paris, where they would capture a larger international one, the Belgians are reminiscent of Japanese designers in their alliance to a stark, conceptual and post-Modern approach to clothing, with a preference for black. They have put Antwerp on the fashion map and inspired a new generation of Belgian designers including Josephus Thimister, Olivier Theyskens, Bernard Wilhelm, Veronique Branquino and Lieve Van Gorp.

Spain, too, has spawned internationally respected fashion houses, mainly in Barcelona. Here, like the architecture of Gaudí that dominates the city, the style is playful and serious, simultaneously colourful and organic in line. Indeed, the biannual Barcelona Fashion Fair is called 'Gaudí Mujer'. Labels of note include: Tony Miro, Adolfo Dominguez, Loewe, Josep Font, Victorio & Lucchino and the young fun-fashion line of Custo Barcelona.

In Germany, Düsseldorf has been dubbed 'the fashion capital of Germany'. It is host to a variety of important textile trade events and home to international fashion houses Hugo Boss, Jil Sander and Helmut Lang.

Long-established manufacturing centres such as Hong Kong and Taiwan in the Far East have added design to their repertoires and hold their own fashion weeks, dominating the markets of the Pacific Rim. Following the Asian stock market crisis of 1998, the Chinese economy is recovering and undergoing exceptional growth; Western brands are in demand. Australia, which has always suffered from the inversion of the seasons down under, is now independent enough to stage its own fashion week, strongly supported by its indigenous wool industry. When it comes to the drawing up of a fashion map, there are still areas of Africa, South America and eastern Europe that are largely uncharted. The fashion world has become a Tower of Babel. The days of homage to Paris are numbered.

Examples of global traders

Pierre Cardin has licences for manufacturing in over ninety countries.

Benetton has over 7,000 shops in over 100 countries, but closed hundreds of stores in the US after failing to make a profit, due to its 'repugnant advertising campaigns'.

The Swedish retailer, Hennes & Mauritz opened in New York in autumn 2000 and sold out within hours. It plans to open 100 more shops before 2005.

British designer John Galliano heads up the Paris fashion house of Dior. Alexander McQueen designed for Romeo Gigli (Italy) and Koji Tatsuno (Japan), followed by the French perfume house of Givenchy before the Gucci group supported his own-name label. Stella McCartney's label, Yves Saint-Laurent, Gucci (Italy) and Céline designed by Michael Kors (USA) are all owned by the French conglomerate LVMH (Louis Vuitton Moët Hennessy).

Italian manufacturers Gruppo GFT, part owned by Gruppo Tessile Miroglio SpA, have production plants in Europe, North Africa and Egypt, and make clothes for Ralph Lauren, Calvin Klein and Dior among others.

The US superstore giant Wal-Mart has penetrated the European market and owns Asda in the UK.

Japanese company Takihyo (which owns Anne Klein) financed Donna Karan to start her label. The British label Aquascutum is owned by the Japanese company Renown. Japanese knitwear company Onward Kashiyama makes Luciano Soprani (Italy), Calvin Klein (USA), Jean-Paul Gaultier (France) and Paul Smith (UK) garments in Japan.

Unilever, a Dutch and British conglomerate, owns Calvin Klein, Karl Lagerfeld and Chloé perfumes.

The American hairstyling giant Vidal Sassoon, who was catapulted to stardom with his haircut for Mary Quant in the 1960s, sponsored London Fashion Week for a decade.

The fashion calendar

Month	Events	Designer's schedule
January	Milan – menswear collections for autumn/winter Paris – women's collections for spring/summer, menswear collections for autumn/winter	Finish production of spring/summer to deliver to stores end of January. Make sealing samples for autumn/winter; negotiate production
February	New York – menswear collections for autumn/winter Madrid – men's and women's autumn/winter collections Florence – Pitti Filati Yarn Show for knitwear Paris – Première Vision Fabric Show Frankfurt – Interstoff Fabric Show	Choose fabrics for spring/summer range and begin designing shapes. Preview autumn/winter to advance customers – refine collection
March	Milan – womenswear designer collections and *moda pronta* exhibition for autumn/winter London – womenswear designer collections and ready-to-wear exhibition for autumn/winter Paris – womenswear designer collections and prêt-à-porter exhibition for autumn/winter New York – womenswear market week for Fall 1 delivery	Complete delivery of last spring/summer orders and take new autumn/winter orders – much liaison with buyers, press and use of research, sales feedback, etc.
April		Make first samples for spring/summer range
May	Midseason shows – for fast delivery to middle market New York – womenswear market week for Fall 2 delivery	Make samples for spring/summer range Production of autumn/winter range
June	London – Graduate Fashion Week; catwalk shows of student work; employers take on new staff	Make samples for spring/summer range Production of autumn/winter range
July	Milan – menswear collections for spring/summer Paris – women's couture collections for autumn/winter Paris – menswear collections for spring/summer Florence – Pitti Filati Yarn Show for knitwear	Make sealing samples for spring/summer range Production of autumn/winter range
August	New York – menswear collections for spring/summer Europe – mills closed for month	Production of autumn/winter range Negotiate production of spring/summer range
September	Milan – womenswear collections for spring/summer Madrid – men's and women's spring/summer collections Paris – Première Vision Fabric Show, womenswear collections for spring/summer	Deliver autumn/winter range to stores Choose fabrics for following autumn/winter – begin designing. Preview spring/summer to advance customers – refine range
October	London – womenswear collections for spring/summer New York – womenswear market for spring/summer Midseason shows – for fast delivery to middle market	Complete delivery of autumn/winter orders and take new spring/summer orders – much liaison with buyers, press and use of research time Production of spring/summer range
November		Deliver holiday and cocktail styles to stores. Design for autumn/winter. Production of spring/summer range
December	Paris – Expofil Exhibition, new colour trends and yarn	Deliver cruise and resort styles to stores. Make samples for autumn/winter. Production of spring/summer range

Time and timing

There is another context that is one of the most powerful forces at work in fashion: time. For the designer of fashion, the key difference between his or her product and that of the designer of almost any other product is shelf life. Fashion has built-in obsolescence. We all require clothing suitable for different seasons, specific events and even different times of day. Even though much of the previous formality demanded for work and special events is breaking down, most of us expect to go to weddings in June, take family holidays in August and attend parties in December. Moreover, clothing is often fragile and subject to wear and tear. It needs washing, changing or replacing. Replacement is both a practical and a social requirement. Clothes can only be laundered and patched up so many times; how acceptable our worn clothing is will depend on our age and status. Commerce has capitalized on clothing's obsolescence, and there is an unwritten expectation that we renew our wardrobes, at least partially, in spring and autumn.

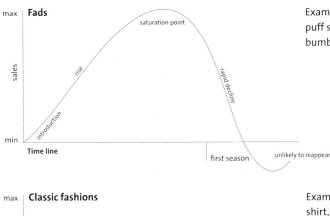

Examples of fads: gypsy tops, hot pants, bondage pants, wind pants, puff skirts, mens' polo-neck shirts, knitted ties, clogs, body piercings, bumbags, fishing hats, skirts worn over trousers, fluorescent colours

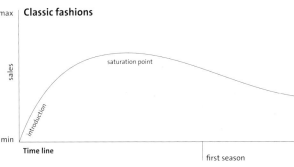

Examples of classics: blue blazer, safari jacket, trench coat, Aertex polo shirt, loafers, Mary Janes, cashmere twinsets, two-pleat pants, Argyll socks, T-shirts and sweatshirts, Levi's 501s. Black, navy, camel and cream

Examples of recurrent fashions and style features: the trouser cuff, broad/narrow shoulders, belted waists, batwing sleeves, bows and frills, platform soles, cowboy boots, the beret, striped knitwear, capes, breeches, animal prints, florals, bias-cutting. Pink, turquoise and green

In order to supply new clothing when there was a demand, and to make book-keeping and stock records efficient, shops traditionally budgeted for two seasons a year: spring/summer and autumn/winter. Each of these was followed by a sale period to clear stock quickly and recoup the financial outlay to offset against the next round of payments to suppliers. Designers at the upper end of the market would deliver new collections to the stores and boutiques in January and August. There was often a further delivery of eveningwear for the winter party season in November. The fashion industry has fixed its calendar around this model (see page 48).

However, in an increasingly complex world, it can no longer be said that there is truly a 'fashion year'. While most high-fashion businesses observe the traditional calendar, chain stores, which sell individual or co-ordinated items and not collections, operate with a tighter turnaround of new items of stock every six to eight weeks, from their factories or **private-label** suppliers. Also, in practice, the seasons overlap, while some styles, such as winter coats and swimming costumes, are repeated annually. Many companies, for example Armani and Gap, repeat popular styles year after year. In fact, every fashion company will have its own **fashion cycle** – the calendar by which it plans its ranges, selling, production and delivery set against the demands of the seasons and the waxing and waning of the popularity of designs. This fashion cycle is a complex interlocking of the wheels of the textile and fashion trades (described in Chapters II and IV).

The show schedule

Timing and distribution are crucial to successful sales of a line. The four main centres for fashion design – Paris, London, Milan and New York – all vie with each other for buyers and jostle for time slots on the international fashion-show schedule.

The twice-yearly ready-to-wear fashion-show schedule for buyers has traditionally passed from London to Milan, Paris and then New York over a period of four weeks. For the spring/summer collections the schedule usually starts in the second week of September, after the shops have received delivery of the autumn/winter lines that were shown the previous March. To complicate matters further, the menswear fashion calendar usually works approximately eight weeks ahead of this plan. Nowadays, however, many designers such as Paul Smith, Yohji Yamamoto and Helmut Lang are producing both menswear and womenswear lines and therefore find it easier to harmonize their shows. Moreover, since the schedule is based on the premise that trends start in Europe, American fashion houses and buyers are increasingly challenging the status quo.

The pressure for time and space on the runway shows during the fashion weeks is immense. Whoever can show first can book their production first, and so gain an advantage by delivering early to the stores. To produce two or more collections a year to meet the show deadlines, the fashion designer has to work fast. Designs must be significantly different from those of the previous season in colour and fabrication, yet must maintain some kind of continuity of **handwriting**. New ideas and trends need to be introduced to entice the consumer and excite the press.

In addition, the runway show itself is increasingly becoming an entertainment to which the public has access. London Fashion Week, for example, has extended its schedule in order to feature gala performances of 'highlights', for which members of the public are able to buy tickets.

'By the time the designers' merchandise has hit their boutiques, the high street will have been there, seen it, done it.' CMT manufacturer Tim Williams

Cultural context

For the designer, knowing what to design and how to present it within the time cycle is not magic or pure intuition, but a matter of good research, planning, experimentation, inspiration and the ability to read cultural trends.

How current fashions evolve

Today, constant advances in communication technology allow ideas and images to race around the globe in the blink of an eye. It is often difficult to tell where a style originated because a silhouette or cut can have a number of variations, created concurrently in different locations. There are many diverse channels for fashion information and influences. Magazines and fashion television are mass disseminators of ideas and looks, but there are some more subtle, yet powerful, influences: for example, clothes worn by popular television actors and the 'viral' buzz created by word-of-mouth and word-of-mouse (Internet) chat with friends and colleagues. Styles associated with bands and celebrities can become part of the culture of groups who are entirely unconnected with the originators. In the new century, fashion has less to do with emulating what the rich are wearing (trickle down theory) or original catwalk styles and copies than it had in the last century. Dynamic cultural shifts are more likely to create consumer needs and desires. The emancipation and earning power of women and the social behaviour of teenagers donning 'street cred' styles such as hip hop, have been key forces for change (bubble up theory). There is an increase in market diversity and the number of style 'tribes' and socio-economic categories, which means that a greater number of styles can be acceptable at the same time and worn by the individual on different occasions. The average individual is more creative in their dress.

Greater fragmentation and an international mix make it harder to predict or spot winning formulae or groupings. Trend analysts like to give names to these categories (Ladettes, DINKYs, Silver Surfers, Tweens, etc.). The way someone lives tends to create their 'look'. People take up trends at different rates according to their lifestyle groupings and their individual personalities; for example, they are labelled as early adopters, sneezers (those who help spread the fashions), laggards, etc. In his book, *The Tipping Point*, Malcolm Gladwell describes how and why bizarre trends catch on and reach the mainstream through social contact.

The traditional methods of analysing and preparing for the next season's fashion are no longer so effective, and many commentators have complained that too much attention paid to the pronouncements of forecasting services has the effect of creating a bland and uniform market. It is unclear as to whether the public continues to be amazed and shocked by the new and extreme fashions that appear on the catwalk. A number of designers feel that such displays are expected of them and are afraid of disappointing their audiences. It is often said that these styles will eventually find their way to the high street or shopping mall in watered-down form. The truth is that only a very few do. Most are daring design experiments, intended to catch the attention of the press, challenge the status quo and make wonderful images. Even the most celebrated designers modify and rationalize the key lines, colours and message of their collections into more accessible styles that sell through their showrooms. A few extremists have a

Trickle down effect

Exclusive high culture; movie and pop stars

Those who associate with them, early adopters

Magazine and newspaper readers. Independent shops – first copies

Middle market – goods available in the high street

General public and low culture – goods widely available

Mass dissemination

Expensive versions appear in exclusive shops

Fashionistas demand special versions

Magazines, newspapers and TV notice the trend

Middle market gives the trend a name

Street fashion and low-culture groups

Bubble up effect

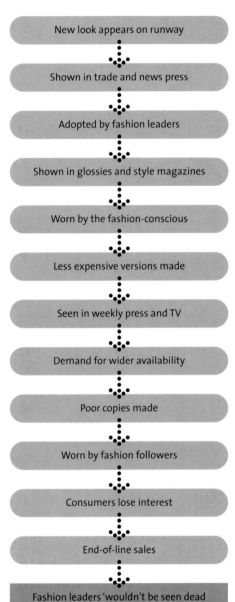

From acceptance to obsolescence

New look appears on runway

Shown in trade and news press

Adopted by fashion leaders

Shown in glossies and style magazines

Worn by the fashion-conscious

Less expensive versions made

Seen in weekly press and TV

Demand for wider availability

Poor copies made

Worn by fashion followers

Consumers lose interest

End-of-line sales

Fashion leaders 'wouldn't be seen dead in it' – move on to the next new look

small band of devoted followers and collectors. The fashion press and forecasters interpret and sift through the ideas, spreading them ever more thinly – a few stick. Ultimately the consumer makes the decision as to what is right for the times.

Fashion forecasting

Fashion forecasters are market-research specialists and analysts who offer financial services and illustrated reports to fashion manufacturers for a fee. Predictions are built up through exhaustive statistical surveys to gauge the relative popularity of fabrics, colours, details and features. Some prediction companies employ trend-chasers or 'cool-hunters', individuals who are especially good at discerning trends in their early stages and predicting products that will fit into them. Forecasting companies also put together style books and specifications of prevailing and emerging styles, with predictions and suggestions for the next season. The largest trend-forecasting companies employ more fashion designers than most clothing companies do.

Media

Fashion journalists and the celebrity-mad news media – including magazines, television and the Internet – all report on major fashion events and designer shows. At one time these were comparatively private, invitation-only affairs. Information leaked out through the filter of the few invited upmarket journalists, and sometimes reached the outside world months later. Nowadays fashion shows are circuses, principally staged to generate interest and catch the interest of the media.

The press

The editors of fashion magazines, such as Anna Wintour, Franca Sozzani and Doris Wiedemann at US, Italian and German *Vogue*, and fashion journalists like Suzy Menkes at the *International Herald Tribune,* have tremendous power and are courted enthusiastically by designers and model agencies. They advise us on how to wear the new styles and frequently show examples of mainstream equivalents. Accessories, beauty, hair and make-up are all adjusted to complete the season's look.

The public usually become aware of the new trends and styles in fashion immediately before the chief selling seasons. The spring (February/March) and autumn (August/September) issues of monthly magazines carry editorials, and often produce supplements featuring the international collections that were shown three months earlier at the Paris, Milan, London and New York shows.

Fashion designers regularly buy the magazines that target the market sectors they are interested in. If their public relations (PR) agent has been successful in placing their garments in features, they will have press cards made and sent to their stockists to encourage further sales. They will also look for lists of the stockists of their competitors' products so that they can make overtures to them the following season.

Trade publications

For designers, trade magazines are more important than the 'glossies'. Although it is important to check who and what is being covered, much of what appears in the general press is already out of date. Trade magazines cover all industry events and fashion shows. In the United States the daily newspaper for the fashion industry, *Women's Wear Daily,* reports in depth on a particular segment of the market each weekday. As well as general news, it also has statistical breakdowns and lists of suppliers and manufacturers, and a classified jobs section.

In the United Kingdom *Drapers Record* fulfils a similar task. Quarterly magazines such as *International Textiles* feature upcoming fabric stories. *Collezione, ModaIn, Fashiontrend, Textile View, Viewpoint* and *View Colour* are beautifully produced colour magazines that are full of reports, fashion forecasting and fabric developments. Some or all of these publications may be in libraries.

The Internet

There are a growing number of fashion-industry resources that are not accessible to the public but are available through colleges that license their limited use by students. The following Internet resources are also useful: live and archived news; virtual collections of costume museums around the world; fashion e-zines; fashion-oriented bulletin boards and chatrooms (good for contacts and job hunting); e-commerce and e-tail sites; promotional sites, which may include information on a company's history, showcase past or current collections, or web-stream its fashion shows. For fashion design or marketing students, using the Internet is a highly time- and cost-effective way of researching, finding fabrics, trimmings and manufacturing expertise. Once a likely supplier has been found, it is usually possible to e-mail the company and place an order.

Further reading and additional resources
History and culture
Caroline Evans. *Fashion at the Edge*, New Haven: Yale University Press, 2003
JC Flügel. *The Psychology of Clothes*, Guilford: International Universities Press, 1966
James Laver. *Modesty in Dress*, Boston: Houghton Mifflin, 1969
Alison Lurie. *The Language of Clothes*, London: Hamlyn, 1983
Malcolm Gladwell. *The Tipping Point*, New York: Little, Brown, 2001
Dick Hebdige. *Subculture: The Meaning of Style*, London: Methuen, 1973
Anne Hollander. *Sex and Suits: The Evolution of Modern Dress*, New York: Kodansha, 1995
Colin McDowell. *Dressed to Kill: Sex, Power and Clothes*, London: Hutchinson, 1992
Angela McRobbie. *Zootsuits & Secondhand Dresses:*
   An Anthology of Music and Fashion, Basingstoke: Macmillan, 1989
Ted Polhemus and Lynn Procter. *Fashion and Anti-Fashion:*
   An Anthropology of Clothing and Adornment, London: Thames & Hudson, 1978
Ted Polhemus. *Streetstyle: From Sidewalk to Catwalk*, London: Thames & Hudson, 1994
Ted Polhemus. *Style Surfing: What To Wear In the 3rd Millennium*, London: Thames & Hudson, 1996
Peter York. *Style Wars*, London: Sidgwick & Jackson, 1980

Fashion industry
Teri Agins. *The End of Fashion*, New York: William Morrow, 1999
EL Brannon. *Fashion Forecasting*, New York: Fairchild, 2002
Gerald Celente. *Trend Tracking*, New York: Warner Books, 1991
Nicholas Coleridge. *The Fashion Conspiracy*, London: Heinemann, 1988
Catherine McDermott. *Made in Britain: Tradition and Style in Contemporary British Fashion*,
   London: Mitchell Beazley, 2002
Colin McDowell. *The Designer Scam*, London: Random House, 1994
Angela McRobbie. *British Fashion Design: Rag Trade or Image Industry?*, London: Routledge, 1998
Faith Popcorn. *Clicking*, London: HarperCollins, 1996
Hugh Sebag-Montefiore. *Kings on the Catwalk*, London: Chapmans, 1992

Contemporary Fashion www.contemporaryfashion.net
Archive curated by the EU and top fashion college collaboration

History in the Making www.historyinthemaking.org
Men's historical costume

Metropolitan Museum of Art www.metmuseum.org/Works_of_Art/department.asp?dep=8
Metropolitan Museum New York costume collection

Industry resources
Womens Wear Daily magazine www.wwd.com
Drapers Record www.drapersonline.com
Dress for Success www.dressforsuccess.nl

From manufacture to market II

Historical background

The mass production of clothing was made possible by the invention of the sewing machine in 1829. Menswear and military uniforms were among the first pieces of clothing to be produced on sewing machines. In 1850 Levi Strauss started making denim workman's trousers for American prospectors. Material was cut and made up into individual bundles and sent out to the homes of machinists to be made up. Later, to save time and costs of delivery and collection, and to ensure the continuity of quality, machinists who were willing to work outside the home were brought together in factories.

However, it was with the introduction of the foot-treadle machine in 1859 by the American inventor Isaac Singer that the sewing machine began to play a serious role both in the home and the workplace. The Industrial Revolution in Britain and Europe had developed working practices for speed and efficiency, especially in fabric production and ceramics. Both industries employed large female workforces. Factory-floor managers soon found that if a worker was shown how to do just one or two parts of a garment it could be made very speedily, as the piece was passed down the line for the next stage of the process. This became known as 'piecework' or 'section work', and is still the most common system of production today.

Electric sewing machines appeared on the market in 1921. This greatly increased the output of women's clothing and enabled mainstream shops to stock the same lines all over the country. Uniformity and perfection of finish was such a novelty that it rendered the term 'home-made' derogatory for the first time. In the United States, the largest proportion of mass-produced clothing was sold through catalogues and mail order.

During World War II, trade was disrupted in Europe and all possible manufacturing facilities were turned over to war-related production. The larger factories were subsidized and organized by governments for streamlined productivity. After the war this left them in a stronger position to continue to produce in high volume. Many smaller factories floundered or died. The United Kingdom has been left a legacy of factories built to handle high-volume, medium-quality clothing rather than small runs. Conversely, in Italy and France, which were more heavily damaged by war, grants from the United States and the Common Market encouraged the growth of family businesses and other small units, which flourished to become a network of high-quality producers.

Manufacture today

In recent years the most dramatic changes in manufacturing have been in pattern-cutting, grading and tracking distribution and sales through computer-operated systems. For example, at the lower end of the market new technology allows the cutting, fusing and stitching of a standard-sized suit in approximately ninety minutes. (By contrast, a bespoke suit, with up to 200 hand-finishing operations, may take up to three days to complete.) Suits can also be made to individual measurements and laser-cut, using computer-aided design (CAD) technology. Some CAD machinery will create hydraulic 'cookie-cutter' dies for garments such as jeans, which will be made in thousands. Similarly, recent innovations in computer-aided 'integral knitting' by Japanese engineers have led to the manufacture of entire knitted garments, complete with collars and pockets, within forty-five minutes. Stretch fibre and fabric development has also led to the shape-moulding and engineering of underwear that is lightweight yet strong,

Top and above The industrial-sample machinist has a broad knowledge of garment-making techniques, unlike the pieceworker who makes the same item many times over.

Opposite The lock-stitch sewing machine quickly became the mainstay of production lines in the fashion industry.

Right Knitting has evolved from the use of two needles to complex computer-driven machinery. A knitwear designer will learn to use both.

Far right All the components for a docket are gathered and delivered with the fabric and pattern bundle.

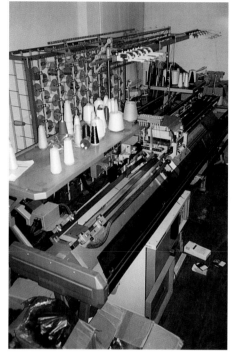

Opposite page, from top
A machine reads the pattern shape and size so that it can be made into a laser-cutting marker.

Trimmings such as zips, tapes and buttons are bought in large quantities.

A stock of regular fabrics can quickly be made into popular styles. Fabric is mounted on spreading machines so that many layers can be cut at once.

A pattern-cutter tests the bias lay of a pattern. There is much more waste fabric than if the pieces were laid parallel to the selvedge.

giving different types of localized support but requiring much less stitching and skill to assemble. The fully automated assembly line for fashion exists, particularly in hosiery and sports-clothing factories. On the whole, however, it is difficult for robots to handle flexible fabrics and they make mistakes when unsupervised.

The speeding up of many small processes has allowed the industry to respond rapidly to market demands; this is known as Just In Time (**JIT**) manufacturing. In the 1990s many of the larger American suppliers worked with store groups to set up computerized electronic point-of-sale (**EPOS**) technology. Using the universal product code (**UPC**) – a bar-coding system that identifies style, size and colour – they were able to track their sales and replace or move goods around speedily and much more efficiently. Better data also results in better financial planning for the following round of purchasing.

A consequence of this is that stores are now less willing to tie up their funds in large stocks, and prefer manufacturers who offer them goods quickly or on less risky 'sale or return' and concession terms. The period between order and delivery to the stores is approximately ten weeks in the middle market. This can be cut considerably, provided there is fabric in stock, and if the factory delivers in drops or sized packages rather than waiting for the whole order to be made up.

Merchandise segmentation

Fashion merchandising has traditionally been broken down into sectors to facilitate manufacturing, design and price targeting. The industry is segmented broadly into three distinct merchandise divisions: womenswear, menswear and childrenswear. However, these sectors are showing signs of fragmentation due to technological developments in manufacturing and cultural shifts which must be taken into account when identifying target markets. Designer fashion represents approximately thirty per cent of clothing companies, but less than ten per cent of overall sales.

Womenswear

Womenswear is the largest segment, taking close to fifty-seven per cent of the market share, and seventy-five per cent of designer companies focus on this sector. A quarter of all wholesale revenues are attributable to a few companies. There is therefore tremendous competition in the womenswear market, and the job turnover for designers and marketing people is higher than in other sectors. Fashions change faster in womenswear than in the other two sectors and the **fashion cycle** puts more pressure on quick response and JIT manufacturing in this segment.

Menswear

The menswear market is worth approximately twenty-four per cent of the market and is expanding. It is undergoing some of the most dynamic changes for a century, making it an exciting sector to work in. In the last century, tailored suits represented half of men's clothing purchases. Now, although men individually are spending proportionately less on clothing and more on gadgets, sports and holidays, more of them are buying fashion more frequently and their preference is for comfortable casual clothing. European designer menswear is more adventurous in styling than that of the United States, but American designers often lead in casual and sports styles, and were responsible for blurring the boundaries between business and casual apparel. Menswear is characterized by more slowly changing silhouettes and fabric choices, but close attention to detail and marketing through logo and brand display.

Childrenswear

Childrenswear is the smallest segment and is delineated by age and size ranges, priorities differ according to the requirements of the age sector. The childrenswear market is increasingly moving towards casualwear, and the requirement for formal party clothes and school uniforms is diminishing. Parents have the highest expectations for safety, durability and versatility in this sector. Children are becoming fashion- and brand-conscious at ever younger ages. Research has shown that four-year-olds are aware of brands such as Nike, Evisu and Tommy Hilfiger. Fashion retailers are entering the market segment. In the United States, Gap has extended its range with BabyGap and GapKids. The strength of peer-group pressure in motivating purchases is much exploited by marketing, which is directed both at parents and at children – who are informed, demanding and value-conscious shoppers. In the UK, the childrenswear and teen market has not developed as rapidly as that in the US and is not as fashion forward or able to command prices as high as those found in the French and Italian markets.

Types of producer

Whatever the market sector or category of clothing, it is essential that the designer and pattern-cutter work together within the framework of the capabilities of the manufacturing available to them. They must be aware of the best that manufacturers or producers can do within the limits of their technological and human resources. There is nothing more frustrating for a designer than discovering too late that a good design cannot be reproduced at the quality or price required.

> 'What's so good about perfection anyway? I don't like it myself. I want to see something a little bit different. I don't want my things to be the same as anyone else's ...' Designer Shelley Fox

From left to right
A multiple lay is spread mechanically and cut with a computerized laser-cutter.

Patterns are often coded, using different-coloured cards for sizes or collections.

Garments are pressed before being prepared for dispatch.

Garments ready for dispatch. Different styles and sizes will be 'pulled' to fill an order.

The pattern lay plan, or marker, is a template for the cutter to follow. In order to keep the profit margin of a garment it must use the least possible amount of fabric.

The fashion industry consists of three main types of producers: manufacturers, wholesalers and contractors.

Manufacturers

Sometimes known as *vertical producers*, manufacturers handle all operations such as buying the fabric, designing or buying in designs, making the garments and selling and delivering the finished garments. The advantage of this method is good quality control and brand exclusivity, but it often creates high overheads. Vertical companies usually specialize in offering fabric, fashion and classic clothing to the larger stores and chains. Some may even have their own retail outlets, but most deal only in wholesale goods.

Manufacturers can grow to a fair size, but many are smaller businesses that rely on the talents of craft-oriented designers. These include haute couture and bespoke tailoring firms, which make their products in-house. In this instance garments are 'one-offs' and may require numerous fittings, so it is appropriate that the designer and cutter work in close proximity to the machinists. Production is limited to what can be managed by a small but skilled workforce and is priced accordingly. Pleating, embroidery, buttonholing and finishes that require specialist machinery are usually subcontracted. Couturiers and bespoke tailors often operate from premises which combine a shop at the front and workrooms at the back.

Wholesalers (or 'jobbers')

Many top fashion-design companies come into this category because, while they produce the designs, buy materials and plan the cutting, selling and delivery, they do not actually make the clothing. This system gives wholesalers the flexibility to make innovative clothing in small runs by subcontracting CMT units (see page 62). However, smaller companies run the risk of being put to the bottom of the priority list by contractors working with larger orders. They also have less control over quality, price and **knock-offs**. On the other hand, jobbers do not have the high wage bills or machinery problems typical of manufacturers. In order to justify the higher prices of their clothing, they need to spend more on advertising, trade and fashion shows, and stylish premises.

Note that the term 'jobber' has a different meaning in the United States, where a jobber is a middleman who buys excess stock or seconds from the manufacturer and resells them to other outlets or through his own shops.

   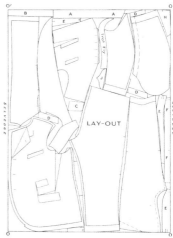

The docket

Before a designer or client places an order with a contractor he or she will want to see how well the design-room sample can be reproduced. The contractor will cut and make one or more samples for approval. Once refinements, details and cost have been agreed, the chosen sample is 'sealed' as the agreed reference garment, together with a specification sheet. In the past, the **sealing sample** had a metal seal affixed to it in order to prevent switches being made in the event of a dispute. When manufacturers or contractors receive a confirmed order from a designer or store, it is called a **docket**, a form showing a breakdown of the numbers of garments required in different sizes. Traditionally this has been rounded up to 'dozens', twelve dozen making a gross – often the minimum for an order. Clothes are usually labelled, given swing-tickets and inspected before the finished order, also known as a docket, leaves the factory in vans equipped with hanging rails. At the wholesaler's warehouse they will be allocated against the shop orders and **kimballed**: that is, tagged with information or price tags before being dispatched to the shops.

Contractors

Contractors vary in size from well-established large-scale operators – often referred to as 'the big boys' – through medium Cut, Make and Trim (CMT) workshops to the lone **outworker**. Large contract manufacturers are located mostly in or near industrial towns, which is helpful for the distribution of goods. They have design teams which work to an agreed framework negotiated by the store outlets that they supply. They are responsible for all aspects of production, from pattern-making, production and trimming to packaging and delivery.

Contractors do not produce collections, but small groups and **stories** designed around a silhouette, fabric or perceived market demand. The design teams produce a great many samples. Some are market tested in flagship stores, and those that show promise are chosen by store selectors or merchandisers. These are finished with the stores' own label and are not offered to other customers. In the United States this is called a **private label**. Contractors take on the risks of design and manufacturing, but not those of failed sales. They negotiate complex rolling contracts with the chains they supply, worked out well in advance of the season, as a lack of orders could put them out of business.

Cut, Make and Trim (CMT) factories tend to be small, family-run businesses employing fewer than thirty people. They are often subcontracted by larger manufacturers at busy times, but they also work for independent design companies. These factories vary enormously in their expertise and reliability. Some have areas of specialism, such as lingerie or special machinery. CMT units do not supply patterns, cloth or trimmings, although they will press, hang, bag or box goods. They do not take on the design or sales risks and may use outworkers when busy.

Outworkers are usually women working from home. They are often very skilled, and set aside a part of their home as a workspace. Outworkers are used by independent designers who have work dockets too small for CMT units. A designer will usually supply them with a set of cut bundles, thread and trimmings, and negotiate and pay for the sewing. If the same style is placed with more than one outworker, consistency of style or delivery can be problematic.

Offshore production

Today many jobbers use offshore production. Manufacturing in the United Kingdom, Europe and the United States is expensive in comparison to production in the Far East and in other regions with low wages or heavily subsidized industries. The quality control, speed of production and care taken over the finishing and trimming can be extremely high. In the 1990s the American designer Calvin Klein moved all his production to the Far East and was quickly followed by other fashion houses. Large companies employ agencies and brokers to negotiate and oversee production and ensure that schedules and standards are met.

There is widespread ethical disapproval of outsourcing labour. Many consumers are uncomfortable with the knowledge that well-known companies sell clothing made by cheap and exploitative labour based in 'sweatshops', although most people still prefer to pay less. Some manufacturers have been the target of boycotts, demonstrations and protests because of their employment policies. This in turn has led to trade quotas, tariff embargoes and 'banana wars' against goods such as cashmere sweaters.

Hong Kong – then a British colony – was the first country to which Europeans and Americans turned for ready-to-wear production. Backed by a social ethos that favoured efficiency and cost-effectiveness, a willing labour market and continuously upgraded technology, it quickly became the second-largest exporter of clothing after Italy. Today there are approximately 10,000 factories of varying sizes in Hong Kong.

With so many companies trading globally today, cost is no longer the priority; the crucial issue is timing. There is such a demand for new fashion that it must be brought to the market fast or perish. Manufacturers in China, Taiwan and Korea can respond with speed, quality and technological organization. American fashion companies look for a turnaround time from Hong Kong agents of about 1,000 hours – from the recognition of a new style to the delivery of some 10,000 garments – and all from 10,000 miles away.

'We do four seasons – spring, summer, fall and holiday – and two lines in the spring and fall. There are 170 pieces per line of which 30 per cent is knitwear made in the Far East. The line gets edited down and about 100 styles get dropped. It's like doing a degree show four times a year. The pressure is intense but with the right people it's fun. The key to it is organization ...' Knitwear designer for Ralph Lauren

The supply chain

With the global trend towards manufacturing offshore, manufacturing has become geographically separated from design, product development and marketing. Specifications, raw materials, trimmings and goods are sent to and from far-flung places to have different processes applied to them. This is called the **supply chain**. Good communication is crucial to a smooth supply chain. Costs can escalate and manufacturing will grind to a halt in the process if components are lost or late, or if production misses its time slot in the booking plan, or shipping cannot be consolidated or sent to the next stage. The logistics of production planning, manufacturing and delivery are a vital aspect of efficient order fulfilment and satisfied customers. The business to business (B2B) Internet has helped to speed up the supply chain by instant communication of orders and pattern data through electronic data exchange (EDI). By connecting to a commercial intranet stock-keeping unit (SKU), data and movement are automatically updated and files are shared by the various parties, with access at any time. It is easier for managers to see or predict bottlenecks and act faster to resolve problems. Companies like Zara (based in Spain) have managed to shorten lead times by several months and can even turn out new products in a week to satisfy consumer demand. Zara employs over 200 designers and operates more than 600 stores in forty-six countries.

Mass-customization and the fashion cycle

The biannual manufacturing and marketing cycle for prêt-à-porter fashion developed over the course of fifty years and until recently was the model followed by the majority of the trade. However, today there are challenges to the sequential formulae as a result of retailers entering the manufacturing arena. The demand for their own **private label** collections and speedy production is contributing to the breakdown of the cycle. In addition, **mass-customization** and **e-tailoring** are entirely new approaches whereby clothing is created from individual consumer measurement data (sometimes generated by three-dimensional body scanners) and e-mailed directly to the factory. In these cases the supply chain is reversed and both fabric and garment can be made after the customer has tried on a sample and placed an order. In the past, a fabric print had to be made in hundreds of metres in order to be commercially viable. Today, ink-jet-printed fabric can be made in very small and unique quantities, allowing for customizable prints and fashions. It is therefore more likely that consumers will want their own 'special' items, and that in future designers and customers will collaborate in the design process. This is already occuring with sports shoes and sportswear, and with men's suits and shirts.

Top As well as providing personal attention, independent designer shops can offer a unique ambience tailored to international tastes.

Above Smaller stores are often willing to risk stocking new or local designers' collections as they need to differentiate their merchandise from that of chain stores.

Identifying target markets

Market analysts consider the following significant factors in identifying target markets:

Age This grouping helps retailers to determine people's buying habits by the life stage they are likely to be going through. Knowing the population numbers within each age group helps to calculate the potential size of the market. In the UK and the US, the fashion conscious 15–24 age range is declining in number, while the 25–34 age range represents the largest market.

Gender Until recently most menswear and womenswear shops were separate. Now that more men are shopping, there is a trend to include both in the large chains and casualwear stores.

Demographics The study of population distribution can track socio-economic groupings, ethnicity, income levels and use of leisure time across a country. Different clothing will be required in a sleepy country town and in a lively holiday resort. Ethnic groups may have preferences for certain colours, brands and accessories.

Lifestyle How people live and travel affects the clothing they require. For example, career women require separates, business clothes and classics. Single men take more interest in sports.

Physical characteristics Size is related to genetic factors that may be dominant in various locations. Surveys show that in the West people are in general getting taller and heavier.

Psychographics Psychographics is the study of fashion attitudes, whether people are fashion-active and early or late adopters of styles. City dwellers will tend to pick up on new styles faster than those living in rural areas.

Social class People like to be seen to belong to a particular level of society, and to shop with their peers. For example, Harvey Nichols department store in London is considered the epitome of upper-middle-class chic. In New York, analysts have designated people as either 'uptown' or 'downtown' shoppers.

Social behaviour Broad changes in society, such as a higher rate of divorce and the increase in single-parent families, can affect people's spending power.

Values and attitudes These are subtle lifestyle indicators that help marketers determine how to fine-tune sales and advertising material. Surveys are done to collate people's responses to many subjects such as dating and sex, movies and music, current affairs and politics.

Economic circumstances Salary is not the same as disposable income – a high-earning middle-class family may spend its money on private education for the children rather than on clothing. The availability of credit or the cost of mortgage repayments will also affect clothing purchases.

Religion Religious observance may influence the buying of modest or flamboyant clothing among certain communities, or create more demand for expensive wedding outfits. It may mean that in some neighbourhoods the shops do not open on particular days of the week or during festivals.

Market segmentation

'Only those retailers who are positioned to serve a carefully targeted market niche with a distinctive and differentiated offering will prosper.' MTI/EMAP report (1999)

Retail managers will deduce the profile of their actual customers or target customers by counting and observing who comes through the door. In the 1980s the use of the newly developed electronic point-of-sale (EPOS) technology enabled the tracking and replacement of items that were selling well. Slow-moving goods were quickly withdrawn so that shops were stocked with desirable merchandise. Sizes that were running out could be restocked quickly. This feedback is known as matrix marketing.

Statistics compiled from national census data, economic conditions, market analysis and shop retail performance can be charted to show broad trends. This kind of work has shown, for example, that sales of suits and outerwear have generally given way to casual clothing for both men and women; the jeans market is in decline; the independent shop is losing out to concessions, in-store designer ranges and high-fashion diffusion lines; there is a growing awareness of branding and brand loyalty; teenagers are much more demanding of street-fashion styles and shoes; women's sizes are getting larger.

In the past the majority of manufacturers and the shops they supplied focused on a particular sort of product such as day dresses, men's shirts or eveningwear. A similar categorization was used in department stores, with, for example, all knitwear grouped together. Now, store merchandisers group garments either by the age, lifestyle and socio-economic group formula, or by fashion houses, which often offer an entire 'story' co-ordinated by colour and fabric.

Types of retailer

Shop reports

As a student of fashion you will learn to do shop reports. This is essentially a technique that will train your interest in market sectors, sales environments, consumers and trend-spotting. It demands a practised, evaluative eye for noting the evolution of trends and manufacturing finishes, colours and styles that are shifting or being marked down, price points and introductions of new fabrics, sizes and labels. The purpose of this kind of market intelligence is not to copy, as the designs are already out there, but to check the time frame for styles, avoid the pitfalls of overexposing a design, check manufacturing benchmarks and gain inspiration for developing the positive trends. Use a notebook, and ask questions of sales staff and customers discreetly.

Today, shopping can be said to be the primary leisure activity. The demand for certain types of clothing and the most convenient or pleasing ways of shopping for them will be reflected by the success or failure of forms of retail. The fashion student needs to be aware of what the different retail environments aim to provide and what the constraints of each are.

Independents

Retailers with fewer than ten outlets make up this category. Most are sole traders with only one shop or boutique. In the United States these are known as 'mom and pop stores' because they can offer the personal touch and often specialize in certain categories of clothing. Independent shops are more pressured by the high cost of

Market Segments

European Segments	US Segments
Womenswear	
The fashion market segments are separated by their price, quality and target customer	*In the US the segments are more fragmented*
Haute couture	High end (no couture)
Designer	Designer
Classic	Missy
Middle market	Young Designer
High street	(fashion forward)
Budget womenswear	Better
	Bridge
	Contemporary / trendy
	Junior
	Moderate
	Budget
	Private label
	Mass market
Menswear	
In menswear the market is not as clearly differentiated by price as by lifestyle	*The US looks to Europe for tailoring but excels in middle-market products*
Bespoke tailoring	Custom-tailored
Designer	Designer
High street	Bridge
Sportswear	Furnishings
Casual	(shirts and ties)
Budget menswear	Moderate
	Sports and active
	Sports
	Popular
	Supermarket
	(e.g. Wal-Mart)
Childrenswear	
Offered in designer, mid-market and budget price points as:	*Offered in better, moderate and popular price points as:*
Newborn	Layette
Infant	Infant
Toddler	Toddler
Girls	Girls
Boys	Boys
Teens	Teens

Top and top right Concessions help to fill a department store with variety. The department store reassures the shopper with its wide range of goods and reputation for reliability and service.

Above Samaritaine, Paris, the historic Art Nouveau department store, opened in 1869. Now owned by the LVMH group, it has been reconditioned and focuses on sales of fashionable merchandise.

business rates and rents than the larger chains. Independent shops are usually not in prime sites because of the cost. There are fewer independent menswear stores, although this is a growing area and is fast catching up with a declining women's independent sector. Independents have to stock different goods than the bigger stores; they have higher costs so they need strong fashion innovation, designer names or exclusivity to draw in customers. Independents have less control over suppliers than department stores with their larger budgets and greater influence to determine when, and at what price, they will buy or mark down stock.

Multiples

These are chains of shops, or several chains owned by a parent company, and they include well-known names such as French Connection and Gap. Some specialize in one particular area, while others provide a wide variety of merchandise. They own or lease prime city centre or shopping-mall sites and therefore generate a high turnover. They are able to buy in bulk or commission own-label merchandise and distribute it to branches. Multiples build brand familiarity and loyalty with corporate images and logos, packaging and advertising. Customers expect to find moderate fashion with middle price points. These shops add value with customer lures such as cafés, store cards and promotions.

Department stores

Department stores offer a wide variety of goods on different floors, or departments, and are designed to keep customers in the store for as long as possible. When they first appeared in the late nineteenth century, they were distinguished by their magnificent architecture and interiors, and their prime locations. Typically, some 70 per cent of the merchandise on sale is fashion. Many stores offer loyalty cards that provide retailers with information for their customer databases and allow them to target specific groups with promotional information. Department stores feature **concession** trading and a wide choice of goods. They also offer extra facilities, such as toilets, restaurants, credit cards, banking facilities and wedding-gift services. Today, department stores are having to work very hard to redress an old-fashioned image and ambience that is unpopular with young shoppers.

Concessions

Department stores used to buy in all their goods from manufacturers and jobbers. The main advantages of buying in goods are diversity of product and no manufacturing costs. Tying up money in stock is expensive and risky; a store must make a profit within a seasonal time frame or it will be unable to purchase the fashions that its customers expect for the following period. If the buyers make mistakes in forecasting, or if the weather and other variable conditions change consumer interest, unsold stock has to be heavily discounted in the sales.

Concessions take the risk out of retail. The store lets out space to a retailer or manufacturer for a fixed percentage of turnover. The agreement guarantees the store a minimum percentage of income. The **concessionaire** employs his or her own sales staff, provides fixtures and fittings and is responsible for stock and changing displays. Concessions work particularly well for the small pitches of accessory and cosmetic companies. Opening a concession in a busy store is a popular way for young designers to get a foothold on the retail ladder and test the market for various styles without the risks and high costs of opening a shop.

Franchises

Franchising is a low-risk method of retailing. Essentially, franchise companies are well-established firms which make the stock, distribute the goods, provide advertising, display material and a company **fascia** or **logo**. The **franchisee** buys the right to sell those goods within a specified geographical area for an initial fee and further royalty payments. The prices are set at the same levels for all the franchises. In return for a smaller proportion of the profits, the parent manufacturing company gets wide distribution of products and a consistent market presence without having to manage local sales and staffing issues.

Discounters

Discounters buy stock at reduced rates from a wide variety of international sources, especially where manufacturing costs are low or contractors wish to dispose of **cabbage** (excess fabric), cancelled orders and overproduction. They have grown to take a fifteen per cent share of the market because they offer very competitive prices. It is customary for the discounter to remove the labels so that shoppers are unable to identify the makers of the clothing.

Factory shops

Factory shops developed from the overstocks and faulty goods produced by a manu-facturer that were offered at reduced prices to employees. Eventually manufacturers opened to the public. The recession of the 1980s saw a steep proliferation of factory outlets, and in some areas they have left the factory premises and grouped together with others to create smart out-of-town shopping 'villages', offering both high quality and low cost. Customers tend to be in the top socio-economic groups, with large cars and high budgets.

Markets

The vibrant and informal environment of the market is where people traditionally expect to find a bargain. The fashion goods sold on market stalls tend to be from similar sources as those of the discounters. Damaged or rejected goods known as seconds are offered cheaply to market traders. Goods are customarily exchanged for cash, and the usual consumer protections concerning 'merchantable quality' are not strictly observed.

Shopping malls offer accessibility and protection from the elements. Many have dynamic architectural and leisure features that encourage people to visit them and stay all day.

Street and craft markets can be an inexpensive way to start trading and build up an understanding of business and consumer demands.

Some alternative markets attract young designers and students wishing to capitalize on their talents and test out their target audience. Flea markets such as London's Portobello Road and the Porte de Clignancourt in Paris, which specialize in second-hand goods, can be rich sources of inspiration and of beautiful antique fabrics for students.

Mail order

Mail-order shopping suits those who cannot, or do not wish to, go shopping. It has been popular since the early American settlers needed goods to run their remote ranches, and Sears and Roebuck filled the demand for workwear and home furnishings. Catalogues were mailed out twice a year and shoppers were offered attractive payment by instalment terms. Mail order is an expanding field; many working women no longer have the time to shop. Many retail conglomerates also run mail-order businesses. 'Magalogues' – catalogues in the form of monthly magazines – are the latest marketing tool of suppliers and department stores.

Electronic shopping

Electronic shopping is a development of mail order made possible by recent technology. Fashion websites are proliferating and are no longer confined to advertising or selling standard garments such as T-shirts. Home shopping through interactive TV is also growing in popularity. Until recently womenswear was poorly represented by these media, but improvements in bandwidth, interactive fashion images, data-protection legislation and transaction security have given people the confidence to buy clothes and accessories online. The increasing number of women using the Internet for holiday, toy and food purchases has led to fashion retailers becoming confident in the Internet as a sales channel. Stores, at first threatened by the Internet, have realized that many people like to browse online before visiting a retail outlet and now offer this facility as well as 'bricks and mortar' stores. Two advantages of electronic shopping are that it is available 24/7 to credit card holders and opens up the market to otherwise inaccessible and/or overseas customers. Fashion advertising and shopping websites are a wonderful research resource; you can learn about a company's history and market approach, and examine how they co-ordinate and style their ranges.

E-commerce

There are two fundamental aspects of e-commerce: Business to Business (B2B) and Business to Consumer (B2C). At present the majority of B2C e-commerce transactions in fashion are via shopping websites. However, apparel companies have collected surprisingly little information about how satisfied customers are and the kind of stock they would like to see. The practice of the designer or store has been to impose fashion on them – not to court opinion. Information is confined to EPOS data which merely records the cost and quantity sold, to whom and when. Today's consumer is a much more sophisticated and informed buyer than her counterpart twenty years ago. The involvement of consumers in product development is logical. A two-way flow of information helps the design room to anticipate the tastes of its market. This already happens in B2B where members of the supply chain or the wholesale customer can contribute ideas, feedback and stock figures to the core company. This gives smaller firms an opportunity for growth and greater evidence of successful styles, and enables them to predict what will strike a chord with their customers. Co-ordinating and transmitting this information to management and designers is set to become an important aspect of market intelligence in fashion. The use of e-commerce in B2B and supply-chain management by electronic means is only accelerating.

Design and visualization software

The apparel and fashion markets are not only about selling products – they are also about creating and promoting dreams. The pattern-cutting and planning hardware and software giants Lectra, Gerber and Investronica (now owned by Lectra) have added virtual three-dimensional design and merchandising software for prototyping garments to their ranges. Virtual three-dimensional prototyping saves labour and money, and allows designers and merchandisers to work together earlier in the design and merchandising cycle. The software tools can be used in a variety of ways, from ensuring that garments fit the customer size-range and make a good design story, to checking that the brand image is consistent in stores. For example, early on, it will be clear if there is too much of one colour or product in a range or order, or if ratios of hanging to folded goods need topping up. The computer-aided visualization systems help designers to show their ranges to wholesale buyers, allowing them to choose items and style an appropriate selection for their customers. Virtual shop layouts allow design co-ordination and in-store mood to be created without the need to buy items or have salespeople handling the merchandise. Garment rails and colour-blocking (arrangement) can be used to create visual excitement or a calm atmosphere. Shop layouts can be easily distributed to different branches electronically.

Kiosks

Shoppers are already familiar with kiosks showing floor plans and orientation information in large shopping malls and department stores. Many people shop just for the pleasure of imagining themselves in new and beautiful clothes, and devices such as kiosks and hand-held RFID (Radio frequency ID devices, similar to bar codes) can solve a host of problems that customers may encounter when looking for clothing. The RFID tagging systems allow stores to locate and move merchandise to where it is most in demand. Goods that are out of stock in one branch can be located and sent to another, or directly to the customer. Shoppers can order items in colours or sizes from larger ranges that aren't carried by the store. Gap and Prada use these systems not only in their warehouses, but also in their stores. Accessories, shoes and make-up can be suggested and demonstrated as if in a virtual mirror. Different ways of using a garment, such as a jacket, for formal or casualwear can be displayed. It is possible for a browser not only to compare prices across brands, but also to mix and match items as in real life – 'up-selling and cross-selling'. These are potentially real advantages over magazine or catalogue images as they are interactive and offer a degree of personalization to make advice relevant to the individual. This is called one 2 one marketing. Computer programs with embedded artificial intelligence (AI) can remember items that have been picked or bought previously, or offer new co-ordinating choices based on styles that have been picked by others with similar tastes. There are new opportunities for design stylists and beauty professionals to work with a brand's in-store technical services to help customers make fashion decisions.

Personalization

The idea of one 2 one marketing is catching hold; it makes individuals feel valued and pampered, and engenders loyalty. Companies that cater to the elite, minority interests or in specialized sports clothing are developing personalized e-commerce sites using AI systems based on consumers' unique profiles, purchase histories, and service histories, and on customer surveys. Women are more apt than men to provide personal information to form a 'relationship', but they must be confident that it will be secure. Trustworthiness has to be gained over time. Commercial websites build trust first and foremost by ensuring that people have a satisfactory shopping experience, with speedy service, delivery and follow-up thank yous. In terms of interface design this means letting them start a transaction with the confidence that they can cancel it later and continue browsing, as in a shop. Shopping bot interfaces (specialized search engines), which combine the technologies of voice and three-dimensional characters tailored to a customer's preferences and lifestyle, can guide consumers through transactions and answer questions. Younger generations are used to interacting with AI characters, from teaching-software and games. Trust and connection are built on by adding interesting fashion news, content and gossip or community features, and asking for feedback. E-mail promotions, personalized offers and targeted advertising are seen as benefits for consumers, as people are made aware of suitable products or special offers that they might otherwise miss. As websites grow in sophistication using them will become like chatting to a friendly and well-informed sales assistant who will help to find, or even design, the clothes the customer wants. The personalization of factory-produced clothes is called **mass-customization**, and is a hybrid of **made-to-measure** techniques and automated production. It is growing in popularity in the mens' tailoring sector and jeans industry, and is starting to gain a hold in womenswear.

Price points

Price points for fashion merchandise are related to the quality of manufacture, availability, design content and the demographic target group. The balance between these diverse factors is not always easy to discern and may turn up some apparent oddities. For example, street-style fashion may be cutting-edge, not widely available and reasonably well made, yet, seemingly against logic, it sells at a comparatively low cost; this is because the people who are interested in it are few in number and do not belong to a high-income group.

> 'Costing is important, you have to run your business properly and make a profit. But you also have to take risks, calculated risks … Our best-selling fabric last winter was £52.00 a metre (about $72 a yard); that is very expensive by the time it is marked up.'
> Designer Joe Casely-Hayford

As a designer you must be aware of the prices set by your nearest competitors. Prices must be fair and reflect the value of the fabric and manufacturing style you have employed. You should also be aware of any extra incentives that are offered to the buyer in the way of credit facilities, sale-or-return privileges, special promotional goods and advertising support. The retail buyers will be making comparisons as they order each season and will also be aware of price resistance in the shop. Retailers must pitch their price bands just right for their customers, even at sale time. Steep mark-ups force the customer to shop around for better value, while dramatic discounts make customers very sceptical of the original price. Establishing an upper and lower level that is acceptable is as important as the designing of the garments.

It is not necessarily the case that the people with the most money buy the most expensive clothes, or that those with the most disposable income spend it on clothes. In recent years there has been a fundamental shift in consumer attitudes towards price and quality, as a result of changing economic conditions and greater consumer knowledge and choice due to the Internet. It is now considered cool to save money on fashion; everyone loves a bargain and offering consumers perceivable value for money is a forceful marketing ploy. Celebrities buying from the UK's Top Shop, designer **diffusion ranges** and **2 for 1** selling are all part of this milieu. It has long been a rule of thumb that the cheaper clothing sells in larger quantities because it is cheaper, but it doesn't necessarily make more profit. It usually makes less profit item for item. Discounting a brand or product can cheapen it in the mind of the consumer and lead in the long run to difficulty in maintaining profitable prices. In order to differentiate their product offering many companies have developed value-added strategies to entice consumers, such as loyalty cards, club membership, discounts, credit arrangements and entertainment.

There are differences between price points at wholesale or retail (such as including the sales tax at retail), but in both cases the price charged will be pitched between one that is too low to make a profit or too high to stimulate demand. These limits are sometimes called the **baseline** and **ceiling** prices, and the space between is the potential profit margin. The profit margin for designer clothes is very high, while clothing sold in concessions (at airport shops, boutiques in larger department stores, etc.) will not only be at a lower margin in order to sell alongside the massive competition, but will have the concession fees to deduct as well. The advantages are in the number sold. There is more information about costing your own designs for a project in Chapter VI and about how to price your garments for sale in Chapter VII.

There are five approaches to setting prices:

Setting prices

1 **Cost-plus** (cost plus standard mark-up pricing, break-even analysis and the target profit)

2 **Buyer-based** (value-based, what the buyer will accept)

3 **Psychological pricing**

4 **Competition-based** (the going rate, undercutting or make me an offer)

5 **Dynamic pricing** (changing the price according to customer status or market conditions)

Cost-plus pricing is commonplace in the rag trade as it simplifies the work of wholesale pricing by totalling the costs of making a garment and adding a standard percentage mark-up, usually between 50 and 120 per cent on materials, labour and a percentage of the overheads for a target profit figure. (Designer outlets will add more.) The sale price is established by the vendor and the figure is then rounded up or down to the nearest acceptable whole number. When the majority of companies in a sector use this method it tends to make prices similar and minimize the competition. There is a belief that this is a fair way to price goods as it is widely understood and sellers do not take advantage of lack of demand or times of shortage. However, this method only works if the expected volume of sales is reached; if garments fail to sell well they will have to be marked down and the company may well lose revenue in the long term. The fashion market is extremely time sensitive, yet to prevent overall losses a company must achieve the break-even (or target profit) point before the mark-down period.

Buyer-based pricing uses buyers' perceptions of value, not the actual costs as a baseline or ceiling. Value-based pricing reverses the cost-based method and the price is established by the customer. Any sales associate will tell you that there are prices that sound 'right' and 'wrong' although there may be only pennies between them.

Psychological pricing is a strategy that uses odd-numbered and fractional prices, usually related to banknote denominations, to stimulate a sale (e.g. £49.95 and £985.00). At retail the higher end of the market usually rounds the figure up to the nearest whole number. The company sets its target price based on what it believes the buyer will think are worthwhile aspects of the product and then works backwards to create items to fit the figure. This way of working takes into account more than the garment alone – service, aftercare, packaging and delivery – and requires a solid knowledge of what the market and the competition are offering. Consequently, design companies adjust the prices and profit margins of their ranges to fit the customers' value expectations. Many fashion products such as leather and silk items have a higher perceived value than is actually the case and can achieve good profit margins. A coat may cost less to make than a man's shirt. Items in a collection or store are balanced and **loss-leaders** are offered to gain an overall effective proposition.

Competition-based pricing is largely established by keeping in line with competitors' pricing, with less regard to costs or demand, and is used where smaller firms follow the market leader or price wars break out. Some contract manufacturers use competition-based bids when tendering for work. This is becoming more commonplace in Internet auctions for fashion contracts.

Dynamic pricing is a new method of pricing which is increasingly used in stores and is frequently seen in **e-commerce**. This entails offering different buyers or visitors to a store diverse prices according to market conditions, the time of day they are shopping, or what is known about their purchase history and budget from their store, or credit card, data. It can be of significant benefit to corporate clients and individual consumers, but the implications of sensitive data storage and use has significant opposition.

As a designer you must be aware of the prices set by your nearest competitors. An important aspect of shop research is to look at the swing-tags and gauge the range of prices that are offered. Prices must be fair and reflect the value of the fabric and manufacturing quality. You should be aware of any extra incentives that are offered: credit facilities, promotional material and advertising. If you are designing for a high street chain, every minute in production can make a difference to the final cost of an item. A large number of people can be needed to approve the production of a garment and many changes may be made to your design before it reaches the rails. Costing sheets will show all the ingredients of a design: interfacing, buttons, labels, packaging, etc. You may be expected to consult buyers or selectors, who give advice from the shop floor, as to what the public are responding to at different price points and what co-ordinates are needed to help the sales of slow-moving items. Retailers must pitch their price bands just right.

The price cycle

Fashion is evolutionary and requires a rejection or phasing-out of the old before the introduction of the new. To some extent this is managed by the fashion industry through the **fashion cycle** and the seasons. However, the public cannot be forced or fooled into buying or dismissing styles; more than ever, the market is consumer-led. Nevertheless, the industry has a powerful persuasive weapon in pricing. At the top of the market there remains a desire to own exclusive and expensive goods as a badge of status. Further down the purchasing chain a garment becomes desirable as it meets the budget of the middle market. A wholesale or designer fashion company will have quantifiable orders, and some sense of how popular a style is likely to be, from market testing and exposure at a trade show or on the runway. When a new style enters stores at the start of the season it will usually be pitched at the highest price the company expects to achieve. At first it will be delivered to their own outlets or only to favoured suppliers on an **exclusivity** basis to create a demand through scarcity. Later it will be delivered to others, and possibly made in alternative fabrics at lower cost and the resale price dropped. Within a matter of weeks, if the style is in demand or is featured in magazines, similar styles and copies will appear in the high street at competitive prices. Eventually, cheap, poorly made versions will appear on market stalls and the market will be saturated with the style, making it difficult for the designer store to maintain the original price. Eventually, as the demand dies down and the style goes out of fashion, or out of season, the remaining garments will be marked down in price and those that are unsold to the public will be offered to **discounters**, warehouse sales or sent for recycling. Designer stores have to keep driving consumer interest by introducing new styles ahead of the field and early in the season.

The price cycle

- Demand for new style replaces fading fashion
- Start of the season
- In at highest price and exclusivity
- High price and versions in better stores
- Price drops with wider availability
- Popular price in high street
- Market stall knock-offs
- Marked down in sales
- Unsold
- Out
- New style appears on catwalk

Company identity and branding

A designer or company can put a great deal of money, time and expertise into the development of new fashions or clothing innovations. When a product and a means of retailing it to a target market have been set up, the company will want to protect its product and give it a unique and recognizable identity.

All fashion companies like to have a **logo**, label or shop fascia (nameplate) to promote their wares and to encourage and reward the loyalty of their customers. Sometimes to be seen wearing a popular brand or label is more important to the consumer than the actual item of clothing. **Brand names**, **trademarks** and logos are registered for a fee, granting the firm exclusive usage. Trademarks can also be registered internationally. Companies can even register certain design features; Chanel, for example, has registered its signature quilted handbag with gilt chain, while Levi Strauss has registered the distinctive double-stitching on the back pockets of its jeans. Registration does not cost very much, and in time the brand or logo can become an asset in its own right, adding considerable value to quite simple garments such as T-shirts and underwear. Nike, which bought its 'swoosh' logo from a young designer named Caroline Davidson for just $35, now pays out millions to promote and protect it – so precious is its commercial and symbolic power. Using a label falsely, or counterfeiting, is a prosecutable offence in the United States and to signatories of the EU Counterfeit Goods Regulation 1986.

Copyright

In the domain of fashion it can sometimes be hard to determine the origin of a design. Very often new fashions evolve as improved versions of their predecessors. Some classic styles such as men's shirts, the six-panelled skirt and hipster flares are so commonplace that they are said to be in the public domain, and cannot be protected. However, from time to time there are innovations in the use of materials or cutting, or a genuinely new arrangement of clothing features, that represent a design worth protecting with copyright or a patent. The creator can register the design as his or her own, unless working for a company, in which case the company owns the rights of use, usually for life plus seventy years. The fashion designer can only register an original illustration of a design, not a finished garment. It must be signed, dated with a postmarked stamp, marked clearly with the copyright symbol and deposited with a bank or solicitor. Others must then ask for permission for a licence if they wish to use the design and pay a royalty on each garment produced. The industry standard is between three and eight per cent of wholesale price. French couturier Pierre Cardin is the king of such licence agreements; in the 1970s he had over 800 licensees producing fashion, accessories and household items, including tinned sardines, under his label. Poor-quality licensed goods may ultimately harm a company's identity.

If copies are made illegally, copyright is said to have been infringed and the case may be taken to court. The copied garment is called a knock-off. Unfortunately, copyright law stops at national boundaries. A design copyrighted in the United Kingdom is only protected within that country. Most pirating of clothing is done in the Far East. In Indonesia, the Philippines and Taiwan, intellectual property is not recognized and very little can be done about counterfeits. In the United States, in spite of well-established copyright law, there was a long-standing tradition of knocking off couture gowns as soon as they were imported to the top stores. Although couturiers granted rights to a few

According to a study by the US National Institute of Child Health and Human Development, released in 2004, American children have the highest rate of obesity in the industrialized world. The study claimed thirty-one per cent of girls and twenty-eight per cent of boys in the United States are obese. Designers and retailers responded quickly, for example by rebranding and offering 'Husky' clothing tailored to overweight girls and boys.

American manufacturers, these were widely abused and the trade took full advantage of the poor monitoring of such practices.

Counterfeiting can be difficult to prove; when is a fashion house following a trend, and when is it breaking the law? In cases where patterns have been stolen or copied from a contractor's factory, original garments found in pieces or fabric printed up to order, the case is clear-cut. Many companies take strong measures to protect their intellectual property; others take the view that imitation is the sincerest form of flattery and move on quickly to new things.

Nevertheless, brands around the world are in danger of being flattered to death by those who produce and sell (and those who buy, too!) copycat versions of their successful products. Not only do they steal potential customers, but they undermine the brand value of the real thing by cheapening its image, removing control over the distribution of original product designs, reducing the return on the investment involved in creating those designs and stealing the revenue needed for future development.

For the budding designer, it is crucial to appreciate the difference between being influenced by the work of others and copying. While you are a student you are expected to study and research historical and contemporary clothing for cutting techniques and stylistic details, and to draw and analyse the work of notable designers. Some projects may ask you to design in the manner of a specific designer or for a specific label. To be inspired by others is natural. It is important to understand the difference between influence, homage and plagiarism. It is not merely a matter of degree; when 'borrowing' from other sources, make sure that they are acknowledged and that you build your own creative propositions rather than presenting the work of others as your own. Educational committees take plagiarism very seriously and you risk outright failure if you cheat by copying designs or having essays or reports written for you.

It is often said that there is nothing new; many designs reappear and get recycled. The truth is that bona fide creative designers use modern fabrics, subtle differences in cut and fit and styling to update a look and create a new fashion. As a student you should place a high value on originality. Occasionally rivalries and similarities between students' work occur when they are working on the same themes or inspired by narrowly defined projects and sources. Sometimes this is malicious and should be discussed with your tutors, but more often it is simply synchronicity. The same happens in the commercial world. Fashions do not happen unless there are sufficient numbers of people excited by the same shapes and ideas. Most colleges will regard the work you do in school as your own intellectual property; however, you should make sure of the policy in place. If others have supplied materials and resources they may consider the work you do to be partly their property. If you are sponsored by a company, or win prize money, you should always make sure you have written agreements in place as to what is expected of you. There may be rules about the archiving and recording of work, or its storage and disposal, that prevent you from removing or selling it. Make sure you make photocopies of any designs that are sent off to competitions; sometimes the work is not returned for months and can be damaged, or elements that may be needed later for academic assessment can be missing.

Further reading and additional resources

J Bohdanovicz and L Clamp. *Fashion Marketing*, Oxford: Blackwell Science, 1995

Margaret Bruce and Rachel Cooper. *Fashion Marketing and Design Management*, London: International Thomson Business Press, 1997

Leslie De Chernatony. *Creating Powerful Brands in Consumer, Service and Industrial Markets*, Burlington: Elsevier, 1998

G Stephens Frings. *Fashion – From Concept to Consumer*, Upper Saddle River: Prentice Hall, 2002

Thomas Hine. *I Want That! How We All Became Shoppers*, London: HarperCollins, 2002

Naomi Klein. *No Logo*, New York: HarperCollins, 2000

Carol Mueller and Eleanor Smiley. *Marketing Today's Fashion*, Upper Saddle River: Prentice Hall, 1994

Paco Underhill. *Why We Buy, The Science of Shopping*, London: Orion, 1999

Nicola White and Ian Griffiths. *The Fashion Business*, London: Berg Ltd, 2004

Marketing and analysis
Verdict Research www.verdict.co.uk
Retail analysis and reports

Key Note Market Reports www.keynote.co.uk
Company and market analysis

European Business Information www.euromonitor.com
Global market analysis

The Department of Trade and Industry www.dti.gov.uk
UK government information on fair trade, imports and exports

Copyright
Anti Copying in Design Ltd www.acid.uk.com
Acid (Anti Copying in Design) is a trade association committed to fighting copyright theft.
Acid supports international companies, students, new designers and freelancers

Copyright Licensing Agency www.cla.co.uk
The Copyright Licensing Agency Ltd is the UK's reproduction rights organization

Fashion shows
London Fashion Week schedule and news www.londonfashionweek.co.uk
London street fashion and shopping guide www.fuk.co.uk
Prêt-à-porter Paris information www.pretparis.fr
French couturiers and designers www.modeaparis.com
New York fashion portal www.7thonsixth.com
USA fashion source bible www.thenationalregister.com

Industry resources
Kemps British Clothing Industry Yearbook
An annual A–Z listing of companies, exhibitions and trade names, as well as listings by categories (menswear, womenswear, childrenswear, fashion accessories, fabrics and textiles, trimmings, machinery and ancillary equipment, and services)

Fashion Monitor
Diary of events and business listings
27–29 Macklin Street
London WC2B 5LX
020 7190 7788

WGSN www.wgsn-edu.com
Fashion imformation, news and resources

Fashion UK www.widemedia.com/fashionuk/fashion/
Business and events

Hoover's www.hoovers.com
Fact sheets on international companies

The body III

Inspiring bodies

We know from the earliest recorded examples that those responsible for making clothes were inspired by the body and its interaction with materials to create new, functional and decorative body coverings. For the coverings to be effective and comfortable and to stay in place, the designer needs an understanding of the mobile structure that is the human body. The evolution of clothing as we know it has taken many centuries. It has gone hand in glove with the ability to measure, map and illustrate the human form and communicate that information to others.

Visualizing the body

To design fashion you need a solid understanding of anatomy – how the muscles are attached to the skeletal structure and how they work in movement with the frame. These are the underlying forms that will dictate how a fabric fits and moves in harmony or at variance with the body. The expression of attitude – frailty, solidity, energy or lassitude – depends on pose and elements such as the tilt of the head upon the spine or how a foot is pointed. The fashion designer needs to be able to visualize the body before working on a collection.

The physical structure of the body is symmetrical around a vertical axis. The head forms a central apex to a silhouette that is triangular, whether seen from the front or sideways, in motion. In everyday life we see and recognize bodies from many viewpoints and in movement; however, in visualizations of the body it is most commonly seen from the front and in a passive pose, with the upper body and face as the prime focus. The contours of the schematic male and female body are significantly different. The female form is more rounded in all dimensions, classically simplified and often exaggerated as the archetypal hourglass figure. The male body has a flat 'inverted triangle' silhouette with broader shoulders.

The more complex, rounded form of the mature female form is easier to draw but harder to dress: it provides a greater challenge for dressmakers. Women have suffered painfully through the centuries, corseting, hobbling and binding themselves to conform to the prevalent standards of sexual attraction. Sociologists and costume historians disagree about whether it is the male or the female who has driven the demand for clothing that flatters or emphasizes the figure and helps to attract a mate.

Body beautiful

All societies form an idea of beauty. We constantly compare ourselves with each other from a young age; we objectify our own and others' bodies. These impressions are reinforced by collective opinion. Thinness and muscularity are seen as indicative of youth, an active life, self-control over the body and sexual ambiguity or freshness. Height literally implies superiority: the tall have to look down on others. The ideal is usually healthy and happy with well-groomed hair and with large, symmetrical facial features. However, throughout the last century there have also been significant trends towards using sickly, flat-chested and miserable-looking models. Twiggy epitomized the look of the underdeveloped, innocent and coltish adolescent that pervaded the plentiful 1960s and represented a paradoxical invitation to male protectiveness that ran counter to women's new-found freedom and financial independence. Her 'pale and interesting' look was the precursor of the waifish models of the 1990s.

Until very recently fashion was a white, Western phenomenon, and black, Asian or oriental colouring was rarely seen in the media. However, today there is a greater presence of diverse and 'ethnic' models on high-fashion runways and billboards.

Above A 1950s mannequin-maker spray-coats a wax model with cellulose gloss paint. Body shapes and materials used in mannequins reflect and emphasize prevailing trends in physical aesthetics.

Opposite Fashion illustration requires an appreciation of anatomy and how a stance is contrived by the skeletal structure beneath the skin and musculature.

Skeletal structure

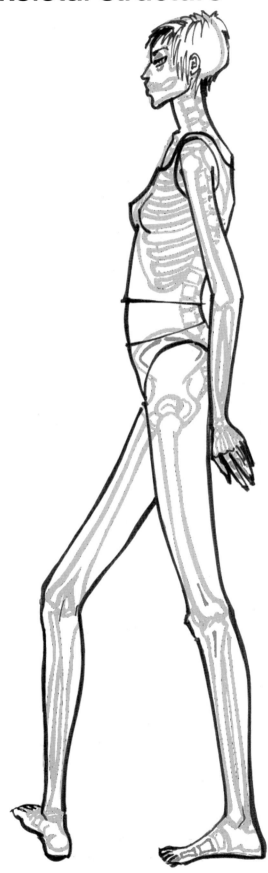
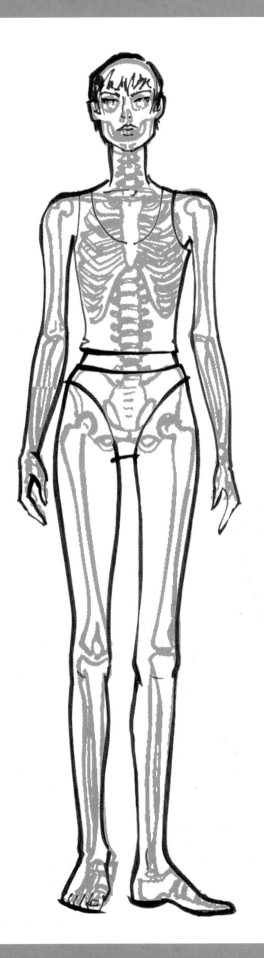

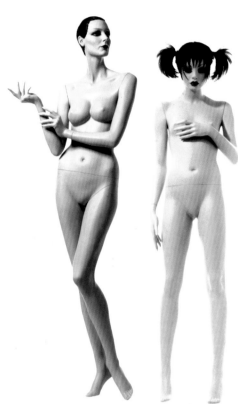

Left Since the 1960s, the Adel Rootstein company has been making display mannequins that epitomize the ideal body, attitude and look of the moment. The sophisticated, womanly look gives way periodically to the gauche adolescent.

Below, left to right:
By clothing only the extremities of the body, you draw attention to the torso.

The hourglass shape of the model is emphasized by the contrasting panels on the dress.

Today, the full range of ages and ethnic types is seen on the catwalk.

Opposite Madonna has popularized various physical traits, such as the belly and the athletic female physique, by resculpting her own body through exercise.

Opposite below Kate Moss models Stella McCartney's designs. The choice of model is important to the delivery of the non-verbal message.

They embody subtle but significant shifts in the aesthetics of physical form. Black models such as Iman and Naomi Campbell have paved the way for the African beauty Alek Wek.

Beauty, by its nature, is a rarity, so those we regard as beautiful are not representative of the masses. Less than five per cent of women have the dimensions of the fashion model. Today's model weighs twenty-three per cent less than the average person. Twenty years ago this figure was eight per cent. We are so used to seeing painfully thin models in magazines and advertisements that people of average size consider themselves abnormal. We are unrealistic about the authentic appearance of the body. Many commentators blame the media and especially the fashion industry for this promotion of the unreal body. Indeed, many of the perfect bodies shown in the media do not actually exist. Advertisers use digital technology to manipulate images of women and create impossible standards: eyes and teeth are brightened, waists are whittled down, legs lengthened and cellulite, wrinkles and blemishes airbrushed out.

Emotion and gesture

Of equal importance to the visual and aesthetic appearance of the body is its attitude and appearance in motion. While nude models have posed for artists for centuries, the nature of painting enforced primarily still or languid postures. Posing for fashion photography has created a new language of gesture. A study of the work of photographers from Cecil Beaton to Juergen Teller, Rankin and Corinne Day reveals the importance of distinct attitudinal poses to each era. Internalizing these gestural exaggerations of the body, the fashion model learns to walk, swagger, pout and express a number of emotional states that can be read non-verbally. Madonna gave voice to this as 'Vogueing'. She reinvents herself and her body regularly with the happy complicity of fashion designers, notably Jean-Paul Gaultier, who made fetishistic corsetry for her 1990 'Blonde Ambition' tour.

The ideal

Designers, fashion stylists and photographers have often identified a model or personality as their inspiration or the epitome of their ideal. They wish their clothes to be presented on the most desirable bodies of the moment, or to find some irresistible attitude that the model embodies. When a model goes to a casting for a fashion show she is asked to 'walk', to take a few paces, turn, pose and return, in a simulation of what will be expected of her on the runway. She may be asked to wear an outfit to see how it interacts with the body in movement. Fabric can behave very differently when worn – it can waft, rustle, bounce and drag, shimmer and dazzle.

What is required will vary with the designer, and perhaps with each collection. Some designers will want to see a confident, sexy swagger, others a slow, lethargic pace; a casualwear collection will demand a different attitude from an eveningwear range. If the collection accents a particular body part such as the back, the designer will want to see long, flawless backs. When Vivienne Westwood wanted to draw attention to breasts and female curves, she found the voluptuous body of Sophie Dahl the perfect vehicle for her designs. Generally speaking, clothing hangs and drapes well from straight, broad shoulders. Long legs dramatize the shortness of a skirt or can carry a greater expanse of fabric in a long dress. Poses are emphasized by long limbs.

From time to time the designer may wish to express some other desirable attitude such as 'naturalness' or 'intelligence'. Issey Miyake has used men and women in their fifties and sixties to add *gravitas* to his collections. Alexander McQueen surprised the

fashion world by championing Aimée Mullins – model, athlete and double amputee. He even designed a pair of hand-carved legs for her which she used to run at full speed down the catwalk.

Drawing and illustration

As a fashion designer you must make decisions regarding the sort of body you are designing for: which features to emphasize, which to diminish and how much flesh to display. A sense of how fabrics drape and stretch across the figure can be learnt by studying works of art and the history of fashion. But better still is first-hand observation of the figure, and the trial and error of sketching, painting and rendering fabrics on a live model.

You can observe and draw people in almost any circumstances. Carry a small sketchbook with you and jot down silhouettes, lines and details that catch your eye. To signal the point of interest you should exaggerate rather than record faithfully. To some extent you will be inventing your ideal figure as well as the clothing. You can choose your own muse and illustrate your designs on that body, sketching the poses and attitudes that best express your designs. Yet it is imperative that you are aware that the fashion market does not exist for perfect bodies. Whatever their ideal, designers need the reality check of getting to know the human body and its interaction with fabric and clothing.

Fashion designers often need to draw fast to jot down a fleeting idea, to capture a transient movement, to generate enough ideas to edit them into a coherent whole. Runway illustrators such as Gladys Perint Palmer and Colin Barnes have mastered the art of expressing shape, fabric quality and mood in a few dramatic lines more effectively than the camera.

Fashion courses devote much time and teaching to life-drawing and fashion-illustration classes, and a great deal of emphasis is placed on the ability to express ideas visually and with originality. Fashion illustration in its many forms is a highly valued tool for communicating both technical and aesthetic information. Drawing and painting for fashion has its own special conventions which must be learnt and practised until a degree of skill becomes natural. You will also be expected to evolve your own 'handwriting': the kind of marks you make, the body you are designing for and, lastly, the garments you design.

Top An illustration class using a live model.

Above The tutor in charge of the illustration class offers advice and encouragement.

Life drawing

In life-drawing classes you have a first-hand opportunity to learn about anatomy and to observe how muscles and bones work together and balance one another in various movements and poses. Studying the model will help you to draw shape and volume, and to use line and shade convincingly. You will be able to try out various media, including soft pencils, pastels, paint and collage. You will find that some of them suit your natural style and gestures more than others, and that you prefer to work at a certain scale or on a particular sort of paper. Do not restrict yourself, and remain open to trying various approaches. Some people prefer neat, detailed line drawings, others the bold and expressive application of colour. The tutor in charge of a class may offer advice, suggesting, for example, that you try a different viewpoint or a harder pencil on the outlines. There is no right or wrong way, however. You must find your own style.

'Some students love to paint and draw, more than designing. It's not an academic thing; it's like playing, having fun, making a mess – it doesn't have to be realistic, you can express yourself on paper and let your own originality come through.'
Illustrator and educator Howard Tanguy

The techniques used in fashion illustration differ significantly from those used in traditional life drawing and painting in a number of ways and need to be taken into account and mastered. There are basically two different approaches: free illustration and schematic drawing. When done with artistry and flair, fashion illustration has the magical ability to capture the intention and essence of a design and how a garment should be worn. To get it right there is no substitute for hard work and practice – not only to render your ideas accurately, but also to hone your own style.

Free illustration

Free illustration is very similar to life drawing, and at college you will probably have timetabled fashion-illustration classes. The fashion sketch aims to capture a mood or 'look' rather than a likeness. Models are notably taller and thinner than the average

Above left Quick pencil and charcoal drawings help to capture line and the volume of drapery.

Overleaf The back and front views of men and women show how proportions are distributed in a fashion illustration. The height of the model is usually eight to nine times the size of his or her head. The last half is at foot level and this depth depends on the height of the shoe heel. The waist is at approximately two-fifths from the top (lower in the male). The length of the female legs is exaggerated. It is important to memorize surface characteristics and where they lie in relation to each other. Indicating key 'landmarks' such as knees, ankle bones and hollows in the neck and inner elbow gives shape to a line drawing.

Proportion for fashion illustration

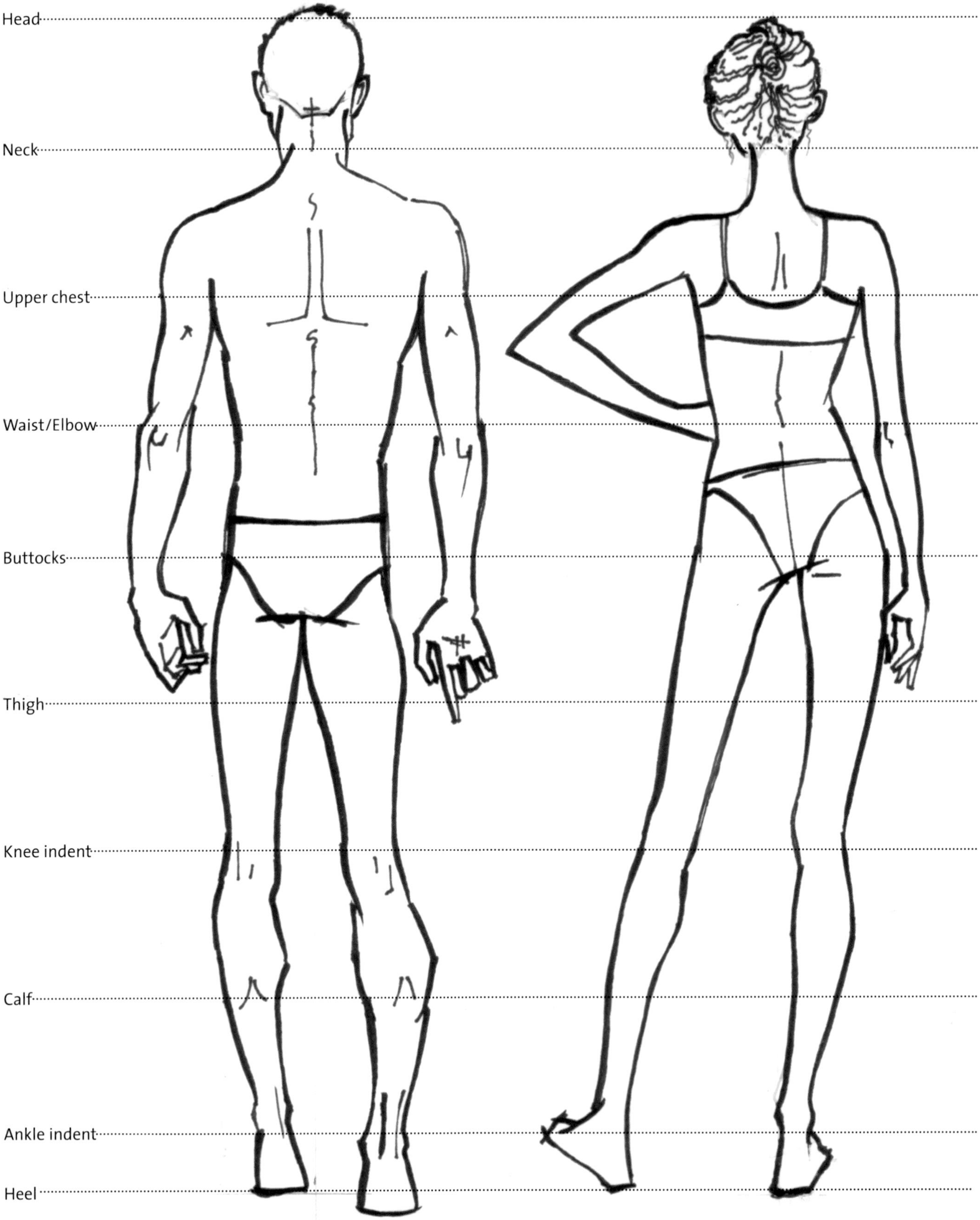

Head

Neck

Upper chest

Waist/Elbow

Buttocks

Thigh

Knee indent

Calf

Ankle indent

Heel

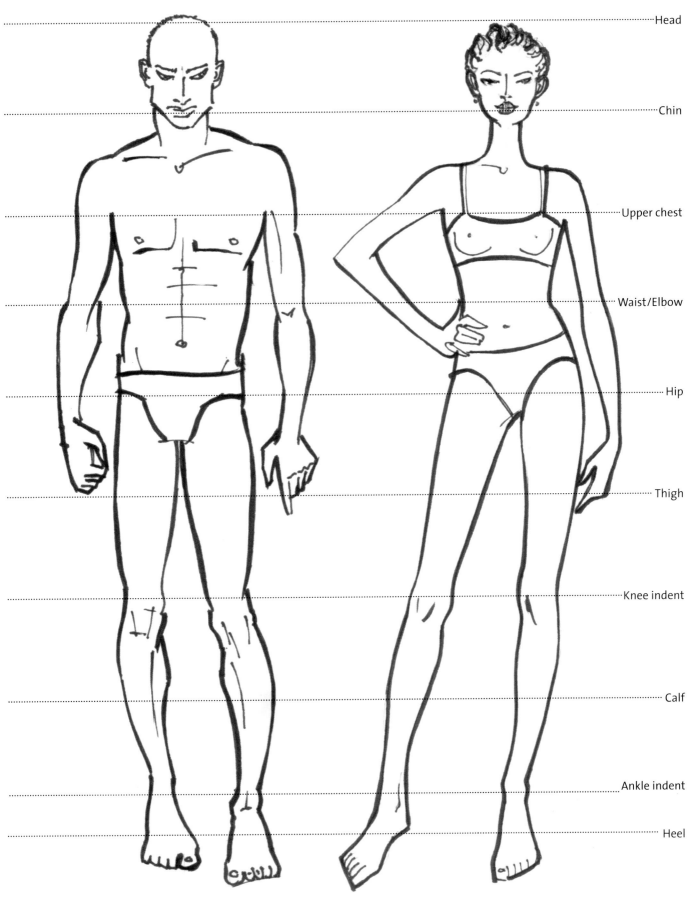

Head

Chin

Upper chest

Waist/Elbow

Hip

Thigh

Knee indent

Calf

Ankle indent

Heel

The model pose

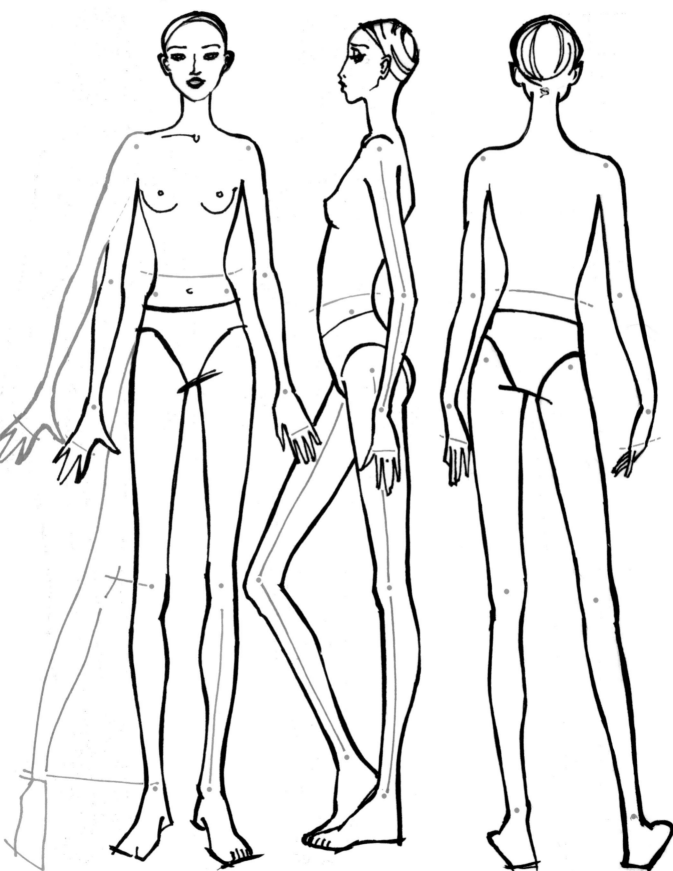

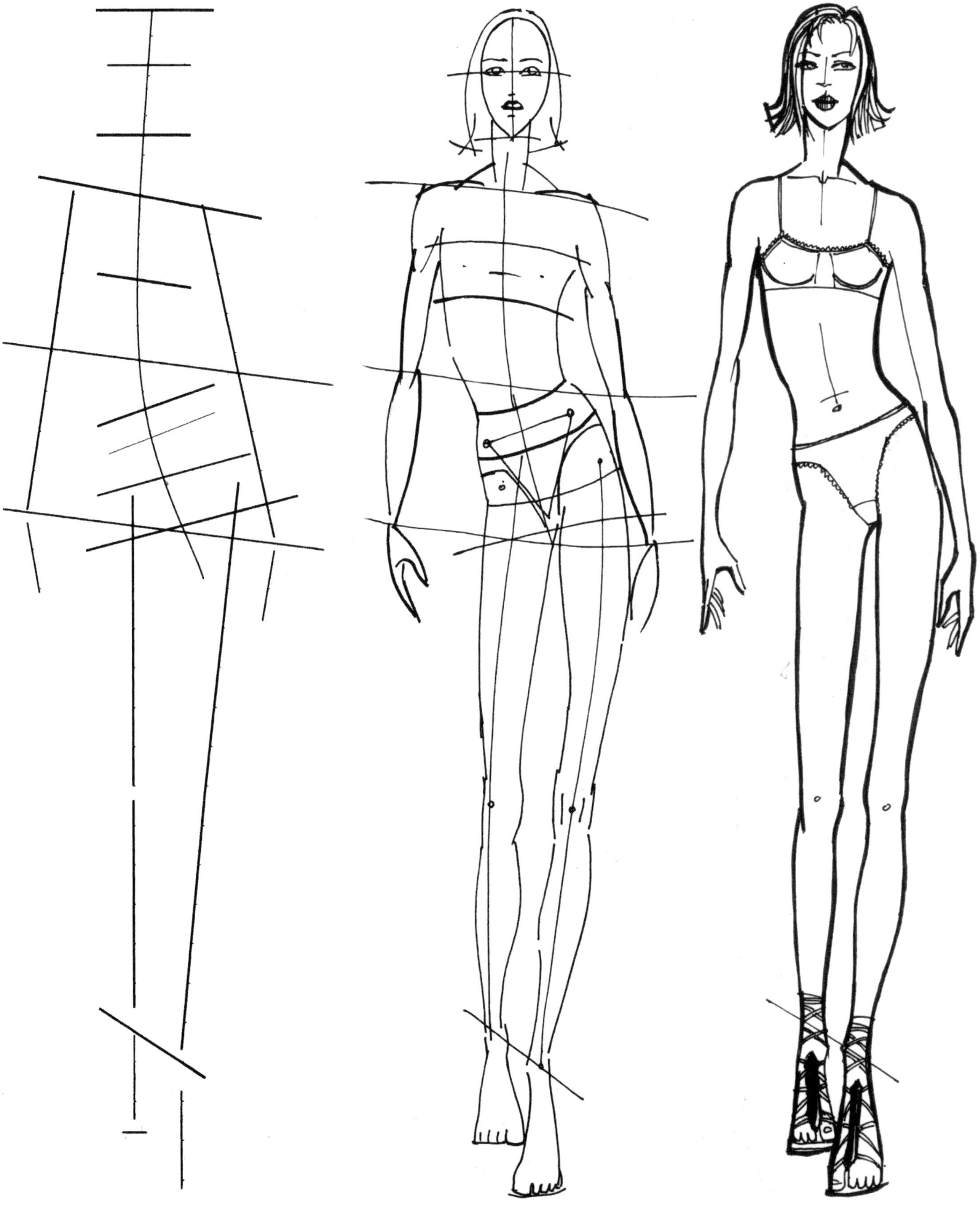

The industry requires all sorts of
are now much clearer about wl
needs of different industry sect
cants is in the choices available
jobs in design is in decision ma
shape, or colour or fabric is hard

Jane Rapley OBE, dean of the School of Fashion and Textiles, Central Saint Martins • Research, re
you have to remember is that
A collection is two-thirds artisti
remember that it is the fantasy
tomers want to buy the straigh
money in the bank Alexander McQueen, designer • Take
colour. You have to see it and ho
and in relation to other colours.
which I keep in big glass jars – m
I've picked up ... it's a total pale

ferent skills and fashion courses
 they can provide to match the
. I think the challenge for appli-
them. One of the most difficult
ng ... Committing yourself to a
hough, let alone a career choice
arch, research ... but then what
ople don't wear research David Kappo, designer •

one-third business. But I always
he artistic side, that makes cus-
orward black pants that put the
olour – you can't really imagine
it resonates on different fabrics
o I have a huge library of colour,
nly ribbons or scraps of material
in jars, John Galliano, designer • Young geniuses do

Previous pages The body can be drawn in many different stances using the joints and pivot points such as swinging hips and shoulders. The head and the weight-bearing foot should be on the same vertical axis so that the model is well balanced. Perspective foreshortens limbs that are in a different plane. A little animation of the shoulders or tilt of the head makes a sketch more lively. Observation and practice will bring speed and style.

Practise drawing the body from many different viewpoints, exaggerating angles to improve your sense of three-dimensional form.

person and their bone structure is often apparent; attention is therefore given to the points where the bones show. These are called 'landmarks' and are emphasized to give form to fashion illustrations.

Be aware of how a tilted axis, such as the pelvis, affects the stance and position of other parts of the body. Limbs must look the same length through perspective and foreshortening. Body proportions are distorted, with heads smaller and necks and legs longer than in traditional life drawings. The head, which stays almost the same size from early childhood, can be used as a measure of age, indicated by its ratio to the body. For example, in the average adult female the head will fit seven-and-a-half times into the length of the body. In fashion drawings this increases to between eight-and-a-half and ten times. The length of the legs is exaggerated more than the torso. Because the emphasis is on the clothing the figure is elongated a little, not only for elegance but also to allow more room for showing details such as pockets and seam lines. Beware of overdoing these proportions or the finished garment will bear little resemblance to the design. Men's leg length is not usually elongated to the same degree as women's, and the upper torso dominates. The male stance is usually drawn with less 'attitude' than the female's.

The body is usually sketched standing and from the front, in a relaxed pose. More dynamic poses are used for casual and sportswear. Three-quarter poses can be

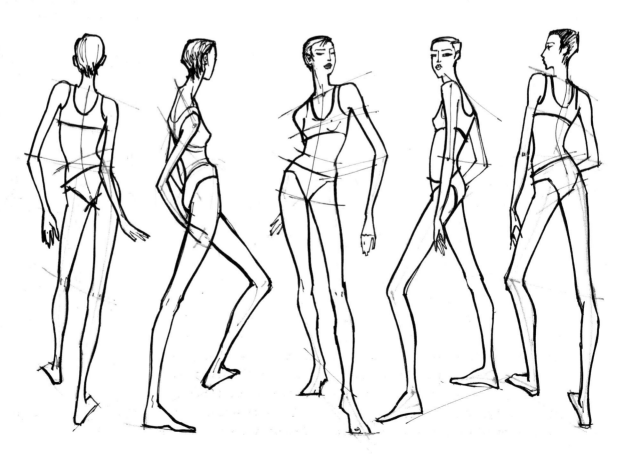

useful for showing side seaming or back details. If the back detailing of a garment is important or differs markedly from what might be imagined, a more lightly sketched back view is included. Arms are usually drawn away from the body rather than obscuring it; face, hands and feet are not shown in detail unless they are crucial to the design.

Simplification is a key element in fashion sketches; shading is not essential except to add depth to drapery or a sense of weight or emphasis to a silhouette. Buttons, zips and important details will be shown, but fabric texture or colour is not usually rendered all over a style, but is only marked here and there. Colour washes, tints and marker pens are often used to differentiate flesh tones and fabric. There are a number of shorthand marks that can be used to indicate folds, pleats and fabric types such as fur, knitwear and denim. Background and floor are often not indicated at all, and are merely suggested by a horizontal line to stop the figure looking as if it is floating.

While you are at college you will be expected to do illustrations and presentations in the form of **roughs**, **design developments** and finished illustrations (also known as **croquis**). Drawings are not laboured over; the objective is to communicate a particular line, feature or mood quickly and stylishly. Speed in drawing adds a certain spontaneity and confidence to the line. For this reason you will be encouraged to draw quick poses and capture the key elements and lines of a design. Fashion photographs and magazines are good sources of poses and are useful for analysing the way folds and fastenings can be captured. Students often arrange to pose for each other for sketches. When you have created a few useful poses you can use them as templates for your rough designs and design developments.

Roughs

Use your sketchbook or a loose-leaf binder to jot down your ideas. Some people like to draw all over a large sheet of paper, others prefer a methodical one-sheet-at-a-time approach. Do not worry about perfection, complete figures or colour at this stage. Aim to get the silhouette and design elements down as with thumbnail sketches, add found images, fabric and ephemera and play around with possibilities. Very often a relaxed approach to drawing roughs helps to create a fluid line that inspires the shape of the silhouette, the fabric used and the proportions of the designed garment.

Design developments

Once you have some strong directional ideas, make a selection of the best and group them into 'stories'. Then methodically work your way through the ideas, drawing and amplifying them, trying out different proportions, necklines, sleeve shapes, fastenings, etc. and considering the front, back and side views. A pad of semi-transparent layout paper is helpful for this process and the most promising designs can be selected for more careful illustration. Design developments should be clear, correctly proportioned working illustrations that others will find easy to read. There is little need to indicate body details such as facial features, accessories or hairstyles. If you are designing a series of items you will probably need to keep an aesthetic design theme running through the illustrations in order to create a '**story**'. This is achieved by focusing on the elements and principles of design, colour and fabric that apply to the body and will create the look you are after. At this point you should also consider the technical issues and skills the garments may demand of you, and ask the opinions of staff. Fabric choices and sampling

The successful rendering of feet and shoes is dependent on the angle of the foot and the viewpoint. The higher the heel, the longer and more slender the foot should appear from the front, and the shorter it should seem when seen from the side. Fashion illustrations often stylistically oversize footwear.

These drawings have a naive charm that reflects the girlish clothing designs.

Drawing the head and face

Fashion design

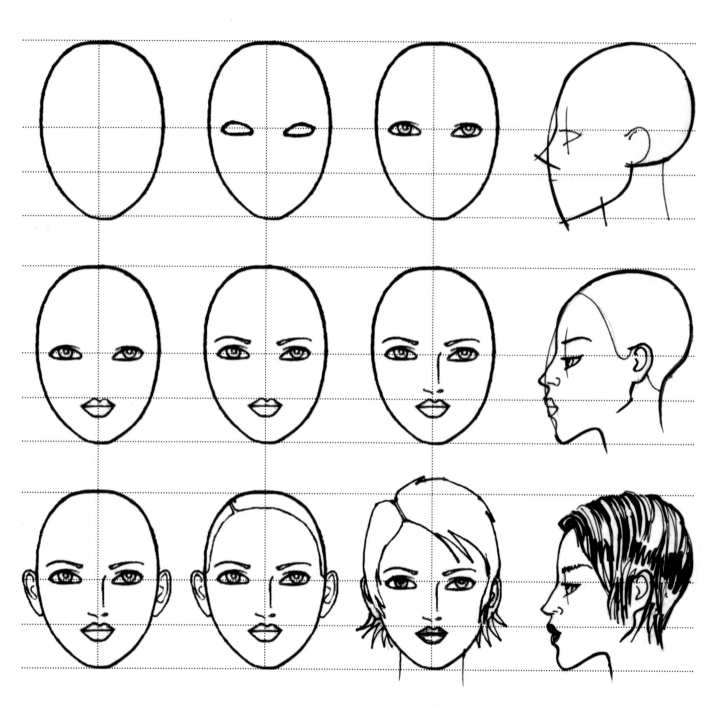

The head is sketched in stages, as an egg shape with the sharper end at the chin. Variations in the width of the oval and the spacing of the eyes give different 'personalities'. The eyes are at the midline with the pupils balanced. The mouth is placed midway between the eyes and the chin; the nose is indicated lightly in the space between. The ears line up with the nose but their positioning can usefully give a different sense of viewpoint. Lastly, the hairline is sketched in and any characterization details are added.

Above Yves Saint-Laurent uses chalk to sketch fashion designs on a chalkboard in the atelier of the House of Christian Dior, where he had just been named as successor to couturier Christian Dior in Paris, 1957. The quick fashion sketch or *croquis* captures the essential silhouette and attitude desired by the designer.

Above left and above Fashion illustrators use different media to express aspects such as fabric texture, garment structure and vibrant colour.

can begin when you are confident about which designs are worth developing into a pattern.

Finished illustrations

Finished illustrations are the highest quality sketches. They are usually done to specified paper or board sizes in order to fit into a professional **portfolio**. Make sure you have a variety of different media and paper to try out different approaches to the style of drawing and the rendering of fabrics. You should allow plenty of time towards the end of a project for finished illustrations as the first attempts rarely succeed. Aim to get across the 'look' or mood of the outfit, in as economic and elegant a drawing as possible. You will need to show sufficient detail, structure and fabric quality to convince the viewer, but without overcomplicating the image. Do not put too many outfits on one page – two is plenty. Colour is not always essential, but is often desirable and sometimes necessary. Bear in mind the demands of the project or client and you will be able to gauge how realistic or impressionistic an illustration you can create. An abstract, finished illustration should be accompanied by a crisp flat or spec. Back- or side-detail views are usually shown in paler outline or labelled to avoid confusion. You may be expected to attach fabric swatches. Avoid using a lot of background graphics or cramming the page as this can detract from the design. Work on developing your own personal style and

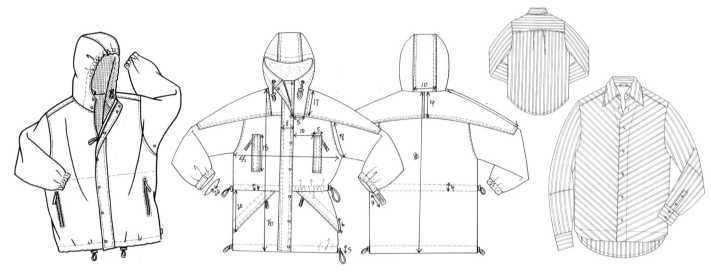

Above, left to right
An 'animated flat' drawn with a thick felt pen and a fine drafting pen. Bending the arms and putting in some lines to indicate fabric folds makes the drawing a little more lively.

A technical drawing, or spec, has measurements added and shows every detail in proportion.

These technical flats of shirts show the use of a striped fabric cut to a chevron in the front and with hidden yoke and cuff details.

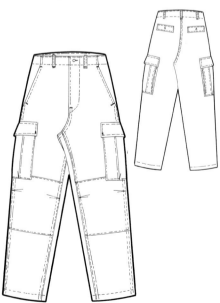

Above Men's cargo pants; trouser flats should show the front fork and side seams, especially if there is top stitching. A bold outline gives emphasis to the drawing.

Above Knitwear flats use a shorthand technique to show stitch textures.

handwriting, vary media or scale for different projects. If you are doing a series of finished illustrations make sure the paper sizes are all the same and that the proportions of the models look correct together. Label and number them in the correct order and protect them with plastic sleeves. Professional presentation goes a long way to adding to your confidence in critiques and interviews.

For a talented few, fashion illustration will be their *métier*. For most professional designers, however, illustration will be used to make roughs, or design developments; finished illustrations will be done only to show a line-up for a fashion presentation or give a journalist a preview of a coming collection. It is easy to become anxious and oversensitive about lacking talent in this area, when in fact the ability to make the clothing may be more relevant.

Schematic drawing: specs and flats

Some students prefer to work with the schematic type of illustration usually known as **specs** and **flats**. These are the least ambiguous of fashion-illustration styles. They are working drawings of a garment that are done in a clear, diagrammatic manner to clarify technical detail. No body is drawn in a spec or flat. It is, however, essential to know what size of body the garment is intended to fit. In this instance it is important that there is no exaggeration of the proportion, and that every seam line, construction and trim detail is indicated by a flat, unshaded graphic to prevent mistakes in production. The industry finds this format easier to interpret than free illustration.

The conventions of drawing specs and flats are still developing and it is a style that integrates well with new technologies. It can be readily scanned and adjusted in a computer, or faxed to suppliers and laser-cutting **CAD/CAM** machinery with no loss of detail. The essence of this form of fashion illustration is to communicate; it is an international language and is especially important in menswear, casualwear, sportswear and knitwear.

Flats are usually drawn by hand to an approximate scale, but the use of computer vector drawing programs allows more precision. For instance, the spacing and actual quantity of buttons would correspond to the correct dimensions to be used. Body, shoulder length, sleeve width, collar size and pocket size should all be proportionately

Line drawings show the salient details of both tailored and casual garments, and can be vectorized and adjusted quickly on a computer. Cutting and pasting allows the designer to create merchandise groupings without having to start over.

correct. Topstitching is indicated by a fine dotted line along the edge of a seam, which is drawn as a continuous line. Any complex detail may need to be shown as a zoomed-in enlargement alongside the flat. Colour can be used, and a little artistic licence is used to indicate softness of fabric, folds or even a 'ghost' body.

A spec (specification) is a more precise version of a flat and includes measurements and technical manufacturing details on the illustration or accompanying spec sheet which details trimmings, linings, threads and labels. Plain or squared (graph) paper can be used. When using squared paper, choose a suitable ratio of squares to centimetres (or inches), start with the grain lines and straight edges, and then add curves. It is a good idea to draw faintly in soft pencil and then go over the design with a drafting pen. Use a series of different nibs: for example 0.9 for outline, 0.7 for style lines and seams, 0.5 for topstitching. When it is correct you can rub out the pencil. You can buy plastic templates for curves and shapes.

Flats and specs have a variety of uses: to accompany the cutting docket, in production processing and the sample room. Seamstresses prefer them to free illustrations as there is less margin for error. They are also used as salespeople's aids when selling collections and for keeping a visual archive of a range or line.

'I normally start my drawings on the back of a bus ticket and then I draw that up and then that is backed up by a proper spec drawing. I don't keep sketchbooks; I just have lots and lots of pieces of paper everywhere.' Designer Joe Casely-Hayford

Using computers

Textile designers, graphic designers and illustrators have long been using the computer as a design tool. Until recently, however, fashion designers have found it easier to create sketches and spec sheets by hand. Vast improvements in the quality, user-friendliness and price of computer systems and software for the fashion sector have gradually changed the relationship between fashion designers and computers.

In the 1980s much of the computer hardware (and software) for the fashion industry was sold as stand-alone systems, often called **CAD/CAM** (computer-aided design/computer-aided manufacturing). These could not only organize and speed up the design process but could also work a piece of machinery such as a weaving loom or laser-cutting device. Often these units were unable to communicate with each other, and software had its own particular sort of interface and required special training. These systems are still very effective and are used in a great many fashion studios and manufacturing plants. You may find yourself using such a machine at college or on a work-experience placement.

Microsoft's Windows environment has become the standard by which most program software is operated. This, together with the growing availability of third-party programs or off-the-shelf applications, means that it is now possible for you to learn how to use the computer in a way that will be extremely useful in most workplaces to generate new styles that would be too laborious by other means.

The use of computers has brought with it a whole new lexicon of jargon and baffling acronyms. This language is not going to go away and it may be necessary for you to absorb at least a little of it so that you can communicate effectively with printers, manufacturers and graphic designers.

Fabrics can be scanned into the computer and scaled to create realistic 2D renderings.

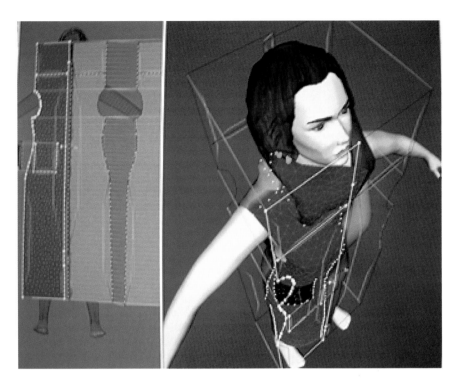

Computer-aided-design (CAD) systems now allow designers to create virtual prototypes of garments with realistic fabric behaviour from flat pattern co-ordinates.

There are two distinct ways in which the computer can deal with visual information: vectors and bitmaps. What follows is a technical explanation of each that will help you to choose the right approach for the task in hand.

Vectors

The most familiar form of computer illustration is technical drawings and specifications. They are necessary to the design process because they are less open to misinterpretation by the manufacturer than a sketch. The most effective way of doing this work on a computer is with a mathematical language called 'object-oriented vectors' or simply 'vectors'. The vector language PostScript, developed by Adobe, is ideal for drawing lines, curves and geometric shapes because it will always produce the sharpest, smoothest lines, with no jagged edges or blurs, that the computer monitor or printer is capable of, no matter what size the image is reduced or expanded to. Vector files are very economical on memory and will not degrade if resized. Patterns and specs can be transmitted across the world, downloaded very quickly and accurately zoomed up to size in this form.

Vector-based illustration takes a little practice but is proving to be a worthwhile creative as well as technical tool. Vector-based commercial programs such as Adobe Illustrator, CorelDRAW and Macromedia Freehand have introduced functions such as colour fills, gradients, text and text-wrapping, seamless pattern repeats and fills, customizable pens and media and hundreds of filters. It is possible to scan in hand-drawn work and convert it to a smooth vector drawing. The menswear sector of the industry is an especially keen user of vector-based illustration and specs. It is also used to make logos and patches for sports clothing and T-shirt design.

Bitmaps

Bitmap, or raster-based, programs are best suited to realistic images such as photographs. A bitmap is a collection of dots of light, also known as pixels. Bitmapped images are resolution-sensitive, which means that the designer must decide before starting

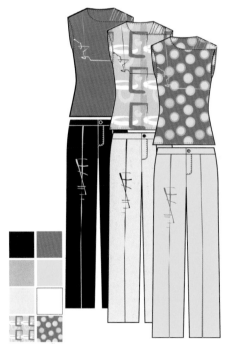

Schematic illustrations can be used by the design room and by salespeople to show how a range co-ordinates and which fabric choices and trimming details are available.

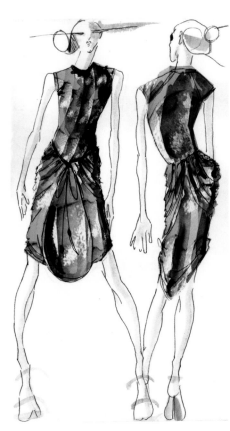

Above These illustrations use a combination of scanned artwork and computer-collaged and manipulated images as fabric ideas.

work the scale at which he or she wants the finished result to be output. Work that is resized upwards can turn out to be very jagged or blurry looking, while reducing it in size can result in loss of essential detail.

Bitmapped images have many advantages, however. Because each pixel can be edited or adjusted, they are good for refined details of tone and colour. Two-dimensional sketches, photographs and swatches can be scanned into the computer, saved as an image file, and then adjusted or combined. Small and fairly flat objects such as buttons, trimmings and yarns can also be scanned, scaled down and used in the artwork. Scanned line drawings can be useful templates to work over and, with the use of a printer, you can run off any number of flipped or rotated duplicates and variations. You can use magazine tear sheets of model poses and materials and accessories as a starting point for quick and effective collage design. Backgrounds can be cleaned up, and textures or exotic locations dropped into place.

> *'I've been illustrating for over twenty-five years and I've always said I'd never use a computer, but now you can't tear me away from mine. There's so much less time wasted on redoing things if the client wants it changed, and you can still charge the same. It's been worth every penny. The big breakthrough was the digitizing pen and tablet – just like using a felt pen or brush.'* Fashion illustrator Neil Greer

Many designers use a mouse or the more responsive graphics tablet with a pressure-sensitive pen to draw and paint directly into the computer. The effect is as intuitive as illustrating by hand without the mess or the multiplicity of materials needed in the studio. There is no waste, no dried-up inks and paints and no further outlay on painting materials. There is also no need to lug around a large box of art materials every day.

Other uses

As a design range grows, the computer can be used to collage the storyboards from day to day. This is especially useful if you are working in a team. The stages can be kept and shown as progress reports and the final artwork used as part of a marketing presentation. Three-dimensional objects and photographs of garments, in stages of production or as finished styles, can be input instantly with a digital camera. Some designers use this technique as an aspect of research and the design process.

As you become more sophisticated at manipulating the potential of the computer, you will have more control over how your work is presented. Not only can fashion marketing or promotion students put together magazine-quality layouts using desktop publishing (DTP) packages, but they can also mount slide presentations. Here the integration of headlines and fashion promotional text, even sound, can make a dynamic and powerful visual message. Web-editing tools can be used to generate not only websites but also interactive stories and video presentations utilizing catwalk or model footage that can be stored on removable media and sent to potential publishers or clients.

The virtual catwalk is not far off. It is already possible to generate three-dimensional models, fully clothed, walking and talking in your own creations. Some students will consider a career in the newer areas of video- and sound-editing for fashion. In future, most fashion students and freelance designers will find it useful at least to have the skills to produce a digital portfolio and curriculum vitae (résumé) to leave for potential employers to keep on file.

The elements of design

Designing is a matter of mixing known elements in new and exciting ways in order to create fresh combinations and products. The main elements of fashion design are silhouette, line and texture. The ways in which these elements can be used are called principles; they are repetition, rhythm, graduation, radiation, contrast, harmony, balance and proportion. Use of these variants causes a response – sometimes strong, sometimes subliminal – in the viewer or wearer. Understanding and controlling this response is essential to good designing. It is not always clear why a design works or not. At times the response can even be one of distaste or shock. However, the element of shock can also be positive in fashion terms.

The ability to articulate and analyse what is happening with a garment allows correction, amplification and development of the design. While a great deal of exciting design occurs through happy accident, it is an enormous advantage to be able to reflect on the effect of your work, to explain what is intentional and to gauge how close you are to achieving your desired result. An awareness of the elements and principles of design will also help you to evaluate other designers' strengths and to spot trends and changes in the market.

Some colleges will teach the elements and principles in a formal way; others will bring them into some project work or allow you to discover and experiment with them yourself without instruction. Good sources of information are listed at the end of the book.

Silhouette

Garments are three-dimensional, and while we may think of the overall outline and shape of the worn garment as its silhouette, this changes as the garment is viewed in 360 degrees – moving, bending and revealing its volume. (In the United States designers even call silhouettes 'bodies'.) Silhouette is almost always the first impact of a garment, as seen from a distance and before the details can be discerned. A collection should not have too many variations on silhouette as this tends to dilute the overall impact and weaken the message. Accentuating the female body with a waistline divides the silhouette into upper and lower shapes, which need to balance visually and proportionally for a harmonious effect.

Closely allied to silhouette is volume. The fullness and bulk, or lack of it, in a fashion style is usually visible in the silhouette. Garments can also have qualities of lightness or weight due to the use of heavy, padded or diaphanous fabrics. The viability of such styles is related to the contemporary idealized female form.

At certain times in history, clothing has taken on dramatic qualities of silhouette. During the fifteenth century, married women wore dresses with a high waistline and large amounts of fabric gathered under the bosom to increase the size of the stomach and therefore give an illusion of pregnancy and fertility. The pannier and farthingale dresses of the 1720s were flat and extremely wide, so much so that it was difficult for women to walk through doorways or pass each other in the street. In 1947, in the aftermath of World War II, Christian Dior shocked the world with his 'New Look', a collection that reintroduced the nipped-in waist and full skirt to women's fashion after the austerity and fabric rations of wartime. Since the 1920s, women's legs have been increasingly revealed by fashion; hemlines reached as high as the crotch in the 1960s and necessitated the invention of tights (or pantyhose) and a whole new market genre.

Silhouettes

Straight column

Natural

Trapeze

Hourglass

Egg shape

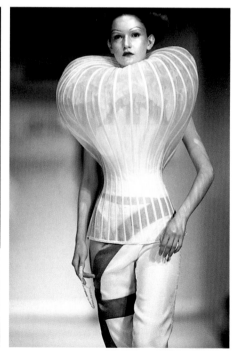

Shoulder wedge

Line

The broad edge line emphasizes the size of this coat

Breaking all the rules for vertical and horizontal lines

A long, lean line with graphic effect

Texture

A crisp cotton trouser suit

Soft knitwear for menswear

Soft mohair and masonry nails make a startling contrast of textures

Proportion and lengths of fashion separates

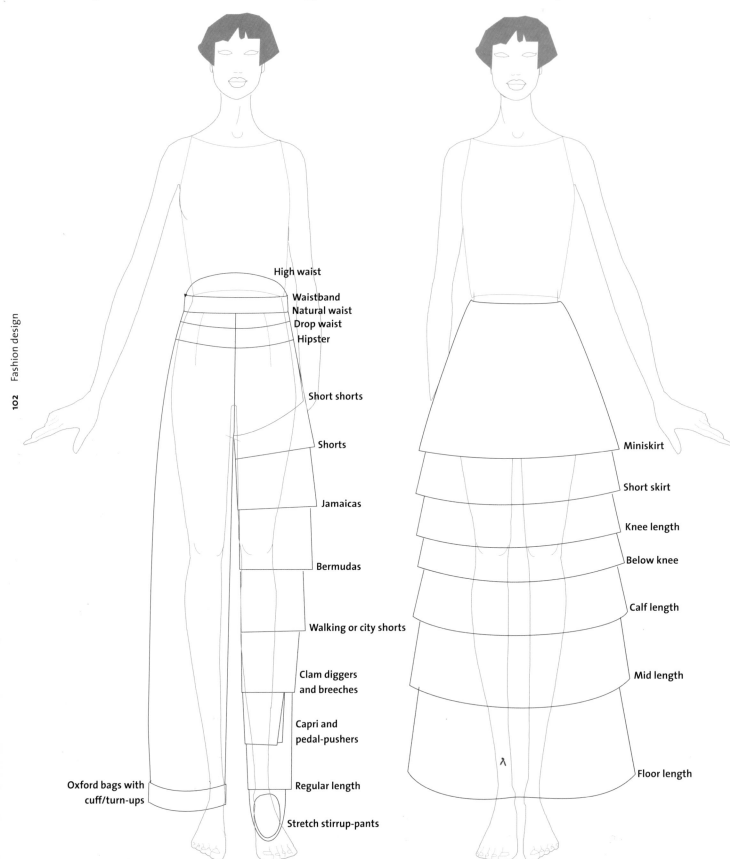

High waist

Waistband
Natural waist
Drop waist
Hipster

Short shorts

Shorts

Jamaicas

Bermudas

Walking or city shorts

Clam diggers
and breeches

Capri and
pedal-pushers

Oxford bags with
cuff/turn-ups

Regular length

Stretch stirrup-pants

Miniskirt

Short skirt

Knee length

Below knee

Calf length

Mid length

Floor length

The visibility of legs and the adoption by women of trousers added to the rich potential of the female silhouette.

Line

We respond in different emotional and psychological ways to the variety of lines that are used in design. A line can be hard or soft, implying rigidity or flexibility. It can move in various directions, leading the viewer to look across, up, down or in a sweep around the body. It can emphasize or disguise other features. It can create illusions of narrowness or fullness. The most common use of line in fashion is in the seaming of the pattern pieces and in fastenings. Vertical seam lines create an effect of length and elegance because they lead the eye up and down the body. Horizontal lines tend to be shorter in span and therefore draw attention to the width of the body. Lines across the body can make the figure appear shorter and wider. In bias cutting, the seam lines travel diagonally across and around the body to give a flowing and dynamic quality to a fabric. Lines can also converge and diverge to give strong directional effects. Curved lines add a certain fullness and femininity to a garment and are often used to minimize waists and draw attention to the bust and hips. Balancing the effects of design lines is one of the first tasks that you will tackle in designing through drawing and sketching your ideas.

Texture

The fabric or materials that a garment is made up of can make or break a style that otherwise looks fine on paper or in toile form. It is both the visual and the sensual element of fashion design. In fact, most designers select fabrics before they make their design sketches. They prefer to be inspired by the texture and handle of a material rather than find the perfect fit for a design sketch. A designer needs experience in how fabric behaves. Fabric is selected for its compatibility with the season, desired line and silhouette, price for the target market and colour. Colour can often be adjusted at a later stage in the process of range-building by changing dye specifications, but the texture and properties of the fabric will remain constant.

The principles of design

The principles of fashion design are not always taught, discussed in crits or consciously employed, but they exist nonetheless. They are an important part of the aesthetic tool kit and are the means by which designers can subtly adjust the focus and effect of designs. Knowing where to find them and change them helps you to view designs objectively. They are usually the key to why a design does or doesn't work. Deliberately flouting these principles is as valid as using them with care if it gets the message across.

Repetition

Repetition is the use of design elements, details or trimmings more than once in a garment. A feature can be repeated regularly or irregularly. This multiple effect can be used to unify a design. Some examples of repetition, such as evenly spaced buttons, are so common a feature that we tend not to notice them until we see an irregular version. The human body is symmetrical, so some repetition is inevitable in the mirroring of one side with another.

Repetition can be a part of the structure of a garment, such as the pleats or panels of a skirt, or a feature of the fabric itself, such as a striped or repeat-printed fabric or applied trimmings. From time to time asymmetrical garments such as single-sleeved tops or skirts that are longer on one side come into vogue as a reaction to the natural rule. Breaking the repeat has a jarring and eye-catching effect.

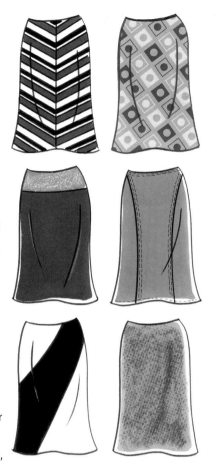

The same garment pattern and silhouette can be leveraged for use with many different fabrics, through daywear to eveningwear and to dramatic stylistic effect, while keeping an underlying integrity to a collection. Some companies keep a successful garment shape in their line for years.

The principles of design

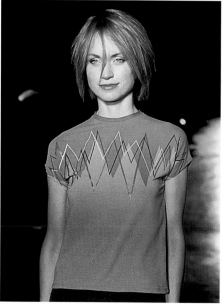

Rhythm   The broken argyle pattern on this top gives it rhythm.

Graduation   The buttons and collar graduate in size, adding interest to this shirt.

Radiation   Ties radiate from a focal point on this parachute blouse.

Repetition   Gathers on the neck and sleeve are a repeating principle.

Contrast A contrast between soft pink wool and hard metal fastenings.

Harmony A rounded top harmonizes with a straight skirt for a subtle and elegant look.

Balance Asymmetry demonstrated in a unique handmade felt top.

Proportion Playing with proportions can feminize a masculine look.

Bodylines and details

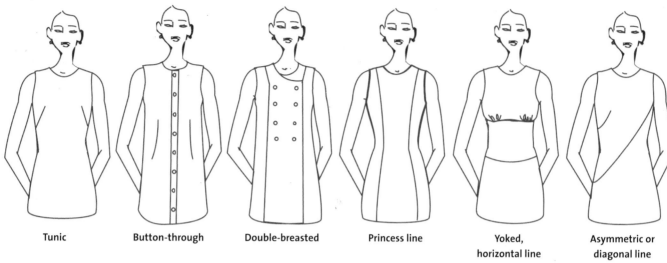

| Tunic | Button-through | Double-breasted | Princess line | Yoked, horizontal line | Asymmetric or diagonal line |

Bodylines

The seam placement and openings of garments can create emphatic visual effect, such as slimming down the torso or drawing the focus towards the chest or face. These are the most frequently seen bodyline design devices for tops, dresses and jackets.

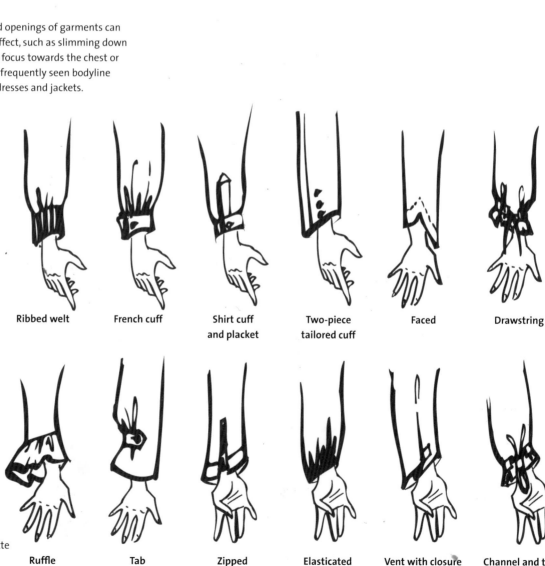

| Ribbed welt | French cuff | Shirt cuff and placket | Two-piece tailored cuff | Faced | Drawstring |

Cuffs

Details such as cuffs and pockets are created to harmonize with the overall style and silhouette of the garment.

| Ruffle | Tab | Zipped | Elasticated | Vent with closure | Channel and tie |

Sleeves

The shape of the sleeve head and its attachment to the bodice is an important means of creating the silhouette.

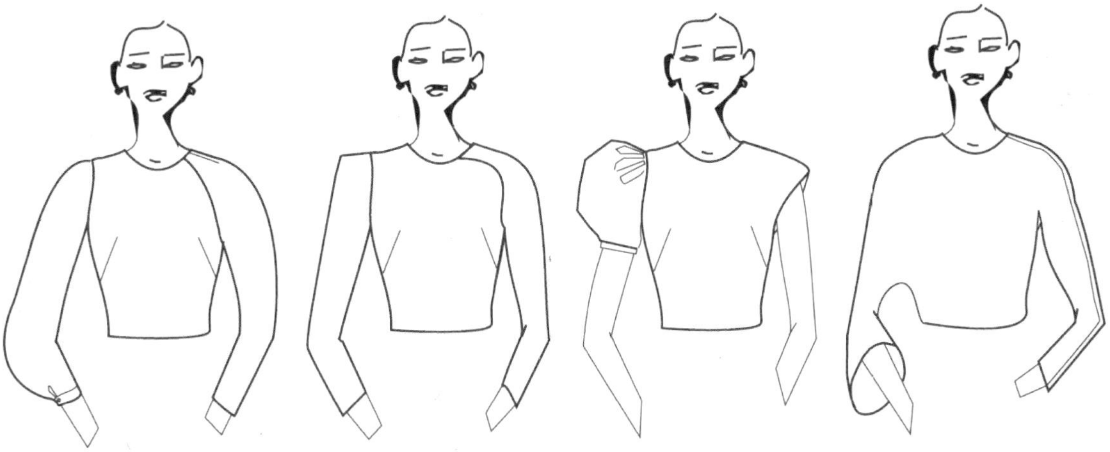

Set-in sleeve   Raglan   Square shoulder   Saddle sleeve   Puff   Cap   Batwing   Dolman

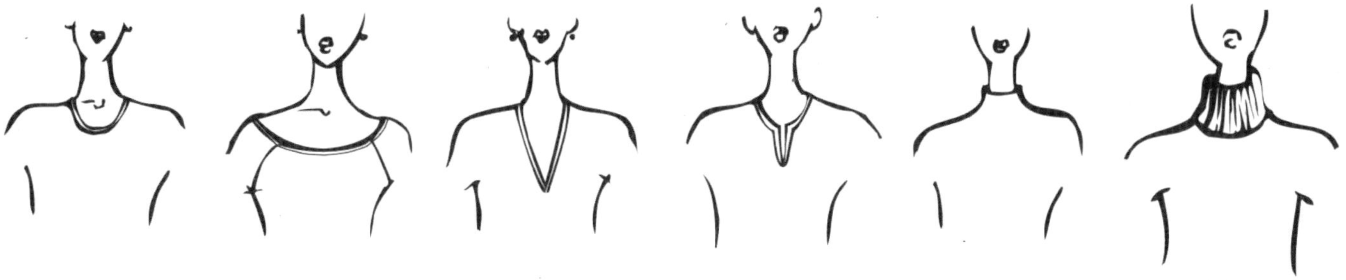

Round   Bateau   V-neck   Slot   Turtleneck   Poloneck

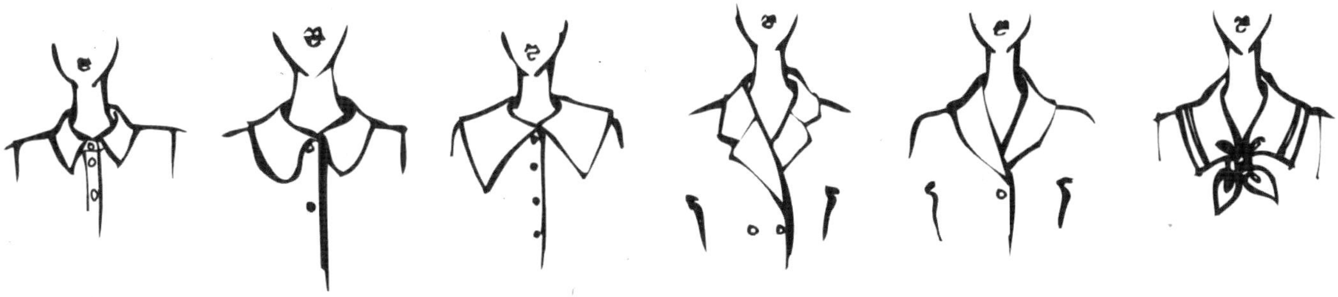

Collar and stand   Peter Pan   Flat collar   Tailored   Shawl   Sailor collar

Necklines

The shape of the neckline or collar may be determined by the type of fabric used, the season or occasion, and how the garment is fastened. Jersey fabrics demand simpler neck and cuff finishes than woven ones.

Cowl   Hood   Jabot   Mandarin

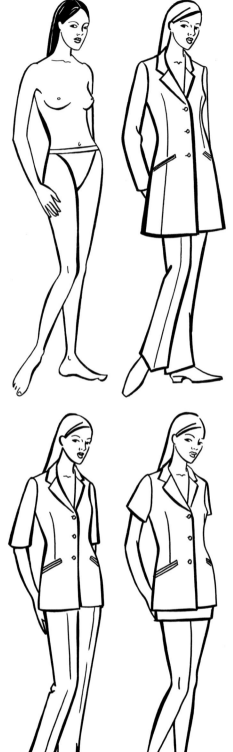

The positioning of horizontal hemlines has a dramatic effect on the proportions of the body.

Rhythm

As in music, rhythm can create a powerful effect, whether through the repetition of regular features or through motifs in printed fabrics.

Graduation

This is a more complex type of repetition where features of the garment are worked in increasing or diminishing sizes or steps. For example, sequins on an evening dress can be heavily encrusted at the hem but fade in number as they travel up the garment. Gathers could be full in the centre of a yoke, diminishing towards the sides. The eye tracks the different degrees of change through the design, so graduation can be used as a way of drawing attention towards, or disguising, body features.

Radiation

Radiation is the use of design lines that fan out from a pivotal point. A sunray-pleated skirt is a good example of this, but the technique can be more subtly deployed in draped garments.

Contrast

Contrast is one of the most useful design principles, causing the eye to re-evaluate the importance of one focal area against another. It relieves the dullness of an all-over effect, for example, if a dress is worn with a contrasting belt. Colours draw attention to themselves and to the features and details they frame. Placement of contrasting features requires care as they become focal points. Contrasts in fabric texture heighten the effect of each material – for example, a tweed jacket worn with a silk blouse. Contrasts need not be extreme; 'subtle contrasts' are created by wearing a suit with either flat shoes or high heels.

Harmony

Harmony is not quite the opposite of contrast, but it does imply similarity rather than difference: hues that do not clash, fabrics that blend well. Soft materials and rounded forms lend themselves better to harmonious design than sharp cutting or pressed garments. Italian fashion is renowned for its harmonious use of soft fabrics and colour mixed with organic and unaggressive tailoring. A collection that is harmonious is easy to mix and match, and generally sells itself without advice from a salesperson.

Balance

The body is symmetrical through the vertical axis, and there is a tendency for our eyes and brains to want to keep it that way. We therefore look for balance in clothing. Vertical balance is created by features mirrored from left to right: matching lapels, aligned and equal-sized pockets, evenly spaced buttons. Horizontal balance is affected when an outfit looks top-heavy, with all the emphasis on the neck, or if it is bottom-heavy, with a skirt that is too large or flouncy. The focus of an asymmetrical design often requires a smaller detail somewhere else on the outfit to echo and balance it. We look at a garment not just from the front and back, but also from other viewpoints. All aspects must satisfy the principle of balance, or say something about a lack of respect for order as in post-Modern Japanese and Belgian fashion.

Proportion

So much has been written about proportion in the realms of art, architecture and design that it seems almost pretentious to apply it to fashion as a rule or tool for achieving effects. However, the same principles apply and will subtly make or break a design. Proportion is the way we visually relate all the separate parts to the whole. This is done by measuring – not necessarily with a tape measure but with the eye. Illusions of body shape can be created by changing the proportions of design features or by moving seams and details around.

As a fashion designer you make decisions regarding the body type you are designing, which proportions to emphasize and which to diminish; how much flesh to hide or display; what the target market will want. You choose your muse and illustrate your garments on this body type, sketching the poses and attitudes that best express your designs. It is imperative to be aware that the fashion market is not only for a few perfect bodies and the fashionistas. Men and women of all ages and shapes want to wear fashionable clothing. To design or merchandise clothes in the quantities required to keep an organization solvent you must be fully aware of the actual dimensions, measurements and needs of 'real' people.

> 'A lot of the time you're not really designing for 'fashion people' but the general public who have some money to spend. People have hang-ups about their bodies so it's no good doing that drapey one-shoulder thing, they are not going to wear it. You can't choose your customer; they choose you.'   Designer Suzanne Clements

The fabrics you choose can make an enormous difference and diverse ones will look or feel very different on the body . A solid-coloured fabric can act as a foil to attractive stitching or fastenings and give the illusion of slenderness; a printed pattern can break up the silhouette. Designers use these tricks to simplify manufacturing and keep the proportions and aesthetic unity of a collection while offering a choice of materials and ways of using them that will flatter the figures of a large number of customers.

Bodily sensation

Clothing is not just a visual experience; it is also a sensory, tactile one. It is essential to handle fabric and test it on the body for how it feels and its properties and associated uses. Contrasts of texture emphasize the difference between the garment and flesh and skin, and can add mood, style and allure. Details on the neckline and cuff emphasize these boundaries. Our sense of touch is stimulated by materials such as cashmere, silk, fur and leather. Very tight or loose clothing can cause sensuous or erotic feelings. The demands of fashion require that the fleshier female body is supported by stretch elastomeric and sheer fabrics that invite touch and flatter the skin. We combine fabrics to playfully extend the feel and appearance of the outfits we wear. Learning how to render different materials is an element worth adding to your illustrative skills. Designers and merchandisers working with separates will need to appreciate good combinations and contrasts and know how to proportion these effectively in a line or store range.

So, whatever the prevailing ideal, designers need the 'reality check' of getting to know the human body and its interaction with fabric. Close observation, the study of fashion photography (and film) and the art of sketching help you to see and understand how the body moves and communicates non-verbally and how nuances of cut, fit and fabric create fascinating and mutable effects of expression with body silhouette, line and volume. Using fabric, texture and colour creatively to work with body shape, skin and hair colouring you can formulate, define and refine your designs.

Further reading and additional resources

Bina Abling. *Fashion Rendering with Color*, New York: Prentice Hall, 2001

Anne Allen and Julian Seaman. *Fashion Drawing: The Basic Principles*, London: Batsford, 1996

Laird Borelli. *Fashion Illustration Now*, London: Thames & Hudson, 2000

Laird Borelli. *Stylishly Drawn*, New York: Harry N. Abrams, 2000

Janet Boyes. *Essential Fashion Design: Illustration Theme Boards, Body coverings, Projects, Portfolios*, London: Batsford, 1997

Yajima Isao. *Fashion Illustration in Europe*, Tokyo: Graphic-Sha, 1988

Kojiro Kumagai. *Fashion Illustration: Expressing Textures*, Tokyo: Graphic-Sha, 1988

Alice Mackrell. *An Illustrated History of Fashion: 500 Years of Fashion Illustration*, New York: Costume and Fashion Press, 1997

Julian Seaman. *Professional Fashion Illustration*, London: Batsford, 1995

Steven Stipelman. *Illustrating Fashion: Concept to Creation*, New York: Fairchild, 1996

Sharon Lee Tate. *The Complete Book of Fashion Illustration*, New Jersey: Prentice Hall, 1996

Linda Tain. *Portfolio Presentation for Fashion Designers*, New York: Fairchild, 1998

Illustration and photography
folioplanet.com/illustration/fashion/
www.showstudio.com

Body image
www.ourbodiesourselves.org/bodyim.htm
www.about-face.org
www.i-shadow.net

New technologies in fashion
www.fashion-online.org
www.virtual-fashion.com
www.snapfashun.com
www.horizonzero.ca

Illustration
cwctokyo.com
art-dept.com
artandcommerce.com

Colour and fabric IV

Colour basics

Research carried out by yarn, textile and garment manufacturers and retailers indicates that the consumer's first response is to colour. This is followed by an interest in the design and feel of the garment and then an appraisal of the price. Choosing colours, or a **palette**, for a fashion range is one of the earliest decisions to make when designing a collection. The colour choices will dictate the mood or seasonal 'tune' of a collection and help to differentiate it from its predecessor.

People respond intuitively, emotionally and even physically to colour. Blues and greens – the colours of sky and grass – have been shown to lower blood pressure, while red and other intense colours can speed up the heart rate. White can make you feel cold; yellow is a sunny, friendly colour; grey can be businesslike or depressing. The 'little black dress' denotes sophistication and elegance, while the little red dress symbolizes fun and sexiness. People brought up in an urban setting will respond to a different palette to those from rural or tropical communities. The same colours can look different or inappropriate in various settings or lighting conditions, for example, in cloudy daylight or under fluorescent shop lighting. Dye technologists recognize this and recommend different intensities of dye and **light fastness** for, say, Manchester, Miami and Bombay.

> *'Pink is the navy blue of India.'* Diana Vreeland, editor of American *Vogue* from 1963 to 1971

The seasons and climate will account for some colour choices. In autumn and winter people are drawn to warm and cheering colours or to dark colours to help retain body heat. Conversely, white (which reflects heat) and pastels are worn more often in spring and summer. There are many social conventions and symbolic meanings attached to colours; in parts of the West it is widely believed that green is unlucky, yet it is also associated with nature and wholesomeness. In India, scarlet, not white, is the colour associated with weddings. In China, white, rather than black, is the colour of mourning. When designing a collection, it is important to take into account the context of the target market.

Defining colours

The average human eye can distinguish some 350,000 different colours, but we do not have names for all of them. In attempting to describe a colour we approximate in the hope that others will see it in the same way. A number of systems have evolved that try

Above, from left to right
The little black dress is always in fashion.
A black-and-white contrast looks chic and fresh.
White can look starkly clinical and dramatic.

to identify and define colour scientifically. The first was devised by the English physicist Sir Isaac Newton in 1666, when he discovered that all colours were present in natural light and could be separated by passing light through a prism. He identified the colours of the spectrum – the seven prismatic colours – red, orange, yellow, green, blue, indigo and violet. He believed that these colours could be related to the musical scale, suggesting colour 'tones' and 'harmonies', and since then colour has often been discussed in musical terms. Newton constructed a six-spoke colour wheel (indigo and blue were merged), which is still used to describe pigments and subtractive colour today. In 1730, Jacques-Christophe Le Blon discovered that mixing two of the primary colours (red, yellow and blue) created secondary colours (orange, green and violet) and, in different ratios, other intermediate hues. Mixing all the primary colours created the tertiary colours: various shades of brown and grey, all the way to black (see colour terms, page 116).

As well as naming the colour itself, we describe its characteristics through the three attributes of hue, value and intensity. Hue refers to the basic colour, such as blue, red or green. There are relatively few pure hues. Value refers to the lightness or darkness of a colour which varies on a scale of white (the sum and source of all colours) to black (the total absence of light). Lighter values are called tints, the darker ones shades. Intensity is the relative strength (purity) or weakness (impurity) of a colour. Diluting a pigment with water will lower its intensity; for example, red becomes rosy pink and then pale pink.

How colour works

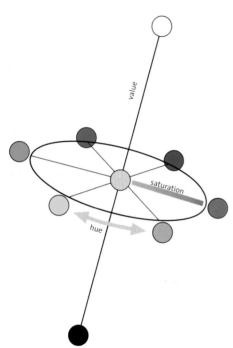

The three dimensions of colourspace: hue, value and intensity of saturation.

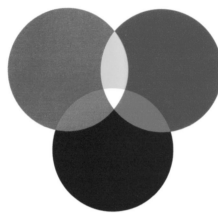

Additive colour System of mixing physical primaries (light). When projected in combination, red, blue and green produce white light.

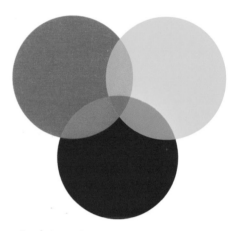

Subtractive colour Mixing the pigments red, yellow and blue creates the secondary colours: orange, green and violet

Colour wheel A
Designers require a wide range of pigments and dyes to achieve a broad spectrum of colours.

Colour wheel B
Attempting to mix colours, such as emerald green and mauve, is not possible using the primary colour pigments.

Simultaneous contrast Characterizes colour as a strongly relative phenomenon; colours change their appearance depending on their context.

In any colour scheme, as important as the identity of a particular colour is the relationship it shares with the other colours in the composition. A dull colour can be brightened, a strong colour can be subdued, an individual colour can change its identity in many ways, depending on the colours with which it is surrounded.

Spectrum Full range of colour, from violet to red, as produced by shining white light through a prism.

Primary colours Red, yellow and blue cannot be made by mixing other colours.

Complementary colours Colours, such as red-green, blue-orange, yellow-violet, which are optically opposed; they appear opposite each other on the colour wheel.

Analogous colours Those colours with a common hue which are adjacent on the colour wheel, e.g., blue-violet, violet and red-violet, etc.

Secondary colours Orange, green, violet – colours made by mixing two primary colours. Yellow and red make orange, etc.

Value The attribute that measures variation among greys; refers to the lightness and darkness of a colour. Any hue can vary in value – red can become light pink or dark maroon.

Vibrating colour When complementary colours of equal value are placed together they cause a visual intensity that exceeds their actual intensity; also known as simultaneous contrast.

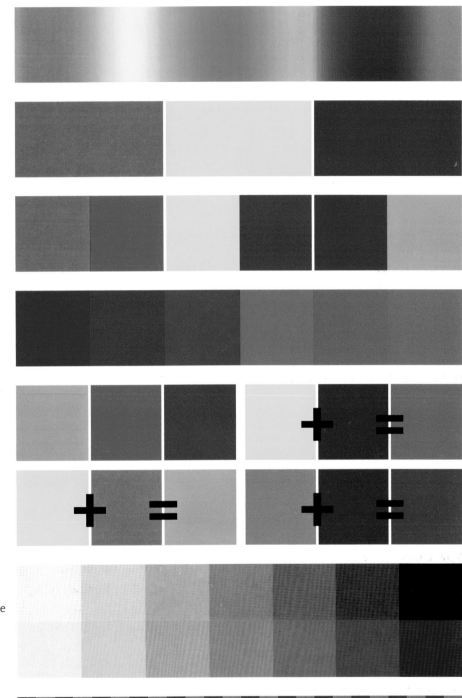

A single colour makes a strong statement.

Colour terms

Below are some common terms used by the dye and fashion industry to differentiate and combine colours.

Tone A 'greyed' colour.

Deep Rich, dark.

Concentrated Intense, saturated colour.

Pastel A colour tinted with white.

Warm colours Associated with fire, sunlight, passion (e.g., red, orange, yellow, purple).

Cool colours Associated with sky, sea, ice, peace (e.g., blues, violets, tints with white).

Neutrals Colours based on the tertiaries (beige, grey, brown, khaki, olive).

Subdued colours Colours shaded up or down by the addition of black, white, grey or a complementary colour (e.g., yellow with a touch of violet creates dark gold).

Monochromes The gamut, or scale, of shades using a single hue from black to white.

Ground colour The dominant background hue, shade or tone.

Accent colour Colour used in a small proportion, which has a strong visual attraction.

Harmonies Two or more colours that look balanced and pleasing together.

Contrasts Colours that strongly emphasize their differences when placed next to each other; often they are directly opposing hues on the colour wheel (e.g., blue and orange).

Complements Almost opposing colour hues; they are more harmonious pairings than contrasts as they use a warm tone with a cool one.

Analogous colours Tints and tones that are close neighbours on the colour wheel.

Subtractive colours Colours mixed using pigments and dyes.

Additive colours Colours mixed using light or light absorption.

Optical mixes Iridescent colours that occur when two different ones are knitted or woven together, usually as warp and weft, so that, viewed from different angles, the fabric appears to change colour subtly. Optical mixes are used in jersey marls, cotton chambré and shot silks.

Fugitive colour Colour that washes out or bleeds (i.e., is not fast).

Simultaneous contrast Effect occurring when the intensity of a colour appears to change based on the value of its background, or within a set of colours; often seen in stripes and prints, and also in contrasts between skin tones and clothing.

Scientific descriptions of colour, however, cannot fully communicate its sensation or emotional effect, so we also name colours based on our familiar and shared knowledge of the world – after animals (for example, elephant grey and canary yellow); flowers and vegetables (lilac, mushroom, tomato red); sweets and spices (toffee, saffron); minerals and jewels (pearl, coral, jade), and so on.

This associative use of colour is helpful for remembering colour shades and naming a palette, but it is not sufficient to indicate to a specialist the exact tone that is required for a match. In order to do this, a number of standardized commercial colour-matching systems have been developed. The most widely used in fashion and textiles are the PANTONE Professional Colour System and the SCOTDIC (Standard Color of Textile Dictionaire Internationale de la Couleur) systems. These were inspired by the method of measuring colours according to hue, value and chroma, devised by Albert Munsell. Pantone has a specialist fabric colour-matching known as the RightColor®. The Pantone method precisely calibrates a six-digit number to indicate the location of the colour on

Left A sophisticated palette using iridescent analogous colours.

Top Layered pastels give this outfit a festive look.

Above Metallic colours such as gold and silver add glamour to a sheer fabric.

Above Colourways and repeating patterns for a screen-printed textile design are worked out and separated into transparent stencils on a light box.

Opposite Dye recipes and pigments are mixed in the laboratory ready for printing onto fabric.

the colour wheel (first two digits) and compares its value to black and white (second two digits) and its intensity (final two digits). The Pantone system is included in many computer design-software packages. Using this system, it is possible to ask a printer or dyer to reproduce your artwork to an exact specification.

Dyes and printing inks have their own chemical names and numbers to indicate strength and variation on a calibrated colour scale. The dye companies are usually subsidiaries of major chemical companies such as, ICI, BASF, Zeneca, Bayer and Ciba-Geigy, and there are a growing number of dyeworks that specialize in 'natural' and eco-friendly processing.

Colour forecasting

Colour prediction has become big business. It impacts not only upon clothing but also cosmetics, home furnishings, lifestyle products and the automotive industry. Dye companies cannot afford to make expensive mistakes, and must be ready to supply the demand for a colour up to two years in advance of the retail sale season. Colour forecasters for the fashion industry collate information from all over the world on sales figures and changes in market interest in colours. They then come together twice a year for conferences in Europe and the United States to summarize and define the broad industry trends.

The principal colour advisory bodies are the British Textile Colour Group, the International Colour Authority (ICA), the Color Association of the United States (CAUS) and the Color Marketing Group (CMG). In the process of analysing data, the forecasters also observe and interpret the underlying social and cultural context and make projections for the future. This informs the likely direction that colours in fashion may take. For example, during the 1990s many consumers were aware and concerned about the damage that chemical dyes were causing to the environment. Colour forecasters warned the dye companies to concentrate on more natural shades and formulations. This provoked a return to the use of softer-coloured 'natural' dyes and to the prevalence of undyed and unbleached materials in fashion.

Colour forecasters do not dictate colours but analyse and interpret the underlying social and cultural events, and various market-sector preferences for *moods* or *families* of colours. There are fashions and long- and short-term cycles in colours and it can be predicted that certain ones will take centre stage for a period and then give way to close relatives or their opposites.

> *'Every season I ask myself: What am I sick of the sight of? What have I seen out the corner of my eye? Like: lime green's a bit out now but watch out for pink for blokes.'*
> Colour guru Sandy MacLennan

The Pantone™ Textile Color System features over 1,900 colors arranged chromatically by colour family. The colour chips correspond to available dyes and are frequently used by the fashion industry to specify lab-dips for yarn and garments.

Forecasters use insight, experience and mathematics to make their predictions. In times of economic prosperity bright and unusual colours sell well, while people choose darker, conservative colours in times of austerity. Observation has shown that there are approximately seven-year cycles between warm-toned and cool-toned colours, and longer cycles of fifteen to twenty-five years between intense, multicoloured fashions and more subdued neutrals and greys. Colour choices move forward more quickly in womenswear than in menswear. Fashion revivals, such as 1950s-style rock-and-roll clothing, usually also entail a revival of the colour family that originally accompanied them. Some colours are popularized, as are fashions, by celebrities or sports. Every four years the Olympic Games can be relied on to put a palette of sporty primary colours into casualwear and the youth clothing market. White is always expected to be in the summer palette, and in the winter earthy and autumnal tones inevitably give way to the most popular fashion colour of all – black. The fresh hues of pastels are associated with revival and springtime.

Colour and the designer

Unless you work within a company where a large volume of goods in production means you can order colours to be dyed to your own palette, you will probably be restricted to ones that are offered by the fabric mills. These are usually the classic popular colours – variations of black, white, navy and red – and the fashion ones as predicted by colour gurus and interpreted by dye houses. It may take between six and eighteen months before the colours you choose at a fabric fair appear as a co-ordinated colour story in the shops. This delay period is called the **lead time**. Recent technological improvements in machinery have shortened lead times by allowing colour choices to be left until later in the season, to respond to customer demand. Computer control of the dyeing process has speeded up colour matching and smaller batch processing. Through a process of 'whole garment-dyeing', solid, single shade garments can be styled independently of their colour. Hosiery, knitwear and sports- and leisurewear without trimmings are most suited to this treatment. Benetton have built their successful brand (United Colours of Benetton) on the speedy supply of desirable colours in knitwear, and produce *Colors* magazine, which is a homage to the importance of colour and culture, and a vivid document of the fashion zeitgeist.

Creating a colour palette

Gorgeous use of colour can be one of the most attractive and emotionally satisfying aspects of fashion design and is particularly important when trends favour more traditional shapes and silhouettes. Build up your own 'colour library' of snippets of fabrics and pieces of paper. This will help you to understand which colours form natural and pleasing combinations, and how to balance the use of ground colours with accent ones.

A fashion colour palette (or *gamme*) usually has between four and ten colours. Some will dominate and be used as base colours, while others will be used more conservatively or within prints. Colours for fashion must take into account the effects on skin, hair and eye colouring. Hues such as yellow and green can reflect colour back onto the skin and are not flattering to many complexions; they are more commonly applied as accent and accessory colours. Beiges and pale pinks can also fight with individual skin tones and make some wearers look washed out. When building your colour palette make adjustments for the age group and dominant colouring of your market sector. Light to mid-tone combinations create a calm, reserved effect. Contrasts and dramatic tones will draw attention to the wearer. Colour can be used in a garment as a design element to emphasize or flatter a part of the body and make or break a focal point. For this reason it is useful to be aware of the 'receding' and 'advancing' effects of various hues in combination. The fashion media is given over to style advice and colour recommendations; it is worth taking note of the key 'rules' and applying this knowledge to your fashion research to see how the top designers follow or break them.

If you have access to a dye laboratory you can experiment with dyeing shades in tones and making combinations to build up your own unique colour palettes, fabric swatches or yarn stories. Keep a book with your colour recipes and dye and print techniques. The introduction of new dyes or colour combinations has often altered the course of fashion.

Different classes of dyestuff have different 'affinities' to fibres when applied. A dye is called 'colour-fast' when it does not wash out or fade. Some fibres cannot be dyed certain shades, as the correct chemical mixes have not yet been invented. Ask how to use various techniques such as bleaching, over-dyeing, tie-dyeing, cross-dyeing and discharging to get interesting multi-coloured effects.

Yarn is packaged in many different forms depending on its end use, e.g., cones, bobbins, cheeses, spools, balls and skeins.

Fibre types

The characteristics of a fibre, its weight, warmth, appearance and the way it behaves, determine the qualities and purposes for which woven and knitted fabrics are made or used.

Acetate A semi-synthetic made with cellulose pulp and acetic acid and extruded as acetate rayon fibre. First marketed as artificial silk (Art-silk) in 1921.

Acrylic A synthetic version of wool made from gas and air, developed by DuPont in the 1940s. A light, cheap and easy-care fibre.

Alpaca Soft, fine hair from the South American alpaca goat. Luxury blends.

Angora Fine, light hair combed from the angora rabbit. Fancy blends.

Botany Top-quality Australian-bred merino sheep wool from Botany Bay area.

Camel The camel sheds its own hair. A durable, heavy and warm luxury fibre.

Cashmere Hair from the fine soft undercoat of the young Asiatic goat. Luxury use.

Cellulosic Fibre or sheet developed from a vegetable fibre or wood pulp extrusion.

Cool wool Worsted yarn for suitings. Dry handle, light summer weights only.

Cotton Fibre from the cotton-plant seed head. A low-cost crop with wide distribution and many varieties. Versatile, soft, easy to dye and launder.

Count Yarn is sized by count; worsted, woollen and metric systems.

Crêpe Fibres can be spun in S or Z torque. Z twist gives a lively crêpe handle.

Elastomeric Yarns usually derived from polyurethane with high stretch recovery.

Felt Dense yarn or fibre that is matted together during processing or in use.

Flame Long strands of fancy fibre added to yarn to give dramatic effect.

Flax Plant from which linen and some durable string qualities are derived.

Geelong Superfine hair clippings from merino lambs under eight months old.

Gauge Term used to describe the spacing of needles in machine knitting and the resulting yarn, e.g., 10 gg denotes ten needles per inch.

Hemp Fibre from the hemp plant. Strong and pliant for sacks and matting.

Jersey Machine-knitted fabric. Flat, tubular, single or double (interlock).

Jute String-like fibre found in aloe plants.

Lambswool Yarn and textiles with a 100 per cent virgin wool content, at least one-third of which is fleece from lambs that have not been weaned.

Linen Durable, cool, absorbent fibre produced from the stems of the flax plant.

Lurex Metallic, glittering fibre, flat in cross-section, for eveningwear fabrics.

Lycra The first synthetic elastic stretch fibre, developed and registered by DuPont.

Marl A double yarn made from two different-coloured single yarns spun together.

Melange Fibre printed or sprayed with different colours and made into cloth.

Merino The merino sheep (origin Spain) produces the highest quality wool.

Microfibre Nylon fibre spun to a very fine denier and textured with a soft handle.

Mineral Asbestos, carbon, glass and metal fibres can be manufactured and are used in furnishings and architectural fabrics.

Mohair Long, lustrous and hard-wearing hair of the angora goat. Luxury knitwear and suits.

Nylon The first completely synthetic fibre. Discovered in 1934, developed and marketed by DuPont as Nylon, Bri-Nylon or Celon. Strong and versatile.

Fibrillated viscose; fibres can be brushed up after weaving to give a soft handle.

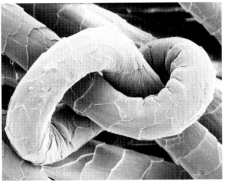

A knot in a wool fibre. The scales on the fibres open in warm soapy water and allow them to lock together to make felt.

The knitted structure of a cotton jersey allows the fabric to stretch both widthwise and lengthwise.

Woven man-made polyester fibre in a plain weave.

A wool gabardine twill.

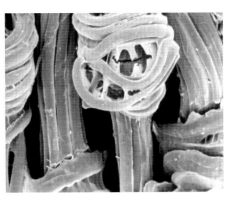

Silk fabric treated with soda to burst the fibres.

Polyamide Nylon is just one form of polyamide – a smooth, strong and stretchy fibre type. Many versions are widely used in hosiery and lingerie.

Polyester Synthetic, cheap, easy-care, petrochemical fibre developed by ICI and DuPont in 1941 and sold as Terylene, Dacron and Crimplene, recylable from plastic cartons as polar fleece. Commonly mixed with other fibres.

PVC Polyvinylchloride, a plastic mostly used as a waterproof coating.

Ramie Derived from plants. Similar to linen.

Shetland wool Once a hard-wearing, inexpensive wool from the Shetland Islands, now a generic term that describes many knitted and woven fabrics.

Silk Fine, strong and lustrous yarn spun as a continuous filament by the silkworm larva. Used for the most luxurious and expensive fashions.

Spandex A synthetic polymer rubbery yarn with elastic qualities.

Tencel A 'green' artificial fibre, stronger than cotton, with a silk-like drape.

Vicuna Fine and resilient hair from the protected vicuna llama of South America.

Viscose Shiny, semi-synthetic, multi-purpose fibre created from wood pulp and soda.

Woollen Full, soft, bulky yarns made from short staple, unparallel spun-wool fibres.

Worsted Smooth, durable yarn spun from longer, parallel combed wool fibres.

Yarn folds The folding, or doubling of yarns, i.e., three-fold or three-ply denotes the size, weight and quality of yarn, and is used in specifying and marketing them.

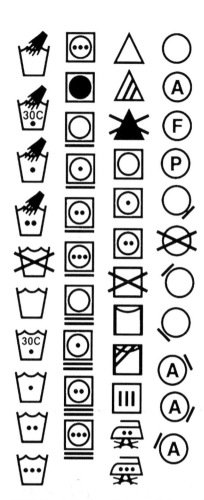

The International Textile Care Labelling Code is a globally recognized standard for consumer information regarding the laundering and handling of clothing. Mistreatment of fabrics leads to waste and returns, which costs the industry dearly.

The Woolmark logo is a mark of quality and guarantees authenticity.

Fabrics

Fabric is to the fashion designer what paint is to the artist: the medium of creative expression. Some designers work directly with the fabric, others might draw ideas on paper and then search for an appropriate material. Choosing suitable fabrics is the key to successful designing. It is a matter not only of what one likes visually, but also of weight and handle, price, availability, performance, quality and timing. The suitability of a fabric for a fashion design comes from a combination of yarn, construction, weight, texture, colour, handling and pattern or print, as well as additional performance factors such as warmth, stain-resistance and ease of care. The designer must have a reasonable expectation as to how a fabric will behave; a material cannot be forced into a style or shape that is not compatible with its characteristics, both practically and visually.

You need to build up a good working knowledge of the different categories of fabrics, their sources, price structures and their suitability for various uses. Keep a notebook specifically for this purpose. Some organizations that can help students to source fabrics are listed at the end of this chapter.

The International Textile Care Labelling Code

All commercial garments must carry a fibre content label by law. In the UK it is an offence to supply or offer to supply textile products that do not comply; the penalties for non-compliance range from fines to imprisonment. The highest fibre content is listed first as a percentage of the total. Any decorative matter that makes up seven per cent or less of the product can be excluded from the fibre content listing. The information on the content label is accompanied by a recommendation for care (sometimes on a separate label). Global manufacturing has led to standardized (ISO) labelling agreements between countries. The European GINETEX labelling scheme consists of a group of symbols called the International Textile Care Labelling Code and is used by all major manufacturing countries. Domestic washing machines and dryers are now being marked with the same icons.

Knowing a fabric's fibre content will help you with future identification, and is essential to learning a material's handling and care characteristics, and whether it is fit for the purpose you have in mind. If you plan to add other finishes such as printing or pleating, the fabric must be suitable.

An increasing number of fibres and modern fabrics are being branded or trademarked by their makers or growers with easily recognizable symbols to denote quality and assure users that they are genuine. The practice of counterfeiting fabrics is a major problem for the fashion industry. If you are buying from source, the manufacturers will give you a header or swatch of the fabric, which will detail the fibre content and weight. This information may be harder to get if you buy from market stalls. Always ask for the name and content of the cloth as well as the price and width. Many fashion schools have fabric libraries, or classes to help you identify materials, but the best option is to start your own collection. John Galliano is said to keep scraps of all the fabrics he has ever sampled in a series of glass jars.

Fibre

Fibre or yarn is the raw material out of which the fabric is made. There are three main categories of fibres: animal (hairs), vegetable (cellulosic fibre) and mineral (synthetics). An experienced designer can often identify basic fibres by hand and sight. Today there are very many sophisticated blends and branded versions of man-made fibres. The length of the yarn fibre (known as the **staple**), the method of spinning it into a yarn and its diameter will all determine the characteristics of the cloth. Blends modify the inherent properties of the main fibre. For example, cotton and linen are absorbent and also crease badly, but when mixed with polyester they dry faster and can be ironed more smoothly.

Fabric construction

The two main ways in which fibre is made into fabric are weaving and knitting. Textiles produced by other methods – felt, net, lace and bonded fabrics – are classified as non-wovens. It is very useful for fashion designers to have an understanding of the basic structures of materials as this indicates how they can be applied and finished. It is important to know how they will wear, stretch and behave when the garment is worn.

Woven fabrics are created by interlacing vertical yarns (the **warp**) with horizontal ones (the **weft**) at right angles to each other. These threads are also referred to as the lengthwise and crosswise grain of the fabric. The tightness or set of a fabric is due to the number of warp and weft threads per inch or centimetre. The edges of the cloth are usually set with a higher number of, or stronger, threads to stabilize the fabric. This is known as the selvedge (also spelled selvage). Because the warp is prestretched to weave evenly, most woven fabrics have good lengthwise stability. For this reason garments are usually cut out parallel to the selvedge so the body follows the lengthwise grain. The additional stretch of the crosswise grain helps the fabric stretch in places like the seat, knees and elbows.

Printed sheepskin combines the exotic with the cosy.

Types of weave

By changing the colour or yarn type in the warp and weft of the weave structure, an infinite variety of fabrics can be produced. In particular, the type of weave will make a difference to how the fabric drapes or behaves.

Plain weave The most common of all weave structures; when warp and weft are of the same size and closely woven, the plain weave is the strongest of all weaves. Fabrics made with a plain weave include calico, broadcloth, flannel, gingham and chiffon.

Twill weave Weave formed by the weft crossing at least two warp threads before going under one or more threads, producing a fabric with a diagonal surface pattern. Gabardine, drill and whipcord are popular twills. Herringbone is a variation that is used in suitings.

Satin and sateen weaves Weaves producing smooth, lustrous fabrics with high drape and a tendency to stretch. The threads are positioned with longer floats on the surface – on the warp surface in satin and the weft surface in sateen.

Pile weave Fancy weave using an extra filling thread that is drawn up and looped on the surface of the fabric. The loops can be left uncut, as in towelling, or cut or sheared as in corduroy, velvet and fake-fur fabrics. High-pile fabrics such as candlewick are made by a needle- or gun-tufting process applied to a woven backing.

Jacquard weave Intricate, figured weave produced on a jacquard loom. Each thread is programmed to lift or stay in place by a perforated card like a pianola roll. Brocade, damask and tapestry are jacquard weaves used for eveningwear and special occasions.

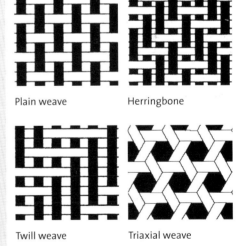

Plain weave   Herringbone

Twill weave   Triaxial weave

Satin weave   Jacquard weave

Fashion design

Integrally knitted whole garments are less wasteful of resources than cut-and-sew manufacturing. Single and customized items can be made quickly to order rather than by fulfilling a multiple docket.

Knitted fabrics are formed by linked loops of yarn. Horizontal rows are called courses, and vertical rows are called wales. They stretch in both directions and have a greater tendency to stretch crosswise. Their elasticity gives them good draping and crease-resistant properties, but by the same token they can also lose their shape with wear and washing. Because the structure is fairly open, knitted fabrics 'breathe' and can keep the body warm or cool, according to the choice of yarn. They are useful for underwear and active sportswear. As fine knits tend to cling to the body they are favoured for eveningwear. As with weaving, knitting can incorporate colour and pattern effects.

Most knitting constructions have been developed from the craft of hand-knitting. Today, modern machinery can produce fabrics and garments that are more complex than could be attempted by hand, at high speed. A fully finished sweater can be made in forty-five minutes. Nevertheless, there is still a place for the unique qualities and charm of the hand-knitted garment in fashion. Machine-knitted fabrics vary from the sheerest of lingerie qualities to heavily cabled woollens. Machine-knitted fabric size is measured by gauge, abbreviated as 'gg'. This refers to the number of needles per inch or per centimetre.

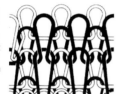

Single jersey

Double jersey

Fair Isle

Jacquard

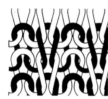

Interlock

Warp knitting

Types of knit

Single jersey In this knit, the face (the knit side) of the fabric is smooth, while the back (the purl side) is comparatively rough and therefore more absorbent. If a stitch is dropped or a hole made, the fabric will ladder or run down the length of the wale. Single jersey has a tendency to curl at the edges when cut. It is lightweight and ideal for T-shirts and lingerie.

Double jersey Also known as interlock, this uses a double row of needles to make a fabric that is smooth-faced on both sides, stable and less likely to bag or run.

Ribbing This is a vertical arrangement of needles that alternately knit, purl and knit stitches to produce a stretchy, reversible construction. Ribbing is used to pull fabric close to the body at the waist, neck and cuffs, and is also used with wovens as a trimming on sports clothing.

Fair Isle A single-jersey knit with small patterns using two colours of yarn at a time; developed from the sweater patterns of the Shetland Islands off Scotland.

Jacquard Double-jersey patterned knitting using as many as four colours in a row; usually programmed and controlled by computerized machinery.

Intarsia Method of producing colourful single-jersey geometric and picture knits. More laborious than the Fair Isle or jacquard methods, until the invention of computerized machinery it was confined to only the most expensive luxury and cashmere-sweater markets.

Warp knitting A hybrid of knitting and weaving that uses a beam of warp threads linked together by a moving rack of needles. The created fabric will not unravel or run and is used for swimwear, sports clothing and lingerie.

The oldest method of making fabrics was by bonding or matting fibres together. When wool is moist, warm and pressed, the fibres interlock to form felt. This process has been extended to the production of thermoplastic man-made fused fabrics. There is no grain to these materials; they can be cut in any direction and do not fray or unravel. Some of the fabrics can be stretched and steam-moulded, as in rabbit-hair felt, to make hats.

In the lingerie business thermoplastic knitted fabric that has 'memory' – that is, it returns to its desired shape after washing – is used for bra cups and the feet and calves of hosiery.

Supporting fabrics such as interfacings and interlinings that add body, shape retention and reinforcement at stress points are often made of bonded fabrics. These are commonly known by their trade names, for example, Staflex and Vilene. **Fusible** interlinings are coated with a glue to allow them to stick to the garment fabric with heat pressing. Wadding is a high-loft fabric of puffed-up, matted fibres used in quilting and padding to give bulk or warmth to a garment.

Net and lace are fabrics made on complex machinery that allows threads to twist and travel diagonally. Lace fabric usually comes with a scalloped hem edge, and lengths are restricted to the width of the machine. Net and lace do not usually fray, but the open and rough surface quality of some lace demands that it is lined. Rubber and plastics are often used in the more esoteric designs. Rubber, derived from the latex (sap) of the rubber tree, can be used in liquid form and painted onto a mould, or even directly onto the body. Rubber sheet can be cut and sewn or glued, and is available in translucent, solid colours, metallic finishes and prints. Plastics, polythenes and cellophanes have all been put to use in the fashion industry.

Fabric development and finishes

The textile industry is continually inventing new fabrics and processes. Tencel, Tactel, Sympatex, Supplex, Polartec, Aquatex, Viloft and Coolmax are all recently developed synthetic materials. Many of the processes are applied after the fabric has been made and dyed, and are known as finishes. Finishing can be for practical and performance

Above, left to right:
The craft of handmade knitwear is an important facet of the luxury market. It gives designers scope for expression with colour, form and texture in creating unique yet long-lasting fashions.

Knitwear can be constructed in three dimensions directly on the machine without the need for seams. Here the technique is used to add drape to a heavy, soft wool.

Very fine jersey drapes beautifully. Here the transparent layers create a changing moiré effect with every step the model takes.

Above Yarn qualities and new colour palettes are developed and offered to fashion wholesalers twice a year.

Below Prototype garments and manufacturing techniques are often developed by fabric and yarn companies in collaboration with fashion colleges to show at trade fairs.

improvement such as stabilizing, fireproofing and crease-resistance, or for embellishment and handle such as brushing, beading or embroidery. Finishes at first devised for the use of military, industrial or household textiles are often used by inventive designers for various sports or fashion garments. Companies patent these new processes and the proprietary trade names are used in the publicity and marketing of the fabrics.

Fabric printing has long been one of the most popular ways of finishing and decorating plain cloth, and there are many methods such as batik, heat-transfer (sublistatic) and screen printing that have their own distinctive looks. Add to this the numerous generic prints, such as florals, geometrics, abstracts, picture prints (known as **conversationals**) and other motifs, and the scope for design is infinite.

> '*Print, I think, you really have to fall in love with, it really is the most difficult decision to make. It can define the whole collection, but also you can see nothing else if it is too obvious.*' Designer Sonja Nuttall

The fabric-development cycle

Modern fabrics and their marketing differ considerably from the past when only natural fibres were available and countries could protect their products and trade. Giant chemical companies have entered the textile business and spend a great deal of money on creating fibres with 'performance' qualities, which they vigorously promote. Natural-fibre 'growers' have fought back by forming associations to strengthen their product innovation and promotional strategies. The process is market-led, and fashion design ranges are now the end result of an intensive process of research and development, within the chemical, dye, engineering, textiles and trimmings industry, that is in advance of fashion by as much as five years. Experts gather information,

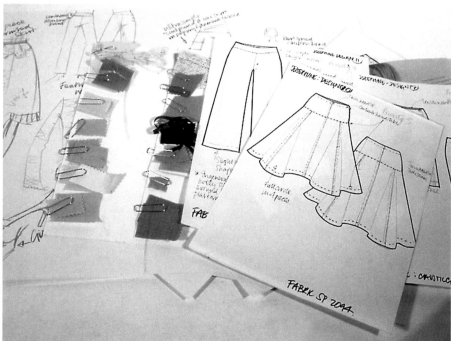

Above After a visit to a trade fair, the designer puts together fabric and colours to range-build and co-ordinate the sampled fabrics. Some materials will then be eliminated.

consult and meet twice yearly to agree forward ranges so that there is some consistency of ideas and directions. Yarn and textile designers present their lines about eighteen months ahead of the fashion market in Europe. Fabric merchants and converters present their ranges approximately three to twelve months ahead depending on volume, ease of production and demand. You may well find yourself involved with fabric development at some stage, and need to appreciate the long lead times necessary to test and approve changes before a product can be launched.

Developments in mechanical and computerized equipment can lead to fresh styles and entirely new categories of garments. Examples are the polar fleece, which is made from recycled and spun plastic waste; seamless lingerie, created on cylindrical knitting machines; and waterproof jackets, sprayed with polymers and heat-set to shape. It is up to you, as a designer, both to invent new garments and techniques using the machinery available and also to demand improvements and adaptations to existing machinery to create the techniques you have in mind. The French, Italian and Japanese textile trades are particularly responsive to the needs of designers, one of the reasons for their supremacy in decorative and technical fabrics. Surface decoration is one of the most effective ways of refreshing a look, with woven colour and texture effects, knitted stitches, patterns and imagery, and by silk-screening or ink-jet-printing fabric. Custom weaves, knits and prints take longer to produce and deliver. Fabrics are usually made in various colour versions called 'colourways'. Fashion companies can request that these are sold exclusively to them or they can specify the colours they want. Fabric samples are referred to as 'lengths' and a short test-run of a print is a 'strike-off'. These terms differ around the world. Learn as many terms and techniques for decorative fabrics as you can, because later in your career you will find yourself buying fabrics, or in discussion with technicians, internationally.

Above With knitwear, a storyboard is built up by trying out combinations of colour and yarn textures.

Below Inspiring techniques used in one-off garments are admired for their individuality, but often cannot be reproduced for mass-manufacture.

Here, rubber has been printed to look like Arran knitwear and Scottish tartan.

Different prints are used to create a stylish and unexpected effect.

The fashion cycle

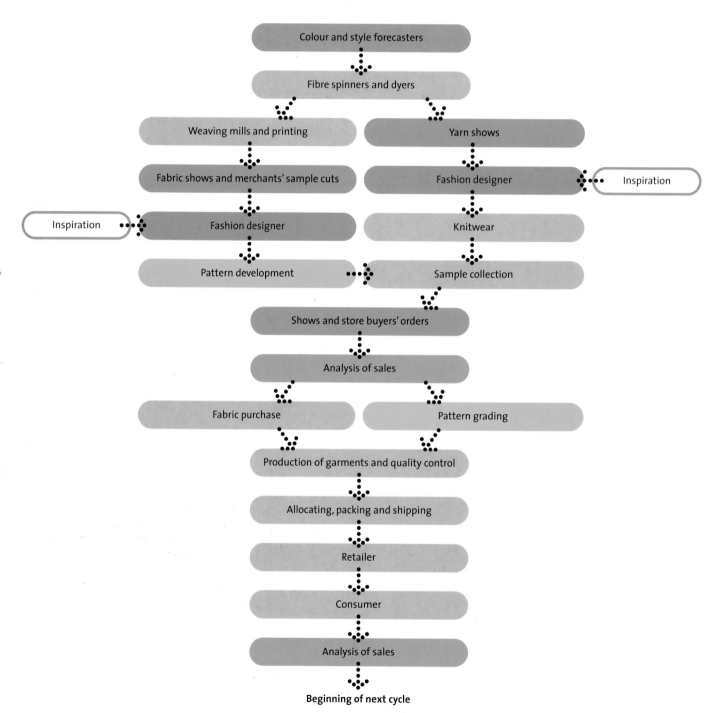

The fashion-design cycle

Fashion is seasonal, time sensitive and works by adhering to a number of interlocking schedules. The fashion business has to manage the design process efficiently and there are timetabled periods for marketing research, prototyping, orders, manufacturing and sales. For each business the timings of these events will depend on the fabric, garment types, market sectors and demands of the outlets that a company provides for. There are some regular dates which peg the calendar in place for the manufacturer, such as the fabric fairs and Prêt-à-porter weeks, and other dates, such as holidays like Valentine's Day, and Labour Day in the United States, which are important to retailers. The cycle will start in different places for different jobs within the industry and not necessarily fit into the annual calendar. This is because the lead times for some types of merchandise take longer to process than others. Most high-fashion businesses observe the seasonal periods discussed in Chapter I: spring/summer and autumn/winter. From March to September they design, range-plan, sample and sell in September for spring/summer deliveries. From October to February they design, range-plan, sample and sell in February for autumn/winter deliveries. This cycle is highly pressured and is being eroded gradually by high street and department stores needing frequent deliveries or 'drops' because consumers like to see new merchandise more often. Computerized systems have also speeded up manufacturing and the supply chain. In the US there is finer tuning of the selling seasons with two 'transitional' periods and additional holiday-clothing times; for example, swimwear is sold immediately after the New Year for the 'cruise' period. The French call September, *la rentrée*, literally the return after the traditional month-long European holiday. At this time they stock the shops with sensible workwear and suits. Therefore designers will often be required to work with others (e.g. knitwear factories) whose cycle times are longer or shorter than their own, and may find themselves planning and working on up to three seasons and cycles at once.

> '*The fashion cycle is relentless. Helen Storey and I referred to this as the "hamster wheel"; sometimes you think you're going round in circles and going nowhere in particular.*' Design manager Caroline Coates

Continuous design and production is a more economic and cash-flow-efficient method of working and keeps the workforce employed, but it is very difficult for designers to perpetually come up with fresh ideas. For the designer, marketing research and design research are particularly important initial phases of the cycle. The design process is born of inspiration, rarely for an individual item, but for a whole mood or look. Design sketches, fabrics, materials and knowledge of processes is necessary to follow through to the next stage of creating prototypes. This is the usual sequence that you will follow through a college design project. For salespeople, buyers and financiers the statistical analyses of sales, profit and budget figures and other market intelligence will be needed before committing to new ranges or investments. Marketing and merchandising students learn how to read balance sheets and interpret the strengths and weaknesses that indicate the way forward.

The first stages of the cycle, marketing and design research usually come together at the fibre and fabric fairs where the forecasts for upcoming trends and colours are promoted by fibre, fabric and trimmings companies and selections are made for

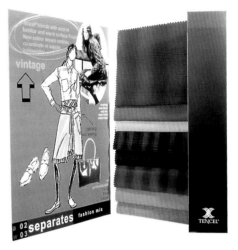

Top Fabric mills and importers are keen to promote their new lines. Swatch cards are sent out to valued customers who may then order sample lengths or cuts to try.

Above Trade publications carry information about new products, market feedback and trends.

Fabric selection guidelines

Crush the fabric a few times in your hand to feel the surface and assess its warmth, coolness, dryness, slipperiness, etc. What is the fabric's personality? What is the fibre content?

How does the fabric recover from your handling? Check it between your thumbs for stretch and recovery. Gently pull it in the grain and bias directions. Fold or drape the fabric to see how it hangs. Tease the threads to see if it will pull apart or fray easily.

Check the selvedges to see whether the fabric is straight. Off-grain fabrics will not hang properly, and in colour-wovens and plaids hemlines and matching seams will be misaligned.

Look for weaving or dyeing irregularities. Hold a fabric up to the light if you think it is patchy. Colours can look very different in shop lighting compared to daylight; if you are trying to match a colour ask if you can take the fabric to another light source.

Knit and woollen fabrics are prone to pilling. Rub the surface and see if fibres come off or roll into balls.

Printed fabrics should be checked for even printing and correct alignment. Hold up the print against the body and also at arm's length to see what the scale of the design looks like.

A starch called 'size' is sometimes applied to silk materials and cheap cottons at the weaving or finishing stage. This washes out later and leaves the fabric limp. Rub the surface to see if a fine powder appears.

If there is information about wash care or finishes, take note. You cannot complain later if you mistreat a fabric.

sampling. Yarns are bought for knitwear sampling. Knitwear requires longer lead times than cut-and-sew garments because the machinery has to be programmed and production booked well in advance of the styles reaching the market. Knitwear designers often dictate the colour palette for the rest of a fashion line because they are first off the blocks. Wovens, solids and prints are selected, ordered and trialled. The range-building starts as soon as fabric headers and ideas start coming in.

Fashion design requires teamwork. A number of meetings are held between executives, designers, assistants and production managers to agree colour palettes, fabrics, design stories, costs and promotions. The sample-pattern cutter and sample machinists usually work closely with the designers to create prototypes (known as 'toiles' or muslins) and first samples. As the toiles start appearing they go through in-house selection processes with management and retail executives in order to validate fabrics, costings and 'stories' that will hang together well. Those selected will then be sent to factories for duplicates to be made to test quality, costings and timings, and for use in exhibitions and showrooms. The design team must work fast and methodically in order to have garments produced at the right times. The items that come through the first filter will go through a selection process by wholesale buyers and retailers at the ready-to-wear shows and through appointments. After orders have been collated, the bulk of the fabric and trimmings are bought and the production management takes over. The garments from the first range will be reaching the shops at the point when the second one is shown to wholesale buyers. At this time the designer starts working on a new range by making fabric selections.

Selection

When choosing fabrics for your design or collection you need to take account of not only the visual and technical properties of the materials supplied to you by the manufacturer, but also its **hand** or **handle**. There is no substitute for feeling a fabric to assess its drape, surface qualities and weight. Selecting fabrics is an enjoyable part of designing, but it takes study, taste and experimentation. Some guidelines are given on the left.

Shops and manufacturers may allow you to take cuttings. Do this rather than impulse buy. It is easy to be tempted by the fabulous or exotic only to find later that a much simpler fabric would have suited your design better.

Jot down prices and widths so that you can work out the right quantity for your pattern lay and budget.

A rich choice of patchworked crushed velvets, bells and smiley buttons adds up to a clever evocation of 'rock chic' fashion.

Range-building

Whether you design a single garment or a whole collection you will need to combine a number of fabric types. This can be as simple as choosing supporting fabrics like **linings** and **interlinings** or as complex as putting together a story of different weights and qualities to build up a range. In designing a collection it is necessary to work out a balance between the number of items you are going to make, the core fabrics and the accent or highlight fabrics that are appropriate. If you use too many fabrics and colours the collection will look uncoordinated; too few and it will risk looking dull or repetitive. Some fabrics need to be simple and classic as foils to the eye-catching items.

Put your fabric cuttings together with your design illustrations or roughs. Always keep in mind the body type and lifestyle of the market you are designing for. In the design room of a fashion company the concept and storyboarding processes are an extensive part of range-building and are frequently reviewed. Fabrics that are too expensive or 'difficult' are eliminated. You will find that you have your own preferences and style for fabrics and trimmings; these choices will establish your image and unique identity, so care and consistency in building your signature choices is advisable. Many famous fashion designers have popularized particular fabrics: Coco Chanel was known for her use of easy-to-wear jersey and braid-bound tweedy woollen suits, while Issey Miyake is famed for his use of felts and pleated polyester.

The garment design and the fabric should not battle for attention but complement each other. The general principles of design – proportion, rhythm and an awareness of the human body in movement – need to be borne in mind and applied not to just one garment but to the whole 'look', when range-building. If your collection is to be shown on a runway, rehearse, in your mind's eye, the order in which you would like to present the outfits for maximum impact. A model line-up helps you to balance the range, swap items around and make decisions about accessories and styling. In commercial ranges the collection is grouped in 'stories' of colour and fabrication to help buyers to merchandise it in their shops. Coloured thumbnail sketches or photographs of your finished items, both separately and worn together as outfits, are useful as aids to range-building and later to selling a collection.

This clear-cut illustration shows how a designer co-ordinates separates in a 'story'. Garments are united not only through colour and fabrics that work well together, but with harmonious stitching and styling details that allow them to be worn in combination and help to simplify manufacturing specifications and retail displays.

Fabric suppliers

Sources of fabric need to be reliable and competitive. Price, delivery times, export and import regulations, fluctuating currencies and consistency of quality are key issues. A good relationship with suppliers is the backbone of a successful design line. Manufacturers and fabric sources vary in their approachability and generosity to students. Happily, you will not be tied into producing multiples of your designs, so it is possible for you to buy fabrics in small quantities, and from unusual sources and at retail.

The major fabric producers have showrooms in the fashion centres of major cities. Sometimes they sponsor students by offering low-cost or free fabric from stock or past seasons. It may also be possible to obtain new lines and developmental fabric ranges as part of their promotion if you credit the source in any publicity. Mills often have their own factory shops to sell excess or damaged fabric. Fabric is supplied on rolls (tubes) or bolts (flat cardboard) so it does not require ironing. Jersey fabric may be delivered 'split' or tubular, and is sold by weight rather than length. Keep a few long tubes handy to roll recently bought or folded fabric onto; it will save you time and effort.

Above Unusual materials call into play diverse sensory effects that can be used to make dramatic fashion statements. As in basket-weaving, this wicker dress was woven as a three-dimensional form. It undulates gently like an octopus in motion.

Above right The use of low-cost fabrics in large quantities gives a rich and dramatic impression, reminiscent of the crinoline.

Right Traditional and unique fabrics such as cashmere and pashmina shawls, folk embroideries and French jacquards can be a rich inspiration for fashion printers and weavers.

Far right As a student you can use special materials, such as brocades and laces, which are unavailable in large quantities, to make unique items.

Textile mills

Textile mills weave or knit fabric that is sold directly to garment manufacturers or wholesalers or sold through agents. Mills tend to specialize in a specific process or type of fabric; for example, cotton shirtings for daywear, luxury woollens for suits and separates, and jacquard-woven silk for evening brocades. Fabric bought direct from a mill may often be less expensive than if it is handled by an agency, but mills frequently demand a very large minimum quantity. A fashion designer can work directly with fabric designers and the mill to produce special or exclusive materials.

Converters

Converters buy or commission unfinished (**greige**) **goods** from mills and have them printed up, dyed, waterproofed, etc. by contractors according to market forecasts. Converters work closely with manufacturers and designers.

Importers

Labour costs, availability of raw materials and copyright mean that certain fabrics have to be imported. Often they have to be ordered in advance on **indent** or **quotas** to suit trade cycles and opportunities. Importers will warehouse these and, while some are paid for at the time of order, some are sold from stock. Working with importers reduces the complexity of shipping documentation and import duties, currency fluctuations, holiday dates and language difficulties.

Agents

Agents are the representatives of fabric manufacturers and do not carry any stock. They will help negotiate and organize the ordering and delivery of merchandise, either locally or through importers. The agent can be a wily salesperson, but he or she can also help you to get a better service from the supplier.

Wholesalers

These suppliers buy finished goods from mills and converters and offer stock while it lasts. Sometimes firms specialize in particular fabrics. Wholesalers do not always have a continuity of colours and textile types. Established fashion companies will be able to place orders and agree credit terms, but as a fashion student you will probably have to visit them and buy on a cash-and-carry basis.

Jobbers

Basic fabrics can often be carried over into the next season, but sometimes orders are cancelled or too much material made. Mistakes, rejected dye lots and fashion fads have to be sold off quickly to turn around the investment. Manufacturers try to keep stock as low as possible as fabric deteriorates, goes out of season and costs money to store. Jobbers are specialists in buying up the excess at discount or acting as agents for manufacturers. They offer fabric to retail outlets, market stallholders and small companies for immediate delivery at low cost. This fabric, and the garments made from it, are known as **cabbage**.

Retailers

Fabric shops and department stores will have obtained their stock from most of the sources listed above. You will be able to buy small quantities of a wide range of qualities but at a price almost three times the wholesale cost with tax.

Fabric fairs

The primary function of fabric fairs and trade shows is to be marketplaces at which to sell products. They also fulfil a secondary role as early platforms from which to promote and forecast the uptake of new ideas. They are events of significant importance to the industry but there are signs that they are losing their hold. Most producers want to make personal contact with their customers and to show their collections in a lively and competitive environment. Most buyers actually want to touch and examine fabrics and fashion before ordering. However, the changes brought about by electronic communications and global manufacturing are creating an increasingly seasonless and fragmented market. As a result of the terrorist attacks of 11 September 2001 (which coincided with New York fashion week) buyers are reluctant to travel and are looking for alternatives. Videoconferencing and cheap courier services mean that salespeople now do business 24/7. Many manufacturers have become wary of showing goods publicly due to the speed with which copies can be produced. The number of large fairs is declining and smaller events are mushrooming. Attendance at these is more expensive or by invitation only, and more people are presenting in hotel suites or at special off-schedule venues and showrooms, at the critical times for their own target markets.

One of the most important fairs is the twice-yearly Paris show – **Première Vision**, also referred to in the trade as PV – held in March and September, immediately after the French Prêt-à-porter fashion shows. Within PV there is a textile designers' exhibition called *Indigo*, which caters to the interests of fabric converters, printers and knitwear manufacturers. Exhibitors show up to eighteen months in advance and some of the most exciting ideas can be found in this arena. Significantly for students, *Indigo* invites European fashion and textile schools to show the work of student designers alongside the professional studios. This is an excellent opportunity to earn some money from your designs without the financial risk of taking a stand, to learn how the trade operates and to benefit from the contacts and ambience of the marketplace.

As a student visitor to fabric fairs do not expect to automatically gain entrance to the fabric stalls or to see garments. Sales representatives show headers, i.e., fabric feelers and swatches, to professional designers and buyers who order sample cuts and lengths. Yarn is ordered by weight or sample cone. Students are unlikely to buy fabrics and yarns this way, but if you are particularly interested in sampling you should contact the company or fabric agent, either with the aid of your tutor or department, or after the exhibition. The show catalogues are invaluable sources of information – they may cost a lot but they will be useful directories for future use and contacts. Use your own business card and address if you want to make a sample order. Never order on behalf of your college or ask for delivery to the college, unless you have made previous arrangements with your department. Some companies give generous discounts to students. Others may have sponsorship schemes in place and will want to see evidence of where you are studying, or require a letter from your college, before taking your order.

You should keep a notebook specifically to build up your working knowledge of the different categories of fabrics, their sources, price structures and ideas for various uses. Sometimes, especially on the last day of shows, you may be given free samples and catalogues that agents do not want to take home. The larger fabric and fibre companies provide fabric libraries and information services, and publish educational materials for their customers. Some also hold free fashion-trend events and shows to demonstrate

Fabric and fibre fairs are held biannually in different fashion cities around the world. Première Vision in Paris and Interstoff in Frankfurt are the largest and most prestigious. Spinners and weavers commission fashion designers to make promotional ranges for their exhibition stands.

how their materials fit into the forecasting analyses. These professional presentations can have a strong influence on future fashions. The PV organization commissions a body of trend experts to analyse and synthesize the themes, colour palettes and trends into displays, audio-visual presentations and daily newsheets of popular purchases. Some commentators believe it is these gurus, not the designers, who have the greatest influence on fashion, while others believe that trend displays create too much banal uniformity in fashion.

Further reading and additional resources

SE Braddock and M O'Mahony. *Techno Textiles: Revolutionary Fabrics for Fashion and Design*, London: Thames & Hudson, 1998

Chlöe Colchester. *The New Textiles: Trends and Traditions*, New York: WW Norton, 1997

Mary Schoeser. *International Textile Design*, London: Laurence King, 1995

Susannah Handley. *Nylon: The Manmade Fashion Revolution*, London: Bloomsbury, 1999

John Feltwell. *The Story of Silk*, New York: St. Martins, 1991

Ezio Manzini. *The Material of Invention*, Cambridge: MIT Press, 1989

Deborah Newton. *Designing Knitwear*, Newtown: The Taunton Press, 1992

Joyce Storey. *Manual of Textile Printing*, London: Thames & Hudson, 1977

Sandy Black. *Knitwear in Fashion*, London: Thames & Hudson, 2002

Magazines
International Textiles Magazine
Textile View
Selvedge

Colour
www.dylon.co.uk   Colour and fabric dyes
www.fashioninformation.com   News and forecasts
www.pantone.com   Colour system and forecasts
www.lectra.com/en/fashion_apparel/products/color_management_fashion.html
Colour reproduction in fashion

Fabric information (also see list of suppliers in appendix)
www.whaleys-bradford.ltd.uk   Muslins, toiles and natural greige cloth for printing
www.fashiondex.com   Global fabric supplier list
www.fibre2fashion.com   Fabric and fashion news
www.thefabricofourlives.com   Fibres and textiles
www.yarnsandfibers.com
www.woolmark.com

Biannual fabric fairs
Première Vision, Paris, France – September and March, Tissu Premiere Lille, France
Eurotuch, Düsseldorf, Germany – March and October
Moda In, Milan, Italy – February and July
Idea Como, Como, Italy – April and November (silks and prints)
The International Fashion Fabric Exhibition (IFFE), New York, USA
Interstoff Asia, Hong Kong
Material World, Miami Beach, USA
Los Angeles International Textile Show (TALA), Los Angeles, USA

In the US there are five 'market weeks' when fabric producers present their lines in their showrooms

Biannual fibre exhibitions
Pitti Immagine Filati, Florence, Italy – February and July
Expofil, Paris, France – December and May

In the studio V

The college studio

The layout of your college design studio may be arranged in a number of different ways. It might emulate a design studio or that of a small factory environment, depending on the course syllabus and the balance of students to technical assistants and staff. Some colleges allow you to have your own workstation and pinboard; others will take an open-plan approach and a first-come-first-served attitude to space. Many colleges are open all hours and the atmosphere in the evening or at the weekend in an open-plan studio can be creatively stimulating. Whatever your preference or your college policy, it is wise to be present at staffed times and to learn to share machine time, tutors and space equably.

Basic equipment

Central to the fashion-design studio is the pattern-cutting table. Tables are usually constructed for the average height of a woman, i.e., 92 centimetres (36 inches) high, and approximately 120 centimetres (48 inches) wide to allow for the widths of fabrics. The length of the table needs to be at least long enough to cut a full-length dress pattern – about 4 metres (or yards) or longer. The table is used both for drafting patterns and also for cutting the sample in fabric. It has a very smooth surface to allow silky and delicate fabrics to roll over it without snagging.

The studio machinery is industry standard in most instances, with some special equipment such as overlockers, seam coverers and binders, and a steam iron or pressing table. Sometimes you will have access to embroidery and knitting machines. Sewing and pressing machines are potentially hazardous, so you are required to have a safety induction and to use them under supervision.

Shears and scissors have traditionally been the sign of the tailor and dressmaker. You will need a variety of essential cutting and pattern-making tools; good-quality tools, well looked after, will last a lifetime.

You may be given a creative space that you can decorate with your own pictures and work in progress.

The pattern-drafting table and the dress form are essential pieces of fashion-studio equipment.

Learning how to make garments to a professional standard using industrial machinery helps you design commercially viable clothes.

Not all colleges have machinists for making up clothes. You may have to learn to do this without aid; most colleges will expect you to have a sewing machine at home. There will usually be pattern-drafting tutors on the permanent staff who give demonstrations in the studio, or through informal appointments, and troubleshoot problems.

The dress form

The dress form (or tailor's dummy) is an essential piece of studio equipment for testing the viability of designs and patterns. It is a solid torso, usually moulded in plastic and covered with thin padding and tightly fitted linen. It is adjustable in height and can be rotated, allowing you to evaluate your work quickly. There are a wide variety of dress forms for men, women and children of different standard sizes and age ranges, and also for trousers, eveningwear, maternitywear and lingerie. Some are made with detachable or retractable arms for jacket styles, and they can be padded or adapted for portly or unusual figures.

You will use a dress form at many junctures of the design development. The effect and scale of fabrics, especially stripes, prints and borders, can be assessed by arranging them on the form before cutting a pattern. You can test the silhouette, fit and grain on the paper pattern before cutting the toile (or muslin) and adjust the fit of seams and darts during toile- or garment-making. A form helps you establish the break point and roll line of a tailored collar and to steam-press it into shape. You can experiment with the placement of details such as pockets and buttons, and insert linings, shoulder pads and other tricky items by sewing them to the garment on the dress form. Bias-cut garments are tacked (or basted) or pinned to hang and stretch before refining the toile or cutting a hem – which can be marked accurately by measuring from the floor and rotating the form. A dress form is vital for draping and modelling techniques. The linen surface of a professional form is usually divided into eight vertically seamed panels which provide guides on which to fit most garments. However you can change the position of the seams with narrow black tape. Attach this with lills (the smallest pins), which come out easily if you want to move the guides. Taping helps you see through the toile to get the darts in the right place and keep the right balance. The neckline and **armhole scye** position can also be tested by draping the tape until a good solution is found. A dress form should not be relied upon for all solutions: many design flaws come to light only when tested on a real body. If you are designing for a particular client or figure shape you must take measurements and adapt the form and pattern accordingly.

Measuring and mapping

In the past, skilled tailors came to observe that people could be divided roughly into body types and fitted by effectively following a few rules of ratio. In the nineteenth century the art of tailoring also became a science. The Victorians were inspired by the writings of Charles Darwin and the new art of documentary photography to catalogue and measure the variety of human forms, at home and in distant lands. The science of anthropometry, the mapping of the body, was developed. Varying methods of measuring the body for tailoring were devised, employing templates, or **blocks**, which were based on the division of the body into symmetrical sections (for example, front torso to centre, top sleeve and undersleeve). Today, new technology, such as three-dimensional body scanners that capture accurate measurements, are improving data and providing the true sizing of different geodemographic groups.

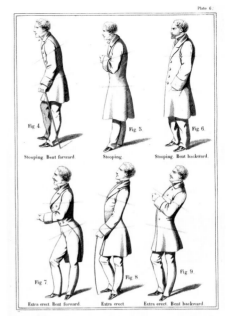

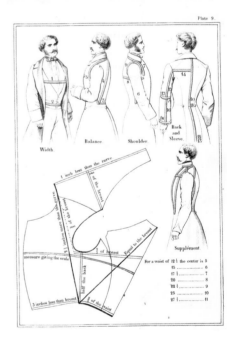

Top The art of the tailor lies partly in the ability to construct clothing that hides the imperfections of the body.

Above Standard measurements are frequently revised as changes in people's health and nutrition continue to affect the average body shape.

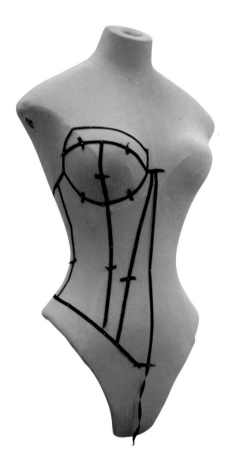

Standard sizes

As manufacturers organized themselves and their products, standardized sizing, pattern-drafting, grading and labelling procedures evolved. Although these methods of measuring still differ from country to country, it is now possible, thanks to the work of the British Standards Institution and the US Department of Commerce, to designate the sizes of garments internationally to help reduce confusion. The United States, where there is a wider range of sizing categories than in Europe, uses the imperial measure: yards, feet and inches. In Europe and the Far East, garments are commonly sized in centimetres. Always enquire whether your manufacturer works in metric or imperial (see the size chart at the end of the book).

The average woman in the United Kingdom, the United States and Middle Europe is 163 centimetres (64 inches) tall (5 centimetres or 2 inches taller than she was fifty years ago), pear-shaped rather than hourglass and wears between a size 12 and 14 (US sizes 10 and 12). Most fashion companies produce women's garments in sizes 8 to 14 (or US 6 to 12), despite the fact that a third of all women are larger than a size 16 (US size 14). Menswear is more broadly defined. Manufacturers sell garments to buyers in a size range that will depend on the market for which they are aimed, with young or middle-aged fashion having different requirements and expectations of fit. Today more suppliers are beginning to offer clothing in 'plus' (outsize), petite and tall ranges, and classic trousers are often sold in a variety of leg lengths. Swimsuits and 'bodies' are also offered in different torso lengths. Hosiery is sold in a wide range of leg lengths.

In spite of two centuries of accurate measurement, however, people still claim to have trouble finding clothes to fit. A survey by Kurt Salmon market researchers found that in the United States, $28-billion worth of clothing is returned to stores due to poor fit. Where the fit is critical, for example in sportswear, it is important to be aware of how the body grows and what sort of movement must be allowed for in certain styles. When a particular fashion such as the hipster skirt or trouser comes into vogue, it also places a demand on the lingerie supplier to cut the line of underwear and tights lower on the stomach, and a 'new' measurement is taken. Such measurements are called specifications, or specs, and are written up on design illustrations to prevent ambiguity in cutting and making.

While you are a fashion student you will probably make samples to a model size 10 or 12 (US size 8 or 10). However, it is as well to bear in mind that, when you leave college and design garments to be graded into different sizes, fashion details such as pockets and seam lines must continue to look right on a narrower or larger fit.

Even if you do not plan to be a master pattern-cutter, you will need to understand the importance of measuring and transferring these measures to a pattern in order to make your sketch, design lines and structure work. It is essential for designers to have a comprehensive grounding in basic pattern-making for the major garment types in order to design well.

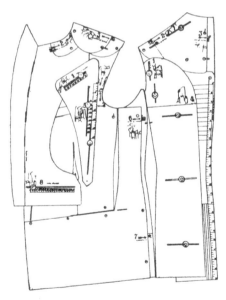

Top The position and balance of seam lines for an evening dress are plotted with tape pinned to the dress form.

Above This patented pattern-maker could be adjusted in two minutes to a customer's measurements to draft a made-to-measure pattern.

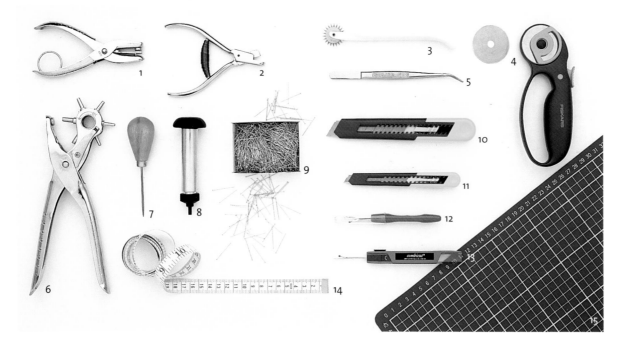

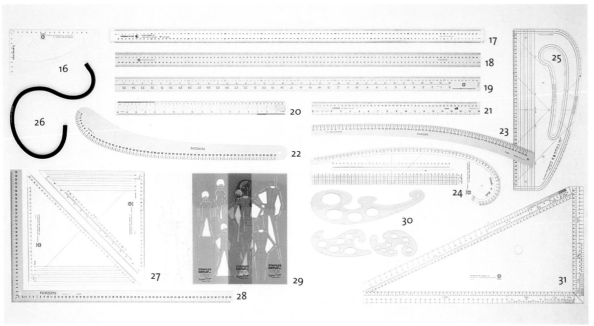

Key of pattern-drafting tools

1 Pattern clippers
2 Pattern notchers
3 Needlepoint tracing wheel
4 Rotary cutter and blade
5 Tweezers (for machine threading)
6 Revolving hole-punch pliers
7 Awl
8 Single-hole punch
9 Steel pins
10 Snap-off blade knife

11 Retractable blade knife
12 Seam ripper
13 Buttonhole marker and opener
14 Dual marked tape measure
15 Cutting mat
16 Quarter scale
17 Yard/metre stick
18 Aluminium rule
19 Dual marked Perspex rule
20 Perspex rule, grader's marks
21 Perspex rule, dual markings

22 Contour master
23 Curve stick
24 Grading curve
25 Patternmaster™
26 Flexicurve
27 Grader's set squares
   (metric and imperial)
28 L-square
29 Drawing templates
30 French curves
31 Set square, various markings

Taking measurements

Measurement chart

Name		Height	
		left	right
A	Neckline		
J	Neck to waist front		
O-P	Neck to waist back		
C-C	Front shoulder to shoulder		
C-C	Back width across shoulder blade		
D-C	Shoulder length		
A-J	Shoulder slope		
D-B	Neck edge to bust point		
B	Bust front to side seam		
U	Under-bust circumference		
B	Chest circumference		
D-E	Neck edge to waist		
F	Armhole scye		
E	Waist		
E-N	Waist to floor		
G	Abdomen		
H	Hips		
I	Leg outer seam		
M-N	Leg inside seam		
E/G-K	Crotch rise		
E/G-M	Seat		
C-L	Arm		
	Shoe size		
	Hat size		

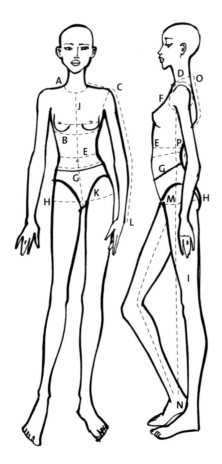

When fitting a model, or making a couture garment, take note that the human body is rarely symmetrical – shoulders and breasts are typically different heights or sizes and you may need to take separate left and right measurements. It is also useful to measure overall height, head circumference and the knee position for hem lengths.

Marking reference points
Use a felt-tip pen or adhesive spots for consistent reference points while you measure. Be sure to check the points of intersection. All horizontal markings should intersect all vertical markings so that you can identify the exact centre front, centre back and side seam locations. (NB: The centre front of the waistline may not be in line with the navel.)

A. Neckline
Identify the natural neckline with a short chain necklace just below the hollow at the base of the neck. Mark the exact centre front of this neckline with a small adhesive dot or pen.

For the nape, mark the prominent vertebra at the top of the spine with an adhesive or pen dot. (Bend the head forward to make the vertebra easier to find.) Mark a point on each side of the neck, in line with the hollow just behind the ear lobe.

B. Bust and chest
Measure across the front of the chest from side seam to seam. Measure the chest circumference across the widest point. Measure under the bust if you are making a fitted garment.

C. Shoulder point
Identify an exact shoulder point by raising the arm until a dimple appears. Feel for the shoulder bone in this depression. Mark it with an adhesive or pen dot.

D. Shoulder seam line
Measure from the side-neck point marked on the neckline, along the top of the shoulder, to the shoulder point. Note the shoulder slope.

E. Waistline
Depending upon body proportions, there are two possible waistlines: a natural waist or, for people who do not have a naturally indented waist, a position where the top of skirts or trousers sit. If it is not apparent, find the natural waist by tying a piece of elastic around the person's waist and have her bend from side to side until the elastic settles around the middle of her body; take the waist measurement here. The waistline is often higher at the back than the front. But the skirt hem must be parallel with the floor.

F. Armhole scye
Measure the curve from the shoulder point, down into the crease formed by the body joining the arm, on both the front and back. The curve should be more pronounced in the front scye than in the back.

G. Abdomen
Measure parallel to the floor across the fullest part of the abdomen. This is essential when making hipster skirts or trousers, which must be fitted tighter than this measurement or they will fall down.

H. Hips
Find the widest part of the lower body by taking a tape measure around the hip area and sliding it down the body. Note that the widest part may be as little as a few centimetres or more than 30 centimetres (12 inches) below the waist.

I. Leg
Measure from the side waist to the ankle bone. Measure the inside leg from the crotch (M) to the inside ankle.

J. Centre front and centre back
Measure from the hollow of the neck to the waist. Measure from the nape of the neck to the back waist point.

K. Rise and seat
Measure the rise from the front waist to the crotch. Measure the entire distance from the centre front waist to the centre back waist.

L. Arm
Bend the arm 45 degrees and measure from the shoulder point to the wrist bone.

Pattern-drafting

Pattern-drafting tools

For pattern-drafting you will need a number of tools, and these can be bought from specialist haberdashers (notions stores) and suppliers to the trade:

- Hard pencils (2H–6H) for drafting
- Pencil sharpener and eraser
- Felt-tip pens, red and black for marking patterns
- French curve (for drawing and measuring curves)
- Grader's set square or triangle (for finding the bias grain)
- Transparent ruler (preferably with slots to measure buttonholes and pleats)
- Metre rule or yardstick (preferably marked with both measuring systems)
- Tape measure
- Tracing wheel
- Paper shears
- Pattern notchers
- Awl or spike
- Hole puncher
- Sticky (transparent) tape and masking tape
- Pins
- Black seam tape

Pattern-drafting can seem a very dry, dull and mathematical subject at first until the magic of it starts to work under your fingers and you realize the infinite possibilities that can be achieved with a snip here and a curve there. Very minor adjustments can make a great deal of difference to the fall of a collar or the balance of a garment. Your design confidence will grow if you can turn your drawings quickly and effectively into the real thing. There are two main ways of developing a garment shape: flat pattern-drafting and draping on the dress form.

Flat pattern-drafting

Flat pattern-drafting is precision drawing that requires accurate measurements and use of proportion, a neat hand and an ability to imagine the effect in three dimensions. Tailored garments have a logical structure of their own and often require stiffening fabrics and paddings. These and garments which outline or follow the contours of the body are most successfully developed from flat pattern-drafting. Flat patterns are usually developed from a set of measured pattern blocks (see below). Flat patterns can also be drafted using computer software that is programmed to plot the entered measurements. Very close-fitting garments such as corsets and brassieres that squeeze or distort the flesh should be flat-drafted and then remodelled on a real body.

Blocks

College courses will differ as to how they approach the art of flat pattern-drafting. The system of working two-dimensionally is fast, economically viable and indispensable to the fashion industry. Some courses prefer you to develop blocks – also known as slopers – from an individual set of measurements; others will issue you with standard-sized blocks for bodice, jacket, trouser and skirt.

The block is a foundation pattern constructed to fit a specific figure. It is used as a basis for interpreting and making a pattern for a new design. It can be used again and again, so it is usually cut in heavy card or plastic to stand up to lots of handling. The style

Top Sports clothing can be a fascinating and inventive field to design for as it is continually evolving. Here an ingenious hidden trouser lies under a skirt that preserves a lady's modesty while allowing her to sit side saddle.

Above The designer drafts a new pattern by using a basic block as a foundation.

Developing the pattern

You are likely to be expected to discuss your design ideas with various people at different stages during the development of your sketches. Sometimes technical staff will point out difficulties or restrictions that you may not have thought of, and you will have to go back to the drawing board.

When you have clarified the design, you will be shown how to draft a first paper pattern. The pattern-drafter copies the block by tracing around it and then superimposes the style lines of the new garment to be developed. It is important to transfer as many details as possible from the basic block to the new pattern, including the centre front (CF), centre back (CB) and the waist and hip lines. Sometimes the pattern will need to be slashed and moved and redrawn, so it is necessary to be aware of how the grain is affected.

The diagrams below show how a basic bodice can have the bust dart position changed in many ways while still keeping the essential fit. The images on the left and right show how the style and seam lines and darts are used to pinch out or 'suppress' fabric to give the garment shape. The same process is used to shape the area between the waist and the hips in a skirt or pair of trousers.

'When we make the pattern, I advise them. I'll say, "Well, you could do it this way or maybe it's better to do it that way", and actually we work together as a team. So I have to get used to each student and help them in their own way – I don't want to influence too much.' Pattern-cutting tutor Jacob Hillel

Fashion design

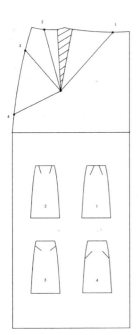

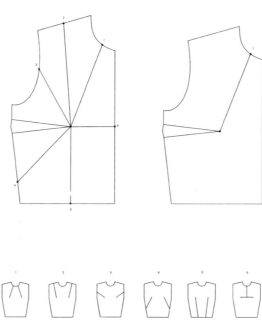

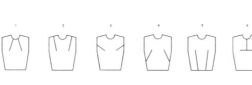

A simple skirt block and the different dart positions used to shape it to the waist.

The bodice block and the most popular dart positions used to give the bodice shape.

A selection of ways in which the front bodice can be fitted using decorative dart positions.

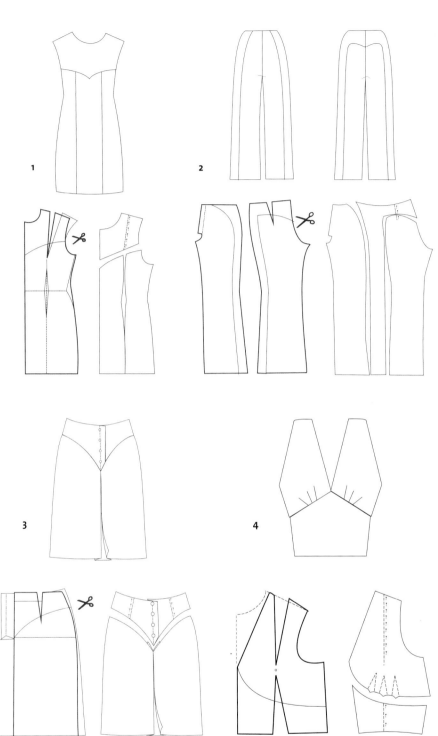

Top and above The development of the pattern and toile for a pleated skirt.

In these four examples, the basic block is drawn in a thick line. To develop a new style, it is traced and the new style lines and seams are drawn; body (dart) shaping is moved or adjusted to create a new pattern.

Altering the toile

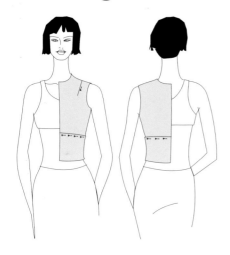

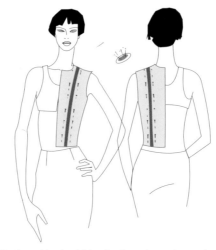

To alter the length of a bodice, pin out the excess, or tape in extra material under the ribcage.

Bust- and back-width adjustments can be made with a vertical addition or subtraction through the bust point to the waist or through the shoulder-blade line.

A flat back will need a horizontal adjustment and fabric taken out under the arm.

Add fabric for square shoulders or if you wish to use shoulder pads.

Excess fabric caused by square shoulders or a forward sloping neck can be taken out of the shoulder seams.

Small darts are used to take excess fabric out of a neckline.

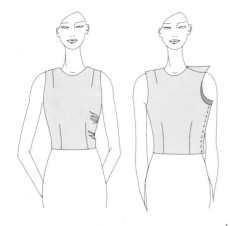

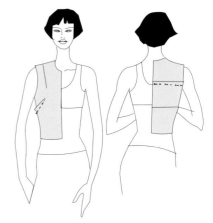

Square or sloping shoulders can affect the fit of the side seams.

A long body will require relocation of the waist and hipline and darts to avoid wrinkles over the stomach.

A plump physique will have a more rounded back and require careful fitting over the bust and belly. Check the balance between front and back pattern pieces.

A tutor helps adjust the toile for a better fit.

A shawl collar edge-to-edge coat.

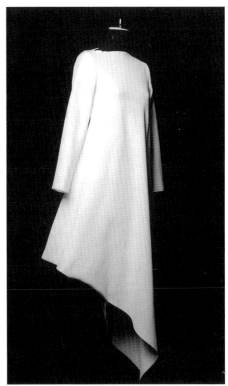
An asymmetric flared dress.

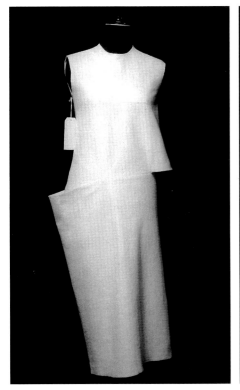
A tunic cut across at the hip to create a pocket.

A tunic with appliqué detail.

A crinoline and corset.

Standard size charts

The charts on the right show the landmark points and measurements that are the averages for the four most commonly sold men's and women's sizes in the UK. Equivalent sizes are given for the United States, continental and Japanese markets. Conversions to metric and imperial systems are not translated exactly, but rounded up to the nearest whole digit. Larger or smaller garment sizes are graded by different increments per body landmark. Basic blocks and patterns are now graded accurately by computer. Bear in mind that women with the same bust, waist and hip measurements can be completely different shapes with variations in posture, back curvature, hip positions, bust shape, legs, etc. Made-to-measure and mass-customized garments are made with minor adjustments to these basic size blocks, whereas bespoke tailoring and haute couture require that all the individual customer's measurements are taken, and their own personal fit block, from which patterns and garments are developed, is drafted.

Women's size chart (metric)				
Size	8	10	12	14
height	157.2	159.6	162	164.4
bust	80	84	88	93
waist	60	64	68	73
hip	87	90.5	95	99.5
upper hip	79.5	84	89	94
neck	34	35	36	37
under bust	61	66	71	76
nape to waist	38.8	40.4	41	41.6
X back	31.8	32	33	34.2
X chest	28	29.8	31	32.2
shoulder	11.5	11.7	11.9	12.1
shoulder to wrist	56.2	57.1	58	58.9
underarm	42.8	43.1	43.5	43.9
armhole (scye)	38.6	40.6	42.6	44.6
bicep	22.9	24.7	26.5	28.3
wrist	15	15.2	16	16.6
outside leg	99	100.5	102	103.5
inside leg	74	74	74.5	74.5
body rise	26.8	27.9	29	30.1
waist to knee CB	61	61	61.5	61.5
waist to ankle CB	94	94	95	95
nape to floor	136	138	140	142

Men's size chart (metric)				
Size	36	38	40	42
height	174	176	178	180
chest	92	96	102	107
waist	76	81	87	92
hip	94	99	104	109
nape to waist	44.5	46	46.5	47
jacket length	79	80	81	82
X back	42	43.5	44.5	45.5
shoulder	16	16	16.5	17
shoulder to wrist	62	62	63	63
shirtsleeve length	84	84	87	87
shirt neck	37	38	39	40
wrist	16	16.5	17	17.5
inside leg	80	81	82	83
body rise	26.2	26.6	27	27.4

UK	6	8	10	12	14	16	18	20	22
US	4	6	8	10	12	14	16	18	20
Spain/France	34	36	38	40	42	44	46	48	50
Italy	38	40	42	44	46	48	50	52	54
Germany	32	34	36	38	40	42	44	46	48
Japan	3	5	7	9	11	13	15	17	19

Shoe sizes											
UK	3	3½	4	4½	5	5½	6	6½	7	7½	8
US/Can.	5½	6	6½	7	7½	8	8½	9	9½	10	10½
Europe	35½	36	37	37½	38	38½	39	39½	40	40½	41
Japan	21½	22	22½	23	23½	24	24½	25	25½	26	27
China	36	37	37½	38	39	39½	40	40½	41	41½	42

lines of the design developed from it may change dramatically, but the fit will conform to that of the basic block used. The standard blocks are usually accompanied by the garment toile that they represent, so you can see what the fit or 'ease' is like and adjust accordingly. Couture and bespoke-tailoring customers will have blocks drafted from their personal measurements, from which all their clothes can be made. Fashion samples are usually made up in the average model size 10 or 12 (US size 8 or 10), sometimes with 3.5 centimetres (about 1⅛ inches) extra length in the back and legs to allow for the height of a fashion model.

The toile

The pattern needs to be tested in calico or a fabric similar in weight and behaviour to the final garment material. The first fabric sample is called a toile (pronounced 'twahl'), from the French for a lightweight cotton fabric – in the United States it is called a muslin. White or ecru material is easier to work with than dark or patterned cloth. Without the distractions of colour or design it is possible to see the cut and fit of the pattern more clearly. The centre front and back should be marked clearly with long, straight lines, using pencil on wovens and felt-tip pen on knits. The waist and hip lines also need to be marked as reference points for fitting and altering.

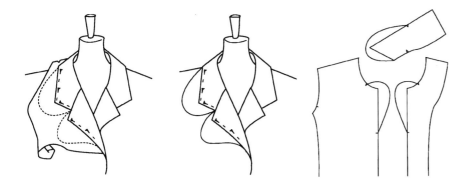

The toile is made up and fitted on a dress stand, mannequin or person. The seams are not overlocked or bound, so the garment can be opened and adjusted speedily. Alterations are made and instructions can be written on the toile in pen or tailor's chalk. Paper or fabric can be attached to the toile to restyle details such as lapels, and style lines can be redrawn and later transferred with a tracing wheel onto the paper pattern. Fabric moves and stretches, and the pattern may need to be adjusted to take account of the nature of the fabric used. This applies particularly to the patterns of jersey or draped styles, which often have to be made up several times to correct the fabric dropping and the inherent bias stretch of lighter-weight materials. In a symmetrical garment it is sometimes reasonable to make only half of the toile.

When you make a collection it is common practice to show your toiles, on models, to your tutors at a 'line-up'. This way the balance and proportion of the whole range or line can be seen, discussed and modified before you cut your fabric. For toile-making you will need fabric shears, small sharp embroidery scissors, a soft pencil, coloured pencils or fine felt-tip pens, pins and a sewing needle, a seam ripper/ unpicker, sticky tape and masking tape, a sewing machine and threads.

Draping on the stand

Draping – also known as modelling on the stand or dress form – entails fitting a toile fabric on a dressmaking mannequin of the appropriate size, or on a real body. When the shape and fit are correct, the toile is removed and copied onto pattern paper or card. Draping techniques work best with jersey fabrics and generous amounts of soft materials. They are also used to work fabric 'on the bias', i.e., across the grain, so that it moulds to the body shape and moves well.

Draping is sculpting with fabric and is most effective when using soft fabrics in fairly generous quantities. Fabric can be draped tight to the body and controlled with invisible stitching, or hung loosely in swags. Real models can be used to work the fabric on. However, because it can take a considerable time to get the effect right, it is preferable to use a dress stand for most of the work. Draping can be very frustrating, yet is hugely rewarding when it works. It is vital to work with the inherent weight and spring of the material. Fabric that is draped on the bias or cross grain stretches and behaves differently to the same fabric draped on the straight grain. Experimenting with the direction of the grain can be fascinating.

It is useful to use a Polaroid or digital camera when draping as it is hard to remember all the permutations you have been through. When you have a pleasing effect, take a picture; then at the end of the day you can review the variations and

Pattern markings and notches

When the pattern is deemed to be correct it should be marked up properly as follows:

Show all the grain lines. These are marked parallel to the selvedge, CF or CB, except in a few cases. Grain lines on sleeves and flared skirt panels are usually marked through the centre. If the pattern is to be used on a one-way print or fabric with a nap, such as velvet, mark the grain line with arrows to show the direction of the nap.

Align and check the lengths of seams. Add and mark seam allowances with the allowance to be taken.

Mark dart points, pocket positions and trimmings with an awl or hole punch. The two sides of a dart must always be identical in length. Sometimes buttonhole positions are drilled with a neat hole that a chalk-mark or cutter's drill can get through.

For the garment to hang straight, notch in 'balance points' at 90 degrees to the edge to mark the grain at CF and CB, and place seam-matching points. Matching points are never put in the centre of a seam, but placed off-centre so that the next piece cannot be attached upside down by accident. This is especially important in styles like slim panelled skirts. Single notches are used in the front pattern pieces and double notches at the back. For multi-panelled styles add more notches for each successive panel, making up to four notches at the centre back (see diagram). Notches are also used to mark off the positions for darts, zipper placements or in curved or bias seams to ease them.

Mark the piece name, garment size and number of pieces to be cut, e.g., pocket bag x 4.

Make sure you give the pattern a name (or number) and put your own name on it.

Place all the pattern pieces in a stack and put one hole through all of them, about 10 centimetres (4 inches) from the top edge. Either put a pattern pin through them and hang them on a rack, or fold them together neatly and put them in an envelope with your name and the corresponding spec or illustration on the front.

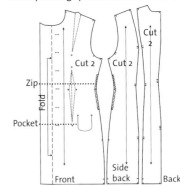

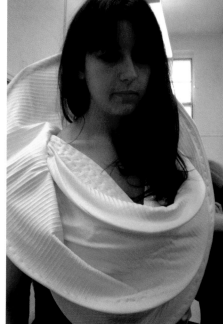

Draping is about working with fabric and body together; it is difficult to master and is therefore a highly regarded skill. The artistry lies in achieving a flattering shape with the least amount of cutting and contrivance.

Draped garments are copied into paper or card and marked with instructions.

return to the most successful. You will also have a record for your sketchbook that proves you have been working.

When the design looks right and has been loosely stitched into place, try it on a real model. Then the fun begins. Drapes have a habit of falling out of place and spoiling everything as soon as a person moves. Alternatively they can do strange and wonderful things and set you off on a whole new path. When you think you have the style tamed, take the toile off the model or form and smooth it out flat. Everything must be meticulously marked. You may need to piece extra fabric together if you are cutting on the bias and run out of material. Use broad sticky tape and felt-tip pens to indicate the direction of folds. Mark the centre front, shoulder line, seams and armholes and snip off any extra bits. Straighten up the grain line and smooth out sketched lines with a French curve or rulers. Then redraw or trace through with a tracing wheel to mark the pieces on pattern paper. Draped styles are often very odd shapes, and you will need to mark in the top and bottom hemlines and probably lots of notches and arrows to show the directions in which to fold them. Try to sew the toile together as soon as possible. It is very easy to forget everything overnight.

The most useful tip in pattern-drafting is to be neat and methodical about marking up your final pattern, however messy the process of arriving at it has been. Fold it carefully and put it in a large envelope with an illustration on the front. Weeks later you will not want to come back to a crumpled piece of paper with bits of old tape stuck all over it.

Most pattern development is a mixture of flat pattern-cutting and draping. Even if you prefer to use blocks, you will find that the form is very helpful for determining the roll of a collar and lapel, or the flare and fall of a skirt. There is no right or wrong way to translate your drawings into fabric. Some styles are very difficult to get right and may take three or four patterns or toiles to be 'just so'.

'It's not as easy as it looks. I start with the idea of a movement, and this season I wanted to have the nonchalance of something falling down. I like to change a movement, change the way something falls. It's like cutting an attitude into the clothes.' Designer Ann Demeulemeester

Fabric grain

In order for a garment to hang well on the body, and to design with the dynamic properties of woven fabric, you must appreciate fabric structure. Different weaves of the same fibre will behave in diverse ways, but the most important thing to observe is the fabric grain. The **grain** (or grainline) of a fabric is the term given to the direction of a woven fabric parallel to the **selvedge** (also spelled salvage) and the long warp threads. In most fabrics the warp threads are usually stronger and under higher tension than the crosswise weft fibres when a fabric is woven. The garment is less likely to shrink in length if the pattern pieces are placed on the warp grain. The **crosswise grain** usually goes around the body. Some commonplace fabrics have the same type and number of threads in the warp and weft, and with these it is acceptable to place the pattern pieces in either direction. Knitted fabrics do not have a grain but will stretch more in the width than the length so the same rule applies. In most garments, the centre front and back (and in trousers the centre of the leg) must be **on-grain** in order for the balance of the garment to hang straight. This **balance** is crucial to standard designs and once you have understood and mastered it you can start to break the rules and make fabric do marvellous things.

The bias

The bias is the diagonal of the fabric (45 degrees to the selvedge and cross grain). Essentially, fabric cut on the true bias stretches, and gives a lively and draped quality to the garment, moulding to the figure like a knit when cut close to the body fit. Fuller cut bias fabric flares out from the body and creates effective flounces and light frills. You can feel the potential stretch of a fabric by pulling it between thumb and finger in a

Guidelines for draping

Mark the straight grain and bias of the toile fabric with different coloured felt-tip pens.

Pin the fabric in the centre front (or back) of the dress form and establish your neck opening. Pin the shoulder seam in place, checking for placement. Pin the side pieces in place and clip the armhole area. Pin or tape folds and pleats into place.

Stand back and observe the results. If necessary, make corrections, readjust gathers, move seam lines, darts, folds, etc. or add fabric where the garment requires it.

When the garment fits correctly mark the neckline, armhole, and waist position CF and CB with soft pencil or fine felt-tip pen. Remove the fabric from the form and transfer all markings to paper. True up all straight edges and curves.

When you think you have the style tamed, take the toile off the form (or model) and smooth it out flat. Everything must be meticulously marked. You may need to piece extra fabric together if you are cutting on the bias and run out of material. Use broad tape and felt-tip pens to indicate the direction of folds.

Mark the centre front, shoulder line, seams and armholes and snip off any extra bits. True up the grain line and smooth out sketched lines with a French curve or rulers. Then redraw or trace though with a tracing wheel to mark the pieces on pattern paper. Draped styles are often very odd shapes – you will need to mark in the top and bottom hemlines and probably lots of notches and arrows to show the fold directions.

Try to sew the garment up as soon as possible. It is very easy to forget everything overnight.

Below Straight grain (A), bias grain (B) and off grain (C – neither straight nor bias).

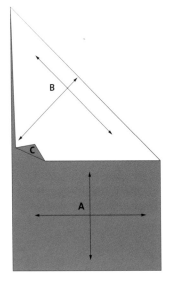

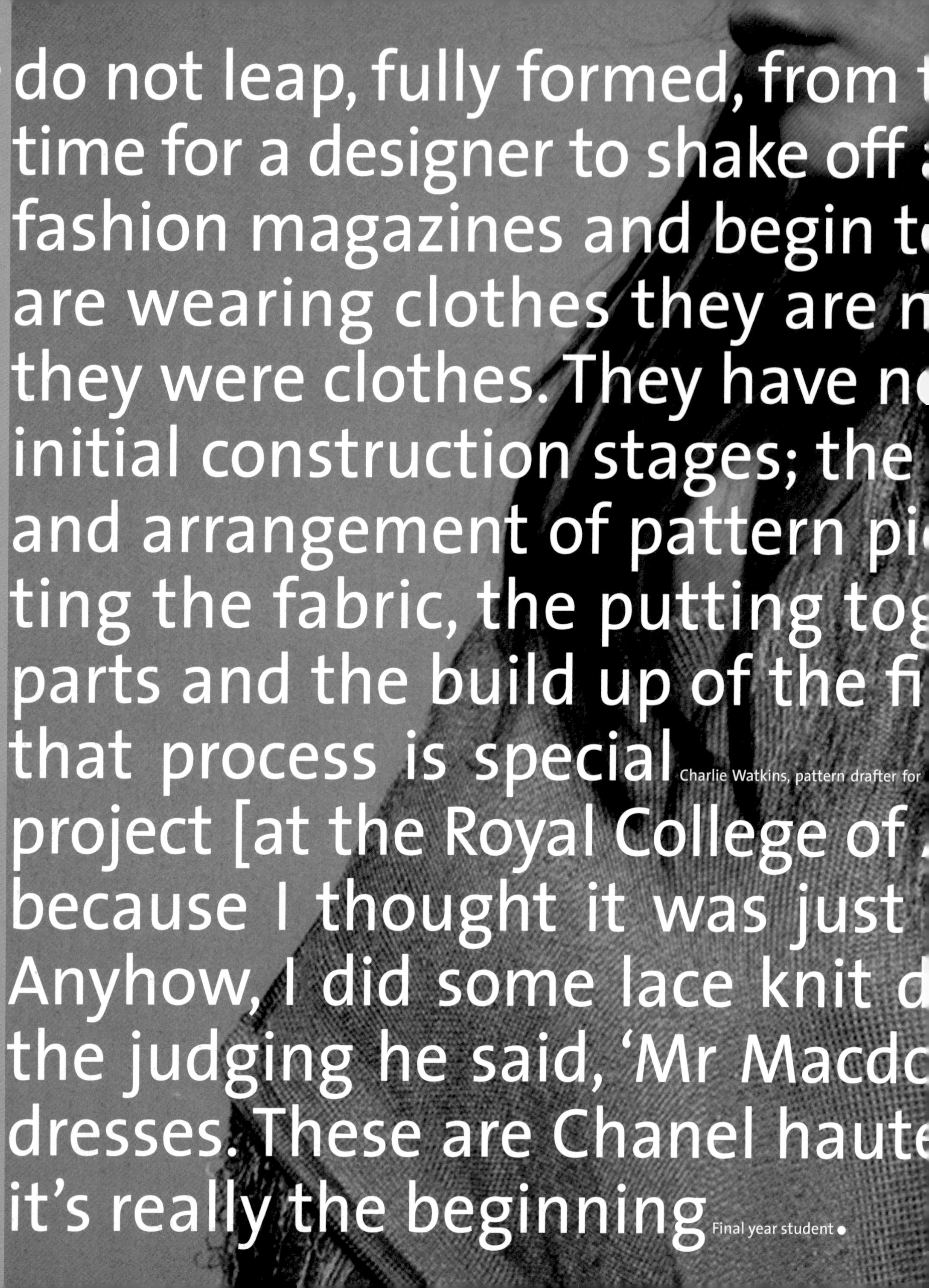

do not leap, fully formed, from

time for a designer to shake off

fashion magazines and begin t

are wearing clothes they are n

they were clothes. They have n

initial construction stages; the

and arrangement of pattern pi

ting the fabric, the putting tog

parts and the build up of the fi

that process is special Charlie Watkins, pattern drafter for

project [at the Royal College of

because I thought it was just

Anyhow, I did some lace knit d

the judging he said, 'Mr Macdc

dresses. These are Chanel haute

it's really the beginning Final year student ●

wombs of art schools … It takes
school, stop pillaging the world's
and alone Colin McDowell, fashion writer. When people
aware of what went on before
xperience of the intricacy of the
ice of fabric and the designing
s, the crunchy sensation of cut-
er of the abstract component
garment. For me each stage of
yan. Karl Lagerfeld set us a dress
. I didn't want to do the project
interruption to my own work.
ses and when Karl came to do
d, these are not Karl Lagerfeld
uture.' Julien McDonald, Designer. It's not the end –

Right This jacket uses a combination of cutting and draping techniques for its fit and flare.

Far right Photographing work in progress with a Polaroid or digital camera allows you to review your work quickly on the dress stand and make minor adjustments.

diagonal direction or holding it at 45 degrees to the grain. Designing for bias cutting is a hard art to master; different fabrics and weaves behave unexpectedly. Slippery satins, silks and sheers like crêpe-de-chine and georgette are gorgeous when cut on the bias, but are very stretchy and difficult to cut and handle. Stripes can give spectacular results but the lay needs to be well planned. Bias cutting can be very wasteful of fabric and you must estimate carefully how much to buy. Plain woven cottons, poplins and stiff fabrics rarely benefit from bias cutting.

Medieval hosiery and gowns were sometimes cut on the bias and the method has been used sporadically throughout history. However, it really came into its own at the start of the twentieth century when Madeleine Vionnet, in Paris, used the technique with slinky silk satins, velvets and newly invented rayons. Bias cutting makes these materials extremely fluid and light. The fabric clings seductively to the body contours, yet allows movement. It is said that the dancer, Isadora Duncan, who was married to Paris Singer, heir to the sewing-machine fortune, inspired her. The garments Vionnet designed demanded light underwear, or none at all, and she presented her first collection on barefoot models. She was revolutionary for her time and the look was eventually taken up and popularized by the Hollywood stars of the 1930s, because it was not only glamorous and curvaceous compared to the boxy, geometric cuts of the 1920s but it also reflected light and photographed well.

Vionnet is an excellent example of a designer working with the natural properties of fabric, not by imposing a drawn design upon cloth. She used a small wooden doll to develop her designs on and scaled up the successful ones. New techniques or fabrics can inspire inventive ways of handling. Bias cutting demands designs with a fluidity of line rather than straight hems and seams because garments continue to drop when worn, becoming longer and narrower. They are left to hang for a few days before the hems are

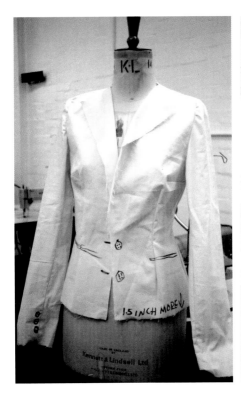

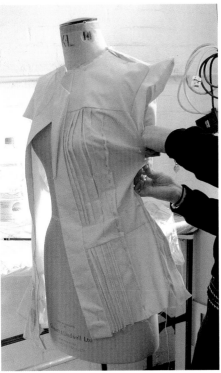

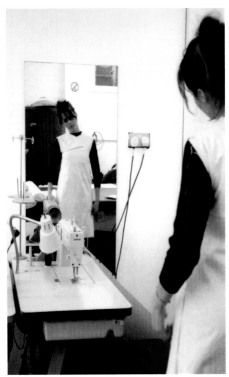

Above, left to right The stages in making a garment include marking the positions of seams and details, making changes and trying the piece on many times.

levelled. Since it is difficult to put zips and buttonholes into stretchy seams, bias cutting is often used in styles that can be simply pulled on or stepped into.

To avoid distorting the fabric, work on a large, flat cutting surface. For better control, cut your garment in a single layer and weigh down, rather than pin, the pattern pieces to the fabric. Sewing also requires a different approach. Work with the stretch rather than against it. When stitching vertical seams, follow the pull of gravity and stitch from neckline to hemline. For necklines and horizontal seams, stitch from the centre outwards. Although bias-cut edges don't fray, the cut edges relax and spread so you need to cut and sew wider seam allowances. Stretch the fabric a little when sewing the seams; it will recover when pressed. To avoid wrinkles, press each seam in the direction it was stitched. Seams will press better if left open rather than overlocked (or serged) and can be trimmed back later. Mixing bias and straight grain in a garment can produce some interesting results, but you need to work on the dress form to check the effect of gravity on the fabrics. To join a bias edge to a straight-grain edge, sew with the straight grain on top: the feed of the machine will fit the bias layer to the straight one better. Hems should be cut narrow and rolled or bound with bias or they will wrinkle. Bias binding is a popular seam-closing and decorative trimming that stretches well around curves and necklines, and avoids the need for interfacing.

Napped fabrics

When selecting a fabric check to see whether it has a **nap**. A fabric without nap has no appreciable up or down direction to the weave, texture or design. It can be cut with the pieces placed in either direction, usually following the **grain**, and is more economical in the use of fabric. A fabric with a nap either has a pile with the hairs smooth to the touch in one direction and rough in the opposite one, or a visible direction to a print (e.g., all flower heads facing upwards); some diagonal weaves and knits also have a nap. Fabrics

Needle	Fabric
60/8	Chiffon, georgette, silk habotai
70/10	Cotton muslin, lining rayons, satins
80/12	Cotton poplin, calico, light crêpes and wools, linen
90/14	Gaberdine, wool, bottom-weight fabrics
100/16	Denim, canvas, coatings, tweeds

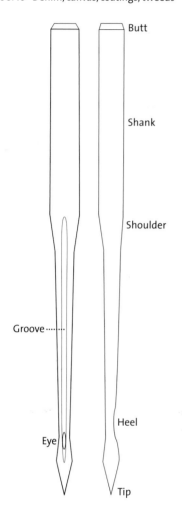

must be cut with all the pattern pieces going in the same direction (napped fabrics look best in styles with few seams). If you cut napped fabrics such as velvets or corduroys in mixed directions you get an effect called 'shading'. Hairy fabrics look and feel better with the nap running towards the hem. Velvets look richer and darker with the pile running towards the top of a garment; velvet curtains are usually cut with the nap in this direction, but garments, especially trousers and skirts, have a tendency to 'creep' up the body. Pile fabrics can be hard to press without damaging the nap. Boards made up of fine needles are available, or you can cover an ironing board with velvet. Always allow for extra fabric if you are using a napped material.

Cutting the sample

When you are satisfied that the toile is correct and that you have made the alterations to the paper pattern, you can cut the sample out in the intended fabric. Plaids and print designs may require careful laying of the pattern pieces so that the final effect is pleasing. Some fabrics, such as corduroy, have a direction or nap that causes the material to shade. The pattern will have to be put down in a single direction. Stretch fabrics may stretch in one or more direction and this needs to be allowed for; cut them in their 'relaxed' state.

Roll or spread the fabric on the cutting table, and lay the pattern pieces flat on the fabric; they may be weighed down with heavy metal bars. There is no time for pins, which in any case may make the fabric wrinkle and cause inaccuracies. You should check the lay of the pattern to see how much fabric it takes and if the fit can be improved. While you have the pattern pieces on the cloth, make a sketch of the lay. If you have to make another sample it will save time as you won't have to fit the lay again. Sometimes a pattern, or even the design itself, needs to be revised to make a difference to the wastage if the fall-out is significant. Where pairs of items are called for (sleeves, pockets, etc.), make sure two pieces of each are laid in.

Outline the pattern pieces with a soft pencil or chalk, and mark the darts and pocket positions through holes in the pieces. Samples and toiles are hand-cut with shears, using the full length of the blades on straight edges and without lifting the fabric. Depending on the garment type, there may also be facings, fusible interfacings and trimmings to incorporate into the finished garment. Cut these and match them up

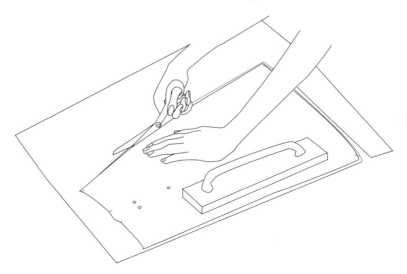

Right Samples and toiles are hand-cut with shears, using the full length of the blade. Hold the pattern pieces down with the flat of your hand as you cut. and always cut the notches as you come to them.

to the pieces with which they are to be fused. Roll all the fabric pieces together and tie them up with a strip of wastage, along with any zips or trimmings and a sketch of the design, ready for assembly. This is called a bundle. Rolling is better than folding as creases are less likely to form. If you give the bundle to a sample machinist, discuss your design and any aspects you need to work out.

Sewing

A crucial aspect of your fashion training will be learning sewing skills. Some students arrive at college having already made a number of garments on their own sewing machines and feeling fairly confident; others will never have threaded a needle. You may imagine that designing can be done at the drawing board, but it is in testing design ideas by sewing a toile, and discovering technical problems such as seam bulk or stretch, that you learn how to design appropriately.

Industrial sewing machines are much faster, smoother and more specialized than their domestic equivalents, and practice is required to use them effectively. Sewing takes patience and dexterity. Not everyone enjoys it, but the greatest motivation is seeing the garment you have designed turn out well. Learning how to sew to a professional standard will also give you credibility with your future colleagues, help you to give specifications to a factory and comes in handy when you are struck by genius after hours, or when something needs rectifying for a photographic shoot.

'I am amazed at how fast I can sew now. I didn't use to believe those stories about John Galliano running up dresses for people in the lunch break so that he could afford to go out clubbing. But I've run up a few things for myself now and it really makes you feel good when people ask you where you got it and you can say, "Well, actually ...".' Second-year fashion student

Certain sewing techniques are associated with different levels of the manufacturing market. Haute couture, because of its use of expensive and delicate fabrics, merits expert sewing, more hand-finishing, bindings and linings. Lower down the market, hand-work is rarely used as it is costly and time consuming.

Unusual materials such as plastics and leather may require you to use tissue paper or silicone spray; for others you may have to invent your own way of making them up. You may need to send garments to a specialist finishing house, for example for pleating or elasticating. Some machines can turn and apply bindings and flat-felled seams or apply elastic around the neckline and armholes. Twin-needle machines strengthen seams on jeans and workwear. Blind-stitch machines turn up hems with invisible stitches. Fashion knitwear students will learn how to put knitwear together with industrial linkers.

Needles and threads

Needles and threads are the simplest and cheapest, yet most important, tools of the seamstress. Using the right ones for specific materials will make all the difference to the quality of your work. Using too large a needle, or a blunt one, can cause puckered seams. Needles come as either sharps or ball-points. Sharps are used for woven fabrics, ball-points for knitted ones. Universal needles are versatile, modified ball-point needles, meant to be used on both woven and knit fabrics. All these needles come in a range of sizes from very fine, size 60/8, to large, size 100/16. The finer the fabric, the finer the needle size you should use.

Straight overlocked seam; pressed open seam; topstitched seam; flat-felled seam.

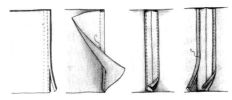

French seam; clean-finished seam; bias binding.

Centred zip; lapped zip; fly-front with zip guard.

Concealed (or invisible) zip; open-ended zip; exposed zip.

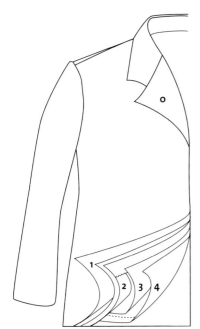

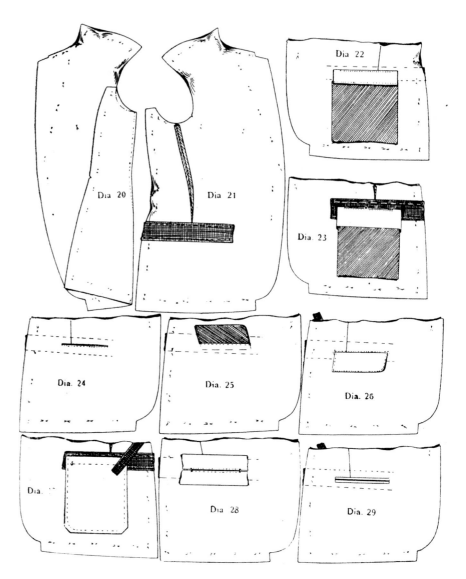

Supporting fabrics

0. *Facing*

Facings are the fabric pieces that follow the cutting line and smooth off the front button wraps, hem, neck, armhole and cuff edges of a garment by turning the seamed edge to the inside. Facings can also be cut in decorative fabrics.

1. *Interfacing*

Interfacings are technical fabrics, either sewn or heat bonded to the facings or fabric to give it greater stability at critical points, such as button bands, collars and cuffs.

2. *Underlining*

Underlining is used to strengthen a flimsy fabric or reduce transparency. It is cut from the same pattern pieces as the fashion fabric and attached before construction begins. Then, as the garment is constructed, the underlining and fashion fabric are handled as a single unit.

3. *Linings*

Linings are used to give a finished look to the inside of a tailored garment, to prevent seams fraying and to reduce wrinkling. Linings are usually cut from a silky fabric to make a garment easier to slip on and off. They are attached only at the garment's waistband, neck and facings, and sometimes its hem – otherwise, it hangs free in the garment to allow the fabrics to move independently.

4. *Interlining*

An interlining is an additional fabric that adds warmth without bulk and which is applied to either the fashion fabric or the lining. Winter coats often have a quilted or removable interlining.

Some specialist needles are available for difficult fabrics. Microfiber and Microtex needles are Teflon-coated to prevent static electricity, which builds up on polyester and nylon fabrics. Static causes the thread to stick to the needle and results in skipped stitches. Embroidery needles have larger eyes and reduce the friction on metallic and fragile silk threads. Metafil needles are specifically for metallic threads and help to reduce the breakage common to these. Leather needles have a sharp flange which punctures the leather without making too large a hole. Use longer stitches for leather than for cottons or wools. Use leather needles or fine Microtex (80/12) needles on waterproof fabrics such as Gore-tex and jacket-weight nylons. Keep spare needles in a small box, wrapped in foil. A needle threader and a pair of tweezers can be useful for awkward machines.

The rule of thumb for using thread is to use the same fibre as the garment. Where this is not possible poly/cotton will do. Spun polyester thread is cheap but often stretches on the bobbin and puckers seams. It is sensitive to a hot iron and can melt, undoing all your work. Polyester bulk thread is good for overlocking (serging) as it covers the cut edges well.

Opposite Jetted pockets, welt pockets and flaps are among the hardest elements to make well, as they must match in position and size. Buttonholes are the last details to be finished on a tailored suit.

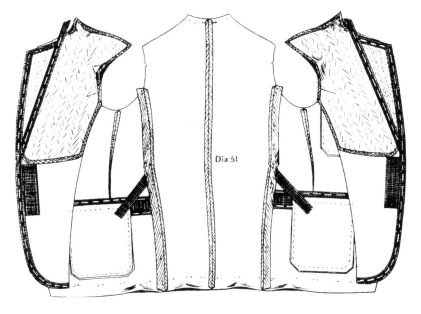

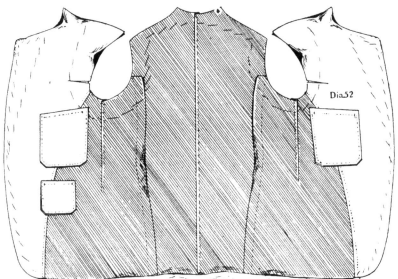

Top right and above right The many linings and interlinings that go into a structured jacket have to be cut and trimmed away carefully in order to avoid bulky seams.

Right Much of the work in a tailored jacket is hidden on the inside; a jacket requires facings, interfacings, linings, shoulder pads and seam bindings.

Tailoring

Tailoring techniques include, and are an extension of, sewing. Tailoring is used most commonly in outerwear for men's and women's clothing. It is a method of combining and moulding fabrics together to create the desired shape on the body. It is in effect a combination of padding, tape stitching and pressing. Supporting fabrics and linings are added for strength and comfort. There is more hand-work and attention to detail, making tailored garments more costly. Worsted and wool fabrics respond well to tailoring techniques as they have inherently pliable stretch and mould properties, although tailoring is not restricted to wool, and diverse fabrics such as linen and brocades can be tailored.

Tailoring work is most commonly seen in men's and women's business suits, coats and outerwear. A jacket can have as many as forty to fifty pieces to assemble. Suits can vary enormously in price depending on the approach taken. A **bespoke** (made-to-measure and handmade) Savile Row man's tailored suit can cost as much as £4,000 (approx. $7,200). However, most suits are sold through department stores and chains in the middle range, at £500–£800 (approx. $900–$1500), or in lower **off-the-peg** price brackets at £200–£500 (approx. $350–$900) respectively. Mid-range suits can be made-to-measure by machine (also called **demi-measure**). This is achieved by hand-measuring the client, or taking a three-dimensional body scan, and altering basic blocks to fit (mass-customization). A single suit is cut and then 'engineered', a semi-automated method developed by Italian manufacturers, and pressed to fit personal dimensions. Lower-priced suits are usually made in multiples to standard sizes. CAD/CAM equipment and automated sewing and **fusible** (heat bonded) interlinings are used to eliminate as many manual operations as possible.

During the last two decades, the rapidly growing men's casualwear and sportswear markets have pressured the tailored suit market, as casualwear is increasingly accepted in the workplace. In order to compete, the price of tailored clothing has been forced down and the manufacture of suits has speeded up considerably. A bespoke suit may require a number of fittings, dozens of different sewing operations and take four months to deliver. A bespoke tailor will baste (loosely tack together) a suit ready for the first fitting. When adjustments have been made it will be sewn with a combination of hand and machine stitching. Hand-stitched buttonholes, the last sewing procedure, used to be the visible sign of a top-quality suit. Assembly line **piecework** is now common in the menswear industry and the skills of the tailor are quickly becoming extinct. Fast tailoring, also known as Japanese tailoring, is a feature of Far Eastern manufacturing. In Hong Kong or Bangkok a businessman can be measured and a suit made up, typically with two pairs of trousers, in twenty-four hours. Fashionable adjustments, for example, to the width of lapels, number of trouser pleats and the positioning of the waistline, contribute to the lack of demand for longevity or robustness of manufacture.

In the last decade the relaxation of formalwear in the workplace and the influence of tailors such as Armani, through exposure in films such as *American Gigolo* (1980) and *The Untouchables* (1987) and Sandy Powell's costumes for *Gangs of New York* (2002), has led to a softening in the style and construction of the traditional suit. Increasingly, flexible and washable fabrics are being used, synthetic and stretch finishes are adding comfort and less padding is needed. Fabric choices and detailing are emerging from an era of sobriety.

Above This is the traditional sitting position for tailoring – despite appearances, it is very comfortable, the fabric can be spread across the lap and the knees can be used to ease and stretch the fabric into shape.

Far left A tailor makes a fitting of the first 'baste' of a bespoke suit.

Left A finished suit hits the catwalk.

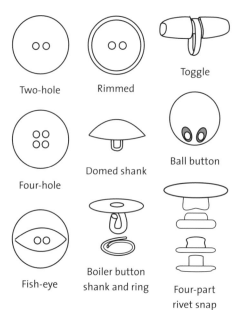

Two-hole Rimmed Toggle

Four-hole Domed shank Ball button

Fish-eye Boiler button shank and ring Four-part rivet snap

Haberdashery

Trimmings and garment fittings are classified as haberdashery or notions. Elastics, braids, ribbons and fringes are also called passementerie. Trends in trimmings and fittings change with the fashions and are crucial to the appearance and the fit of garments. Trimmings can make or ruin a garment and choosing them requires care; there are technical, aesthetic and economic considerations.

Buttons are the most commonly used trimmings; the size, number and quality can be critical to the effect of a design. Fancy ones can significantly increase the retail cost of a garment. In the early twentieth century the price of buttons dropped with the invention of casein, a milk protein derivative, celluloid and plastics. Two- and four-hole buttons and standardized sizes allowed the sewing of buttons and buttonholes onto clothing to be automated, lowering the cost and speeding garment production. They were able to compete with the popular, new-fangled zipper as a garment fastening, and replaced time-consuming ties and lacing on women's and children's clothing. Buttons that are too heavy for a fabric can pull the garment. For fine or medium-weight fabrics it is best to use light, flat buttons. When making a tight-fitting garment test the button positions on a real person. Shirt, blouse and dress buttons must be effectively secure at strategic points and placed so that the fabric does not gape. Lingerie requires small delicate buttons as comfort is important. Heavy fabrics require larger buttons with shanks to penetrate thicker layers and withstand more force.

For close-fitting garments and trousers the zipper is the closure of maximum efficiency. It was the patented invention of Whitcomb Judson in the United States in 1890, but did not take off until 1923. Zippers became more popular in the 1960s when nylon ones could be dyed to match garments. Thousands of miles of zippers are produced daily. Methods of applying zippers (see page 157), and styles of slider, can enhance their effect. Zippers are usually put into a seam or hidden behind a placket; sometimes fashion demands that they are visible. Jeans need metal studs and rivets to complete the utility look.

Buttons are sized in a curious measurement derived from a French word *ligne* – the inside diameter of a 'round wick folded flat' that became the standard reference used by German button manufacturers in the early eighteenth century, and which is now an internationally accepted standard. A ligne (L) measurement is inches divided by .0888, or centimetres divided by 2.2558. Buttons are available in sizes as small as 4 millimetres and as large as dinner plates.

Common button sizes

Ligne	mm	inches
18	12	$3/8$
20	13	$1/2$
22	14	$9/16$
24	15	$5/8$
28	17	$11/16$
30	19	$3/4$
32	20	$5/6$
34	21	$6/7$
36	23	$7/8$
40	25	1
60	38	$11/2$

Right These oversized buttons and comb inspired a striking visual joke that makes the model look like a doll.

Far right Fringing has been used in abundance, even on the shoes, to create an outfit that shivers sensuously with every step taken.

Velcro™, the name for the (1942) trademarked closure of Swiss inventor George de Mestral, comes from the French words *velours* (velvet) and *crochet* (hook). This practical product was first used in skiwear. It is now available in a large number of tape widths and shape forms, and is particularly useful for giving a modern and utility look to children's clothing, sportswear and shoes.

Trimmings such as elastics, braids and ribbons are sometimes called 'narrow fabrics' and can be used integrally for utilitarian and decorative purposes. Many require special machinery and skilled application. For most garments the trimmings and fittings must be able to withstand the high temperatures and abrasion of repeated washing and pressing, or dry cleaning. Delicate trimmings such as sequins, diamanté, beads, feathers and fringes are suitable for eveningwear and may have to be removed from garments before laundering. Decorative trimmings can attract high tax tariffs and contribute to the expense of importing and selling luxury clothing.

Fit and garment presentation

The successful presentation of a garment depends on the final touches of fitting it to a real body and pressing or easing it into shape. Many seams, facings and darts need to be properly pressed with a jet of steam as the garment is put together. This is called underpressing. Some colleges have industrial flatbed finishing equipment. Tailors' hams and sleeve boards are used to add curvature and stretch by steaming fullness into wool and suiting fabrics. Suits can be steamed over lightly while on the dress form. Bound buttonholes, jetted pockets, hems and seams need to be flat-pressed to give a crisp, straight edge. Collar points, cuffs, mitred corners, patch pockets and waistbands need to be turned out with a pointed tool while they are being pressed. Take extra care ironing around buttons and trimmings. Knitwear can be fluffed up with steam. Casual and sports clothing should look natural. It is not a good idea to iron knife creases onto shirts and knitwear. Be careful with trouser creases; check where you want them to fall on the body as it is difficult to remove them once they are pressed in.

Knowing the content of a fabric and understanding its care requirements is a good guide to making a finished garment look good (see appendix for fabric types and the international care code). Easily creased fabrics such as cotton and linen will not look finished until they have been flat-pressed. Nylons and some synthetic mixes have a low melt threshold and some surface treatments can cause a particular fabric to scorch easily. Leather and suede can be gently ironed. You might need to spray starch, silicone or waterproofing onto some fabrics to finish them. Always test the heat of the iron on a scrap of material first, and press sensitive fabrics on the reverse side to minimize shine. An iron that is not sufficiently hot to produce steam will leak water onto a garment. You may need to devise your own techniques for unusual materials and complex styles, but in most cases pressing through a thin, damp muslin cloth is the safest approach. Do not pile up warm ironing as it will set in folds; hang it to cool.

When you have pressed the garment check what it looks like on real bodies, and ask your models to walk about, sit and stretch, and give you a verdict as to comfort and fit. Some people like a generous cut and others prefer a closer fit. Active daywear is usually cut with ease of movement in mind. Evening dresses and straps may need to be checked on more than one model for décolletage and slippage. Draped styles need to be seen in movement and often require some adjustment or stay stitching to keep the

Simple and flat-pattern pieces slotted together and wrapped around the body form the basis of this collection, which was developed on a wooden doll. Unusual materials must be checked for flexibility and comfort.

Some styles should be tried on the body to check for fit and stretch.

fabric in place. Any style that is avant-garde or unpredictable certainly needs to be fitted to see what surprises may be revealed. But classics, too, need checking on a body as there are clear benchmarks as to how these styles should hang and fit.

When you are satisfied, make any alterations, hang the garment on a suitable hanger and cover it with a garment bag. Adding your own labels and a swing-tag will give a professional look to the outfit and prevent it being lost, or confused with the work of others.

Further reading and additional resources

Cutting and making
Martin M Shoben and Janet P Ward. *Pattern Cutting and Making Up*
    – *The Professional Approach*, Burlington: Elsevier, 1991
Injoo Kim and Mykyung Uti. *Apparel Making in Fashion Design*, New York: Fairchild, 2002
Edmund Roberts and Gary Onishenko. *Fundamentals of Men's Fashion Design:*
    A Guide to Casual Clothes, New York: Fairchild, 1985
Debbie Ann Gioello and Beverly Berke Fairchild. *Fashion Production Terms*, New York: Fairchild, 1979
Connie Amaden-Crawford. *Guide to Fashion Sewing*, New York: Fairchild, 2000
Karen Morris. *Sewing Lingerie That Fits*, Newton: Taunton Press, 2001
Gerry Cooklin. *Bias Cutting for Women's Outerwear*, Oxford: Blackwell, 1994
Claire Shaeffer. *Sewing for the Apparel Industry*, Upper Saddle River: Prentice Hall, 2001
Francoise Tellier-Loumagne. *Mailles – les mouvements du fil*, Paris: Minerva, 2003
Harold Carr and Barbara Latham. *The Technology of Clothing Manufacture*, Oxford: Blackwell, 2001
Hannelore Von Eberle. *Clothing Technology: From Fibre to Fashion*
    Haan-Gruiten: Verlag Europa-Lehrmittel, 2000
Robert Doyle. *Waisted Efforts: An Illustrated Guide to Corsetry Making*, Stratford: Sartorial Press, 1997
Sian-Kate Mooney. *Making Latex Clothes*, London: Batsford, 2004
RL Shep and Gail Gariou. *Shirts and Men's Haberdashery (1840s–1920s)*, Fort Bragg: RL Shep, 1998
Ernestine Kopp. *New Fashion Areas for Design*, New York: Fairchild, 1972
David J Spencer. *Knitting Technology*, Cambridge: Woodhead, 2001

Patterns and sewing information
sewingpatterns.com Sewing patterns
www.freepatterns.com Free patterns
home.earthlink.net/~brinac/Patterns.htm New York City Costuming Resources – Patterns
www.mccall.co Vogue, Butterick, McCall patterns
www.costumes.org/HISTORY/100pages/18thpatterns.htm The Costumer's Manifesto

Historical patterns
www.yesterknits.com Yesterknits

Vintage knitting patterns
www.shapelyshadow.com/html/scan.htm Shapely Shadow
Dress-form production using body scanners

Top Once you have mastered the basics of pattern-cutting and sewing, you will be ready to mix unusual combinations of cut and material. Here, shattered mirror pieces are being attached to a crinoline-like frame.

Above The finished dress, inspired by sparkling diamonds and worn to celebrate the eclipse at the millennium.

The project VI

Top A contrast between classic tailoring and an extravagantly feminine skirt wins Miguel Freitas the L'Oréal Professional Competition for the Total Look Award 2004.

Above 'Doing Smirnoff was a laugh. I was out to enjoy myself. I really thought I never had a chance of winning it. I've never won anything in my life, so getting the award was one of the biggest honours, especially in front of such a famous cast of judges.' Nick Darrieulat, winning student.

What is a project?

The most popular and successful way of teaching fashion is by means of the project. A project is a sustained piece of work, usually lasting two to six weeks and incorporating both research and practical skills. Its title, tasks, aims and objectives are set out in a project assignment. You will probably be asked to carry out your first one before you start your course. This assignment is an introduction to the process of designing and later, during the assessment critique or **crit**, to the presentation of work in front of staff and fellow students. The scope of a project varies according to the specialism you are studying and also the stage of the course you have reached. The teaching staff will hold a briefing to present the project and discuss what is required of you. The brief will set out the task, tell you what work is to be submitted and who will teach and mark it, give the criteria for assessment, and say when and how the crit will take place.

The purpose of a project brief is to develop your ability to respond creatively to a particular set of requirements. It is often a simulation of what may be required of a fashion designer within different market sectors. The project gives you a chance to practise skills that you will need when you leave college and enter work. There will, however, be some significant differences.

Types of project

The individual project

The individual project can be set either by permanent staff or by visiting lecturers. It may be a problem that all those in your year group are set, or a task you are given personally in order to improve particular skills. You will be expected to respond to the requirements of the project in your own individual way. Your response will be assessed and any marks given will be an indication of the progress you are making.

The sponsored project

The sponsored project is set by a company – usually (but not always) a fabric or fashion company. It will discuss what is required with the teaching staff, and the results will be judged by a mixture of staff and company members, with marks and prizes awarded accordingly. Sometimes marks given by college staff do not accord with the choices made by the sponsors because they are looking for a different outcome from the project – academic versus commercial considerations.

The competition project

The competition project is set by a company or external organization. Fashion competitions are a popular promotional ploy and are usually offered to colleges nationally. Prizes can include travel bursaries and placement awards. The results will be judged by the company team, and, unless you are a winner, it is unlikely that you will know how your work has been appraised. Submitted work is not always returned so it is vital to make photocopies for your portfolio.

The team project

A team project requires you to interact with a group of students, some of whom you may not even know. Team projects are large in scope and frequently require you to consider marketing, labelling and costing issues as well as designing. Your role may be defined by the group, and you will be expected to have brainstorming discussions and to co-operate with others within a simulated work environment. The pressure is intense, and sometimes you will be asked to mark your own or others' contributions. Team-project briefs are set by associated college departments or, more frequently, by companies and sponsors in collaboration with the college.

What the project asks of you

The project aims to inspire you but also asks you to consider various conditions and constraints, some of which are related to real-life conditions within the fashion market and others that are to do with academic requirements. You will probably not enjoy all projects. The brief will usually tell you what the overall aims of a project are and the objectives you should be able to achieve, to enable you to measure your own progress.

Aims and objectives

The emphasis on different aims and objectives will vary with the project, but broadly speaking the common criteria for assessment are that you should learn and be able to demonstrate:

The ability to research and apply what you learn in a creative, independent and appropriate manner;

The ability to analyse and resolve design and communication-of-design problems;

Creative and intellectual enquiry, and risk-taking in design solutions;

Skill, imagination and originality in exploring techniques, materials, imagery and colour;

The ability to synthesize your own ideas within your chosen fashion pathway;

A grasp and understanding of industrial/professional roles and methodologies;

The ability to work as an individual or as a team member;

Good working practices and presentation skills in visual, oral and written form;

Time management, self-direction and self-evaluation;

The fulfilment of your creative and intellectual potential, and resolution of your interests and design aspirations within the parameters of the brief and the curriculum.

The brief will ask you to do a specific task or choice of tasks. Sometimes it will be very clear; at other times it may be fairly difficult to understand – a significant part of the exercise is interpreting it. The project brief will state the conditions or parameters you must observe. Some probable examples are described below.

Occasion and season

It is necessary to have an idea of the occasion for which you are designing, and this can be defined by the situation, time of day or season. The brief will often state the required season or event. A fashion student is expected to see around the next corner; fashion designers must create and confirm trends rather than follow them.

> *'When I used to read about Yves Saint-Laurent I thought, "What's he got to be so neurotic about?" But now I understand. Every six months you go through hoops of fire.'* Designer Paul Frith

Top Winning outfit for an Adidas-sponsored sportswear competition.

Above 'What's been good about this project is that you get to do a bit of everything. Not one outfit is any one person's, we were all involved, and we really got to know one another. We're practically a family now.' Josh Castro, second-year student.

Street markets in some cities can be good sources of beautiful and inexpensive ethnic fabrics. Expect to buy a whole sari or batik piece rather than a cut length.

A streetwise outfit made valuable with collectible stickers and badges.

Muse or customer

A project sometimes asks you to imagine that you are designing for a specific type of consumer – of a certain size, age and gender – an individual who is a physical ideal or a source of inspiration. This can be a friend, model, film star and so on. You may be expected to build up a customer profile, including such elements as background, work, home, lifestyle and spending power. The point is to choose someone you can imagine wearing your designs with the maximum impact.

Target market

Becoming aware of the different market sectors is an important part of design education. You will frequently be asked to make market analyses and to place your designs within context. Designers vary widely in their interest in designing for different target markets (see Chapter II). For some it is a pleasure and a creative challenge to design well to middle-market **price points**. Others enjoy the subtle shifts that take place within the classic clothing field, building up signature styling and customer loyalty over many seasons. For a few the interest lies in a niche market such as sportswear, lingerie or eveningwear. Project briefs are frequently set in collaboration with stores or designers who can give first-hand feedback as to the suitability of designs for their market and customers.

Choice of material and fabric

This element is often set out in the title of the project. It is the 'problem' that you are asked to solve. Sometimes you are given a choice of themes to investigate, a list of contemporary exhibitions to see or a particular fabric to inspire you. Effectively you are restricted in some way in order to narrow the focus of your thinking and foster your creative ingenuity. The most common restriction is within a genre of clothing or the choice of materials and fabrics to be used. For example, you might be set a 'shirt project' or 'the little black dress'. The first requires you to learn the technical skills of sewing regular shirt features such as plackets and collars but in an unrestricted styling and fabric choice. The second is to design an outfit that must work in one colour for a specific occasion. Alternatively the choice may be open.

Costing

The price of a fashion item in the shops will usually be determined by fabric price and making price, plus the profit margins that the retailer applies. In costing a garment, a few centimetres in the width of the fabric can make an enormous difference to the overall outcome, and patterns may need to be adjusted. Trimmings can increase the cost dramatically, quadrupling it by the time the garment is sold at retail and pricing it out of the market. While these financial considerations are not a major part of the design process in fashion schools, they are usually taken into account. You should be able to work out how much an item would cost to produce and thereby gauge whether it fits the marketing requirements of the project. You may be asked to produce costing sheets and **flats** and **specs** to clarify production issues.

In the designer sector the mark-up is usually in the region of 120 per cent. (The retailer will add a minimum mark-up of 160 per cent to this.) Calculate the probable retail price so that you can estimate whether the garment seems to look right for the price. In pricing a collection there is always the need to fix on an amount that strikes a balance between the value of the garment and what the customer will be prepared to pay for it.

Necessity is the mother of invention. Project briefs rarely require students to part with much money, and inspired design with budget fabrics is more highly rewarded than dull design using expensive ones. Recycling, charity-shop and market-stall buys and clever changes of use are all devices that students use to great effect. On the other hand, if you plan to work in couture and high-end fashion, it is helpful to become used to handling luxurious materials without fear. It may be possible to find sponsorship for your fabrics from manufacturers, who have an interest in getting their wares in front of the public.

Practical tasks

The complexity and scope of a project varies according to the syllabus you are studying and the stage of the course you are at in your college programme. The brief will usually state the processes that will be expected of you, the number or type of items, the technical work to be carried out and the form of illustration or presentation that is expected. Marking percentages may be given for these different aspects – check these to understand where the emphasis of study is for each project, and determine which aspects are going to be a challenge. Sewing, pattern-cutting and other making-up skills may need to be learnt before the project can be completed. Professional designers very rarely simply draw their ideas. Learning practical skills impacts tremendously on your ability to design well. Find out the amount of help you can rely on from technical staff. Also important from a practical viewpoint is effective communication, both visual and verbal, so that alterations and mistakes are minimized.

Time management

The timetable or project schedule will show the periods when tutors and technical staff will be available to advise you on the project, and when and where you can use studio space. Keep it safe and refer to it often. It is vital not to miss these occasions as changes to the project schedule may be announced and practical information is often given. You may be seen individually or as part of a group. If you have an appointment to see a member of staff, bring work to do while waiting as tutorials often overrun. Some colleges have arrangements for collecting project timetables and information electronically, and for e-mailing staff, and there may be strategies for learning at a distance. Illness and absence must be notified and circumstances validated or you will risk loss of marks and credits as well as credibility. There are periods of self-directed study to familiarize you with the discipline required to organize your time for research, designing and work after graduation.

When you receive a project brief check your personal diary and decide how to divide your time effectively. Try to stick to this. You will need to factor in mundane housekeeping time. Gain an understanding of your own creative process and the time of day and conditions when you are at your most inspired or practical, and when and where you can best work without interruption. Bear in mind that other students will also be making demands on staff and technical sewing time, and that overambitious or unfinished work loses you marks. The period set for a project is a training in delivering on time!

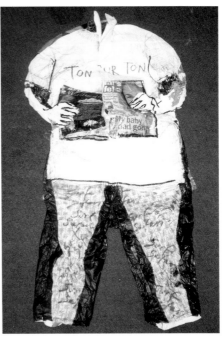

Top These hand-embroidered tunics are inspired by old cross-stitch kits.

Above Recycling second-hand clothing, unravelling and knitting new sweaters from old, and customizing are all popular ways for fashion students to make ends meet. Here, cheap paper overalls have been customized for a 'trashy' look.

Inspiration

Fashion expresses the zeitgeist, or spirit of the times, and therefore mirrors changes in society. In their search for inspiration designers must learn to keep their eyes and ears open: to visit shows, shops, clubs, cafés, galleries and films; to read magazines, newspapers and novels; to party and to listen to music; and, above all, to people watch and absorb the subtle and incremental aesthetic changes that take place in society. The key to creating new ideas is to jot down and mix the influences together in a sketchbook, then to blend this inspiration with your growing knowledge of fabrics, fashion details and target markets. With this constant fine-tuning of signals, you are in a better position to answer the brief and bring to it your own individual and intensely contemporary viewpoint.

> '*A good designer mirrors the times ... I never party, but I watch people and I read –
> about how people's lives are being dominated by technology, for example –
> and I'll respond to that.*' Designer Joe Casely-Hayford

Colleges encourage students to paint and draw from life and nature as primary sources of design. Through close observation you gain a real appreciation of what you personally find inspiring, disturbing or beautiful in your environment. Popular visual research subjects include flowers, animals, landscape and urban themes such as architecture, city decay, bright lights and reflections. Sometimes a still life or a model and environment will be set up in the studio as a focus for abstracting colour and line studies.

Resources

The following are frequently used resources and starting points for project research:
Museums, galleries, costume collections and libraries; historical and folk costumes can be particularly fruitful areas.
Crafts, folk art and hobby interests – e.g., toys, embroidery, flora and fauna.
Social influences – e.g., cult movements, music, film, literature, theatre and dance.
Lifestyle themes – e.g., architecture, interior design, social events.
Prêt-à-porter and haute couture shows, magazine reports and forecasts, style books.

John Galliano's final-year collection was inspired by costume research into the 'macaronis' and 'incroyables' of the years after the French Revolution and led to the New Romantic look that swept London in 1984.

Designs inspired by the blue morpho butterfly, Japanese fans and retro punk.

Above Researching a project may involve background reading, as well as historical and practical research into fabrics and trimmings.

Above right The concept for this outfit began with reading Patrick Süskind's novel *Perfume*. The model is wearing a cabinet jacket with perfume bottles on shelves; the fan on her head wafts scent into the audience.

Personal creativity and style

A fashion-design student learns how to create new fashion by first understanding classic garments and their detailing. To become a fashion designer, however, you must do more than merely master a body of knowledge. You must look beyond that which already exists and find new combinations of ideas and materials that can satisfy people's needs and desires. Innovation comes with having the vision and courage to change the rules playfully.

When you first start to design your tastes, like your personality, will have been partially formed by your background, social standing and experiences. This will be the core of your unique expressive spirit. What staff will be looking for in your response to a project is your own honest style, not a copy of your favourite designer's. This will evolve gradually, formed over the years by a passionate immersion in your work and by a keen appreciation of the work of your fellow students and professional designers.

While originality is prized, there is a balance to be struck; fashion does not find its mark if it is too far ahead of its time or outrages to the point of disregard. In creative surroundings you will find that you can discuss, show and achieve your ideas and be supported and stimulated by others.

> *'People do their own thing. Some do romantic things, some do conceptual, some do commercial. You can't compare us because we are doing what we want. If you are too competitive, you can drive yourself crazy because there are such a lot of good students here.'* Second-year student

Left This eclectic look was inspired by the cheerful mixture of charity-shop sweaters and indigenous clothing that the student saw on a work placement trip to Africa.

Tapping creativity

There are many techniques for tapping into your creative spirit. Some of them can be taught, and some have to be experienced personally. Psychologists have identified two kinds of thinking that are useful for problem-solving: convergent and divergent thinking.

Convergent thinking focuses the mind on aspects of the task that are already known and reduces the problem to one that you can manage, through skill, assembly and organization. Sometimes creative problem-solving depends on using the right tools, tricks, procedures or methods of analysis.

Divergent thinking requires a softer focus, dipping into the unconscious at will and utilizing the imagery to transmit ideas. It is not the same as daydreaming, more an ability to keep an open and aware mind. Have the courage to venture into the unknown, even if you don't understand where you're going or why these new paths will lead you to your solution. Try out ideas that look unlikely to work as well as the more defined ones. Many fashion designers spend time just handling and getting to know fabrics in this meditative way. Later, how to use or place a fabric may suddenly spring to mind.

It can be creatively useful to 'put yourself in someone else's shoes'. A project may require you to design in the style of a known designer or a specified period or cutting method. This frame of reference allows you to try out already successful techniques and combinations of cut and detail, it can give you insights into the talents and tastes of others, and the confidence to push your creativity further. Try to balance this approach with your own input.

Avoid an emotional or ego fixation on your own style; you are learning and need to be flexible. There will be design themes and qualities, or intellectual ideas, that particularly intrigue you and become the basis of your creative strengths and identifiable as your 'signature'. Your illustration and presentation techniques should also mature and develop into a personal 'handwriting' to complement the type of clothing you are designing.

'Good taste' in fashion is a very mobile concept. It is time- and context-sensitive, partially instinctive and partially learnt through some ground rules. It is often sensed intuitively rather than logically analysed. You may wish deliberately to flout good taste, to shock or amuse. Alexander McQueen is an example of a renowned fashion designer who has consistently challenged ideas of taste and yet been fashionably of his time. Remember, the cutting edge moves extremely fast.

Right Florals are always in fashion, sometimes small and discreet, sometimes large and dramatic. Here they are 'storyboarded' for cosy knitwear designs.

Opposite Used here in this halter-neck dress, the rose motif looks fresh and summery.

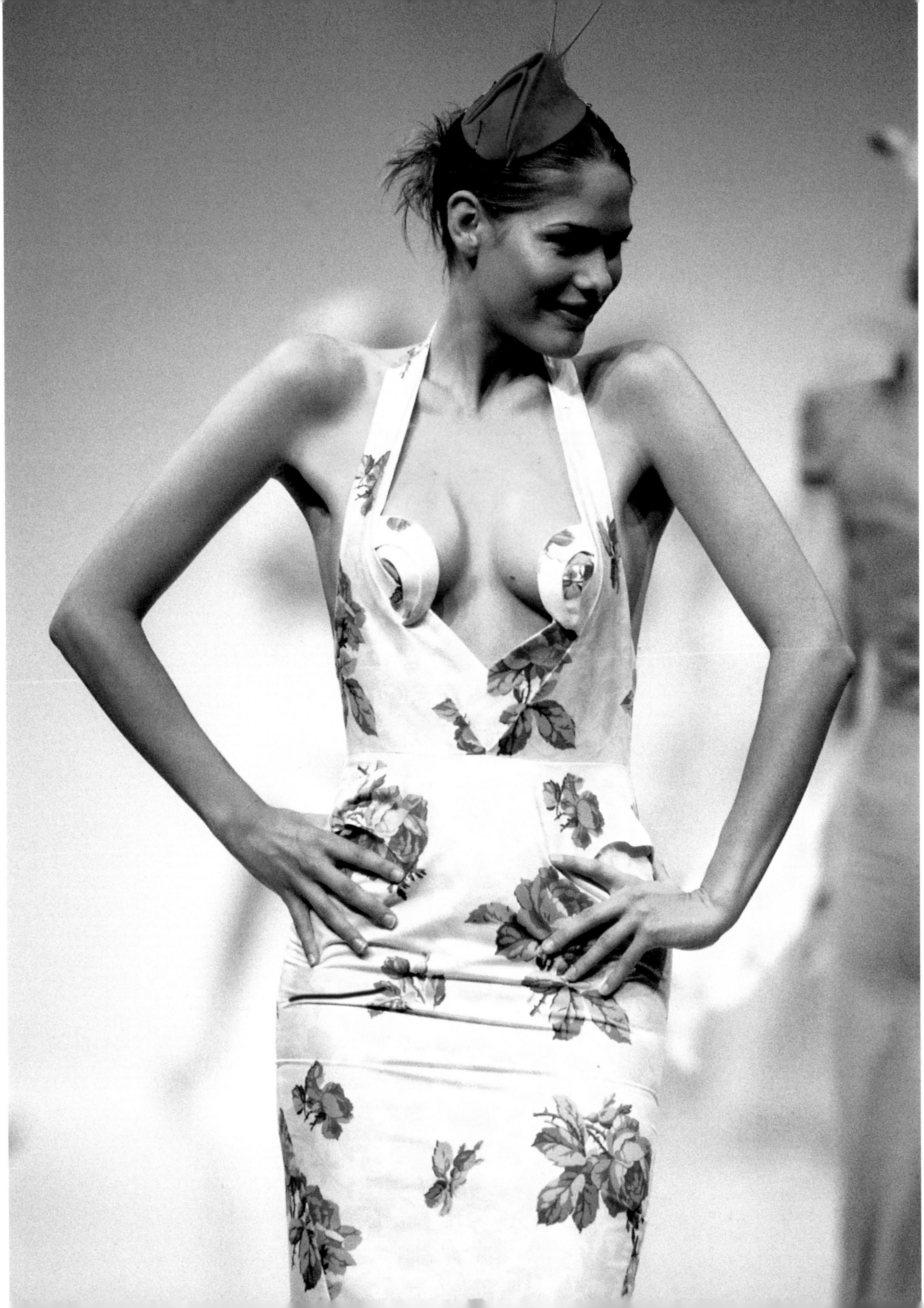

'When McQueen was at college they were trashing Galliano. When I was at college they were trashing McQueen. And then I went back last year and they were trashing me.' Designer Andrew Groves

Stay positive

Criticism and judgement are important to progress and are the means by which you will improve on your performance. Do not confuse a critique of your work with personal abuse. Keep your ego under control. Designs cannot be imposed on people; they must be accepted by them. The ability to bounce back from disappointment is as much a part of the creative armoury as drawing and making.

And don't work too hard. Pace yourself – you need energy to be creative. Prolonged, intense focus and lack of sleep or nutrition is counterproductive and can stall the creative flow. It can be upsetting if you find that you are at a standstill or unable to make decisions when all around you others are busy working. Sometimes you need patience, help, a break or a breakthrough in inspiration to set the wheels in motion again.

Above Humour has its place in fashion. This tailored collection was inspired by ventriloquists' dummies.

Right Hussein Chalayan took a considerable risk with his final-year collection in 1993. The clothes were made with paper, metal and magnets and then buried in earth for six months to rot and rust. Electromagnets underneath the runway made the fabrics vibrate and pull unexpectedly.

Presentation

Sketchbooks

Sketchbooks and visual notebooks are an essential part of the fashion student's kit. Used regularly and in conjunction with a camera, they form a portable and personal resource file of all that you find inspiring and stimulating. Your sketchbooks should record your evolving interests: impressions of artefacts, people and body poses, clothing and detail notes, colour and aspects of the environment. They can build over the years into a vast archive and supply of ideas that you can dip into.

It is worthwhile to keep a variety of sketchbooks on the go at any one time. Vary these in size and paper quality for convenience. Keep a small book with you for thumbnail sketches and entering scraps of fabric and interesting design details seen in shops or on public transport. Larger sketchbooks can be used to draw or paint from life or to work out more complex ideas. Sometimes the use of a larger scale gives weight to an idea. Layout pads are useful because of the almost transparent quality of the paper, which allows body stances and silhouettes to be traced over quickly and details changed.

A good sketchbook will give those who see it a window onto your thinking processes, and clues as to the origin of your design ideas. Your tutors will expect to look at your sketchbooks occasionally. They may also be assessed at the end of projects or at certain points in the academic programme. At times you may be asked to produce books with a more defined purpose: for example, a visual diary when you are abroad or a sourcebook that follows a particular line of research or theme. Knit- and print-design students will be expected to keep notebooks of colour and dye experiments.

Tear sheets

Tear sheets (or swipes) are pictures torn out of magazines and newspapers, exhibition programmes, postcards, flyers and so on. Collect images that you like in order to help define a mood or look that engages you – but don't directly copy them. Tear sheets need not necessarily be contemporary. Second-hand bookshops, for example, are a rich source of unusual visual and reference material. Photocopies are useful, but beware of using too many or your work will take on a very 'secondary source' look.

Mood boards

Once you have collected sufficient images and ideas from your research, it is possible to start the design development. You might be asked to do a 'mood board'. This is a more formal statement of your concept and intentions through pictures and scraps that you have carefully arranged and collated as if for a magazine page. Items are often pinned onto polyboard (foam core) rather than stuck down permanently. Polyboard is light and portable but can stand the weight of fabrics and trimmings and form a flexible focus for discussion of your ideas with your tutors.

Design sketches

During the early stages of a project you need to sketch a number of ideas quickly in your sketchbook or on a layout pad. These are referred to as **roughs** and **design developments**. Mark or select the roughs you are happiest with and those that have elements you wish to explore further. You can group designs according to various criteria such as the use of fabrics, silhouette, detail and so on. Some designs pop out of the pencil ready-formed; others you have to grope for. Some happen in the moment of draping fabric on a dress form or seeing a silhouette toile on a body. An instant Polaroid

Toys and dolls are popular inspirations; sketchbook pages and storyboards show how colour, materials, details of scale and the pattern of a teddy bear are worked into designs.

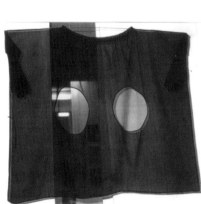

Left An idea is tried out in a drawing, then made in miniature and finally made up full-size.

camera can be very helpful at this stage for capturing variations. Some ideas develop by accident. Do not throw away work you are dissatisfied with; a week later you, or your tutor may find it more compelling than you expected. Design tutors and technicians will help you to make choices that clarify and justify your ideas. Remember that the opportunities to talk to them informally in the studio are also moments when you can learn a great deal; and staff will be observing your working methodology and application to the tasks in hand before the presentation of the project.

Storyboards

A project will usually require you to make a presentation of your ideas through artwork as well as a prototype or garment. Storyboards are a series of finished presentation sheets or polyboards, which represent the whole 'story' of your solution to the brief. They will usually include a mood board, final illustrations and co-ordinated fabrics and trimmings, with a small amount of text to explain the theme, colours and market. Fashion courses have different approaches to this sort of presentation and may give students quite a lot of freedom when it comes to putting together artwork for a crit. This work often forms the core of a portfolio.

Opposite Intriguing photography can help to finish off the presentation of an outfit or collection. Styling, location and accessories can distinguish or change the look. Here the mood, caught between takes, is charged with atmosphere.

The crit

The **crit** (or critique) is the occasion when staff evaluate your response to a project. It is both an objective and a subjective assessment of how you have fulfilled the requirements. It is also an exchange of ideas. The crit can be managed in a number of different ways, according to the type of brief. Sometimes it is a private assessment with a panel of teaching staff. At others it is a mini fashion show to which you bring your dressed model. On these occasions the crit can be attended by the entire student group or a selection of students and staff, technical staff or invited visiting tutors. The members of the panel will be looking for a design that has not only solved the problem set by the project, but which also has balance, harmony, originality and a good choice of fabric and trimmings. Additionally, they will want to see that you have developed your design and practical skills.

Now and again only selected designs will be discussed in full, in order to speed up what can be a very protracted process. The main points of success and failure that have come out of the project will be discussed and clarified. You will be given marks on the presentation of your work, both in its practical form and in the way that you explain and support your answer to the project brief.

> *'During a crit students need to listen hard and learn to extract the useful information and facts from personal opinion … A crit situation has all the dynamics of group therapy; it's usually very positive but often there are also confessions and tears. We all learn from it.'* Second-year fashion tutor Sally Calendar

Most students and staff find that the crit is an enjoyable finale to a project. It is very satisfying to see your design finished and being worn, and also to see how others have tackled the same themes and yet come to very different conclusions. There will often be conflicting or varied points of view as to how successfully you have arrived at and achieved your objectives. If you are well prepared and have rehearsed your presentation, this should not be a worry. The purpose of the crit is to help you to appreciate your progress and resolve potential problems in your future work.

> *'If you know what you want to do because you have thought it through, it should have an inner logic and conceptual rightness – where all elements fit, dictate form and colour. Then you are away and it is straightforward production. Sweating over it for days can spoil it.'* Final-year student

Opposite Preparation and discussion of modelled designs and artwork at a critique.

Right A line-up of toiles shown before the garments are cut and made in the correct fabrics helps the decision-making process. It also allows the designer to spot items missing from the collection and to make alterations that improve the overall presentation and balance of the line.

Far right Photographing work in progress is useful as a record for your portfolio, especially if the design mutates significantly during the process.

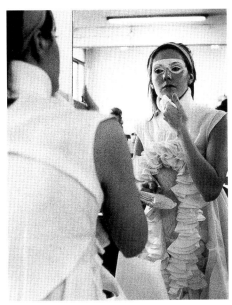

Assessment

The grading scheme used for all marked projects varies between colleges and courses. Some colleges use an 'alpha-beta' system and their equivalent percentage marks. The course handbook will explain what level of achievement the marking bands represent. Some courses award credits, marks which you accumulate to allow you to progress to another or advanced **module** (unit) of the course. You can chart your progress by keeping a note of these marks and defining the strengths and weaknesses that can be addressed in your portfolio. Most colleges will assign you a personal tutor who will guide you and give you written and verbal feedback in a variety of progress tutorials. If you are unhappy with your marks at any point during your education you should make arrangements to see your tutor and discuss the problem. There is usually also a formal assessment of your progress at critical junctures of your course. You will be informed when and where these will take place so that you can prepare yourself. You may be asked to put up a display of your work or show a portfolio to the staff team. Assessment is a matter of judgement, not simply of computation. Projects are commonly marked by a number of different people on different occasions, who will use their own objective discretion moderated by discussion. The moderation process is an important aspect of the assessment, and circumstances that may have affected your attendance or performance in projects or during the year can be taken into account providing you have reported them. At the final stage of a degree course you are marked by a panel of tutors, most of whom have been familiar with your work over an extended period. In most colleges the panel consists of at least one **external examiner**, who has been invited from the industry or academia to ensure that there is a fair assessment of all students and that the required standards are observed. Usually marks for written work, such as a **thesis,** business report or **dissertation**, are computed into your final grade. The balance and percentage given to contextual studies varies in different institutions. Some courses offer a variety of ratios of practical work to written work from which you can choose to be assessed. Faculty members are always keen to see their students do well.

Further reading and additional resources

Carolyn Genders. *Sources of Inspiration*, London: A&C Black, 2002

Oei Loan and Cecile de Kegel. *The Elements of Design*, London: Thames & Hudson, 2002

Penny Sparke. *As Long as it's Pink – The Sexual Politics of Taste*, London: HarperCollins, 1995

Petrula Vrontikis. *Inspiration = Ideas: Creativity Sourcebook*, Rockport, Mass: Rockport, 2002

Galleries and portfolio sites
www.artshole.co.uk/arts/fashion.htm
www.arts.ac.uk/ntouch
www.dresslab.com
www.wgsn-edu.co.uk
www.showstudio.com
www.zoozoom.com
www.sowear.com
www.firstVIEW.com
www.inMode.com

The final collection
– and beyond VII

The final collection

Your last project, often called the 'final collection', should build on the individual successes you have achieved over your years at college. This is the range that will launch you into the professional world. Essentially, it is you who write your project for your final collection. You may be expected to write a rationale, or explanation, of your intentions to help you to resolve your ideas. This, together with your drawings, fabric selections and any other relevant data, will be presented to the teaching staff and possibly also to external examiners or others invited to discuss your presentation and help you make your final garment selection. It can also function as a 'press release' to send out to the media, potential employers or buyers.

By this stage of the fashion course you will have identified the market and the type of person for whom you would like to design. Over the years you will have established a design identity. You will have an appreciation of the complex and competitive industry into which you are stepping, and the supporting work, photographs and illustrations in your portfolio will indicate that you are ready for your first professional project. Fabrics, colours and your decisions about silhouette and design details will all be handled with a confidence that has grown and blossomed. You will have gained a variety of skills and technical knowledge, to produce clothing appropriate to your specialism.

Your final-collection designs should look strong and include both important directional ideas and less dramatic pieces. When your designs have been approved in the presentation **crit**, you are ready to go to the pattern-making stage. A number of adjustments and changes to your plan will probably be needed before the collection takes form and the toiles meet with approval at the **line-up**, or review, of your collection before the styles are made up. For some, the practical making of their collection is the most enjoyable aspect of all.

'A collection can end up looking quite different from what you had in mind. It is quite hard to control; it has a life of its own; it jumps out of your hands. You look at it on the day of the show, when everything is put together, and it has changed. You think: "How did that happen?"' Designer Suzanne Clements

The college fashion show

The fashion show of an established designer differs markedly from that of a student collection. The professional show gives retail buyers and the press a first view of a new commercially available collection. It is also a public relations exercise that fuels the supply of pictures and stories to magazines and, increasingly, it is an entertainment in its own right. The chief members of the college fashion-show audience, by contrast, will be staff, along with students, parents and a sprinkling of sponsors and manufacturers on the lookout for fresh employees and ideas. Some colleges feel that it is educationally decisive for fashion students to have the simulated experience of the catwalk show since many will meet with it later in their careers. The critical pacing of your workload, and the ability to focus and present a cohesive range that is both creatively exciting and relevant to your future aspirations, are assessable outcomes of the final-collection project.

You will have worked very hard on your final collection and will naturally have strong ideas about how you want it to be styled and worn on the catwalk. Remember, though, that a student show is a vehicle for a large number of people and that it is not possible to mastermind it as if it were a production for a single designer. Colleges have limited funds, and while most will try to take account of individual students' wishes, it is necessary to streamline the use of models. You may have some choice over the casting of models for type, colouring and height, and also over music and accessories.

Not all fashion-college programmes feel it is appropriate to test or showcase their students on the runway. There are many aspects of fashion design that do not lend themselves to this form of exposure. All fashion courses, however, stress the importance of having a good, professional-looking portfolio over the momentary spectacle of the catwalk. Colleges usually hold an exhibition of end-of-year work to which interested parties and manufacturers are invited. Increasingly, courses are looking to new technologies, such as digital video and the Internet, to help students to promote themselves more widely.

Tips for styling your college show

Try to keep your concept simple. A clear silhouette, colour and design message comes across most effectively if it is not overwhelmed by styling tricks or models who look vastly different from one another.

Visualize the effect you want. Do you want your models to appear singly, in pairs or as a group; to walk fast or slow; to take items off or pose?

Tell your tutors what you plan to do well in advance – you will lose marks for last-minute theatricals. A show with some unusual features as high points can work well, provided it is organized in advance and planned into the running order for maximum effect.

Below Each student supplies shoes and accessories for their outfits.

Bottom Students help with make-up before the show.

Below right Checking the line-up for fit and details backstage.

Rehearsing the models for walk and timing before the show.

Graduate shows are often held in temporary exhibition sites.

Even at student shows there is a hierarchy of seating, and security is necessary.

The crowd gathers outside.

Models who are not professional – however beautiful or beloved – can often spoil a presentation by being in the wrong place, walking badly or self-consciously or attempting to upstage one another. Rehearse them so that you can spot and iron out any idiosyncrasies.

They have their own ideas about what they are prepared to wear. A few will refuse to show very short or revealing garments; others will baulk at putting on an outfit they think makes them look foolish or ugly. Be diplomatic: swap clothes around; if all else fails, cry! It is necessary for models to change their outfits very quickly between 'runs'. Beware of using complicated accessories – tights (pantyhose), belts and jewellery all take time to put on and remove. Change times need to be checked or the flow of the show may grind to a halt. You may have to beg, borrow, hire or put down expensive deposits on accessories and items for the show. Organize this well in advance.

Show producers usually have a team of professional dressers. You may not be allowed backstage to check that everything is perfect just before your designs hit the catwalk. It is important to name and number your outfits, and to have drawings and lists of what goes with what and how it is worn. Make sure the dresser and models understand what is expected. Have extra pairs of tights at the ready as these can be ruined or lost in rehearsals. Attach or pin accessories onto garments where possible. Explain complicated fastenings to the dresser. Some 'conceptual' fashion will need demonstrating to both model and dresser.

If you want elaborate hairstyles, don't forget that the necks of your garments must go easily and quickly over heads. Some colleges insist on simple, sleek hairstyles throughout the show. It is possible to style with wigs and hats, but take care – nothing looks more foolish than a slipping hairpiece. You may have to compromise with make-up that suits all the students, unless you have your own models or are the last to use a 'set' of models and they have time to apply extra effects between changes.

If you are borrowing shoes or having them made, find out the models' shoe sizes. Most tall models have larger-than-average feet. It can be useful to pick a style that is adjustable or one where a bad fit does not show: for example, slingbacks, boots and brogues (Oxfords). Contact suppliers well in advance and make sure the shoes arrive well before the show so that the models can try them on and be comfortable walking in them. Cover the soles with masking tape to prevent them being marked, making the shoes non-returnable. Simple choices such as flip-flops are cheap, stylish, easy and understated.

You will probably be allowed to select your own music track for your collection. You will be given a finite length of time, so make sure it is neither too long nor too short. Start listening to potential choices at least a month beforehand, and try 'walking' to the track. Monotonous, loud or atonal avant-garde music can irritate more than please.

Special effects can heighten your designs, but can be disastrous if done badly. Dry ice, for example, can make an audience suffer from coughing and sore eyes or obliterate the clothes completely. Health and safety regulations may not allow what you have in mind, so check these before hiring expensive equipment. Showers of water, glitter, thrown flowers or 'accompaniments' such as dogs are best left for the finale or models will be stepping in debris left on the catwalk throughout the show. After the show quickly collect any accessories. It can be chaotic backstage, and small items can be damaged or lost.

'It's all over very quickly. You study for three or four years and then it's all over in three or four minutes ...' Final-year student

Top The press arrive early. The show will be videotaped for the exhibition.

Above A student anxiously checks her outfits before they go on the runway.

Top The dresser has a moment of peace before the show.

Above Whether you are showing garments or helping behind the scenes, experience of a college show is good preparation for the cut and thrust involved in professional shows.

The show ends with a
dramatic show-stopper.

If they have been helping backstage, students do not see the impact of their collections on the runway until they watch the video playback.

Student exhibitions

A commonly required part of the fashion and textile academic degree is a small exhibition of your final project and portfolio to assist in the assessment of your work. Over the years these assessment shows have grown into delightful exhibitions, which are initially just for parents and invited luminaries but which are later opened to the public, sometimes for a fee. The standard of display and presentation skills is very high, and much of it must be planned well in advance.

You are often given only a day or so to prepare a stand and put up your element of the show; any special fittings, lighting and shelving must be discussed beforehand with college staff. Photography, graphics and elaborate slide shows or video pieces should all be organized weeks ahead. If you are required to show your garments, make sure they have hangers that complement them. Clothing will be less likely to go missing and looks more professional if you put on name tags and swing-ticket labels. The graphics for these and your business cards should have an overall identity that helps someone to remember your work. Textile swatches can also be headed with the same information and displayed in a way that makes them enticing to handle. There is usually a shelf or cradle for your portfolio.

Try to get your personality across, but beware of cluttering up the display – the smaller the space, the simpler it should be. Sketchbooks and technical work should be piled up neatly for the assessment, but are often removed before the show opens to the public for reasons of space and security. You are usually expected to be present at times during the exhibition in order to keep your area safe and tidy, answer enquiries and promote your work and that of others. After the exhibition, follow up on any enquiries that have been made, reorganize your portfolio and start looking for your first job.

Graduate showcases

Most colleges also belong to associations that showcase their students' work to industry. Graduate fashion-design exhibitions are an excellent opportunity for making contacts, getting feedback about your work, and seeing and learning from the work of others. Prestigious prizes are awarded by panels of sponsors and industry observers, and the shows are attended by the press, television, fashion scouts and designers. This is not a time to relax; you must be there and on your best behaviour if you wish to stand a chance among the many hundreds of hopeful talents.

Selling your collection or artwork

If you are exhibiting your work in public, keep business cards and a small notebook for comments beside your display. You may have some contacts and sales enquiries to follow up. It is wise to give some thought to prices beforehand. It is difficult to cost and set a price for your garments or illustrations when asked outright by an interested buyer. You may feel flattered, especially if the buyer is a celebrity or model, and under-value the piece (celebrity buyers will wear your outfit in the right places, but may also expect to receive items free of charge). To avoid awkwardness and later embarrassment, there are a number of factors you should consider before agreeing to a sale. In most cases you do not need to give an answer or a price immediately, but take contact details and do not delay overlong. Your collection garments are unique and the love, time and money spent on their development can rarely be balanced by objective pricing. Your bank account will have suffered during the run-up to your

Above TV and press journalists interview students whose work has caught their eye.

Opposite Winning an award is a wonderful endorsement of your hard work, and listed on your CV or résumé, can open doors when jobseeking.

collection and the chance to recoup some funds is tempting. It is wonderful to have your work appreciated, but you may be reluctant to part with the fruits of your labour and set too high a price. Months later, when fashion has changed, you will have lost the sense of attachment and wish you had taken the cash.

If the buyer has a store or company, you may be concerned that the garment will be bought as a sample and put into production. Alternatively, you may be asked if you can take an order for dozens of items. You should discuss the request with your tutor as there may be college property rules or agency arrangements in place. He or she will be able to advise you on how to set or negotiate a price that suits both you and the buyer, and can explain the need and the protocol for a written order or paperwork where reproduction, intellectual property rights or conditions apply. It is unwise to hand over artwork or designs until the end of the exhibition, or even a few weeks later. Your work may still be needed for assessment, interviews or the press. You should make sure that you have photographs of it in your portfolio. Consider making an arrangement with the buyer to 'borrow' the piece back if it is needed for publicity. Be professional about the transaction; agree terms (cash and electronic transfer are safer than a cheque), give a receipt and pack the item/s so they will not be damaged in transit.

Your portfolio

It is essential to have a professional display portfolio from the very start as a way of keeping designs and artwork flat, orderly and portable. If you can afford to do so, buy two – one for carrying about day-to-day, one to use for interviews. An A1 (84.1 x 59.4 centimetres, 33 x 23½ inches) portfolio is appropriate only if you have excellent large-scale work; otherwise it is easier to travel with an A2 (59.4 x 42 centimetres, 23½ x 16½ inches) or A3 (42 x 29.7 centimetres, 16½ x 11¾ inches) one. Avoid carrying bulky work or sketchbooks; although these may be interesting, they do not look professional. Photocopy any especially good pages and put them in one portfolio.

The central spine of spring clips holds transparent sleeves; this makes it faster to rearrange your work. Estimate how many pages you need. A portfolio that is too empty or too full can look amateurish. It is a good idea to sort the work into order and lay out all the pages before you slip them into the plastic sleeves. Think about which designs will appear on right-hand pages as there is a tendency for people to pay more attention to these.

In some colleges you may be expected to put work into chronological order for assessment purposes. However, for maximum visual effect you should sort it into best, secondary and 'maybe' piles of projects; edit these and arrange them as if they are articles in a magazine, with the most eye-catching work at the start, following on with good work and tailing off towards the end. Finish with a strong 'conversation piece'. Try and keep the orientation of all the pages the same. It is very tiring if you have to to keep moving your head or turning the whole portfolio around to view the designs. Don't clutter up your pages; you will be familiar with your work, but others will be seeing your portfolio for the first time and too many designs will confuse them. Each section should tell the story of how you went about researching, creating design developments and resolving the brief. Separate each section with one blank page.

Make a decision as to the overall layout and style. The portfolio should look like the work of one person and show up your strengths, not your weaknesses. Sleeves often come with a sheet of black backing paper that can set off your artwork well. It is not a good idea to change the background colour too often. Neutrals are usually smartest, but too much black can have a depressing effect. Use the paper that comes in the sleeves as a size guide and trim other papers to this size.

Keep the effect uncluttered by including a border around your work. Glue only the corners of the artwork down, as you may want to move it in the future. Loose or light fixing allows you to reposition pieces. Not everything looks good in transparent sleeves; the polythene can dull vibrant colours. If you have made beautiful fabrics, it may be better if they can be freely handled.

Each project should be clearly defined; titles will help make clear what each section is about. Make sure you write these on separate pieces of paper, not directly on artwork. It is embarrassing to be told by your interviewer that you have spelt something wrong, so check everything carefully. Handwriting can look relaxed, but it will look more professional if it is done on a computer. Keep notes and titles short, but write enough to give an idea as to what was intended, in the event of your absence. Do not put dates on the work as this can make designs look passé.

Collages of research work can look good as an introduction to a project, but if the pieces are bulky it is best to get them colour-photocopied. Curiously, colour copies sometimes look better than the original artwork. Some people like to laser-copy their entire portfolio, as an archive and also for continuity, although this can lead an interviewer to doubt that the work originates with you. Large drawings can look neater if reduced, and bringing sketches down to one size can add a more professional uniformity. A portfolio should contain a balance of clear and considered design developments with some roughs and finished illustrations that show more artistic spirit. Vary the number of figures in a layout, and the scale and media in which they are produced. You should aim to show styles that indicate your versatility in designing for different seasons and colour palettes.

Check the order by looking through the portfolio a number of times to see how it reads – there should be features that keep you turning the pages. It can be useful to have a dramatic fold-out presentation piece to pull out of the portfolio sleeve if conversation starts to lag, as well as a copy of an illustration to leave behind with your business card as a memory-jogger.

There are other ways of presenting work. You can show slides on a portable light box, or you could make a digital portfolio and résumé to hand over as a CD-ROM. Do not put all your best work on this, but do include something memorable and significant.

When applying for a particular job, your portfolio should be organized to maximize your appeal and fit the advertised role. Research the company, find out what it has produced in recent seasons and its marketing objectives. Go through your work and review it in the light of who will be looking at it.

Following spread You are unlikely to be asked to take garments to an interview. A professional-looking record of your work will give your portfolio display the edge. Colleagues and friends interested in fashion styling can advise on appropriate hair, make-up and lighting to create a high-quality studio shoot.

Below left Portfolios are laid out for people in the industry to browse through.

Below Knitwear is difficult to display yet tempting to touch.

Bottom Business cards are an essential contact tool to remind buyers and potential employers of you and your work. They should include the following: your name, university or college course, telephone number (home and mobile if possible) and e-mail address. If you have an exhibition stand, the more people pick them up the better.

Work placement and internships

For a graduate, sudden exposure to the world of work can be daunting. It need not be, however, and the key here is preparation. Start networking early in your college career, find work experience or take a **placement**. At the very least you can try finding holiday jobs with a company that interests you. Some colleges offer sandwich courses, which include a sustained period of work experience within the industry as part of, or in addition to, the curriculum. This is called a placement, or **internship**. It is a useful way to test out and view at first hand the different career paths and roles available.

Although placement work is often not well remunerated, the experience should prove a valuable investment. Usually you will be taken on in the position of a studio junior. Typical tasks may include everything from modelling toiles and sewing on labels and buttons to answering the phone, making the coffee and running out for sandwiches. You are unlikely to be asked to design or contribute to the collection while on a placement, but if you are alert you will be given more complex jobs and responsibility as you prove your competence.

Your personality and self-presentation will be under scrutiny in these circumstances; you can be easily replaced. Timekeeping and orderliness, hard work and good manners are valued. Contacts and friends can be made who will form part of your future network and who may be willing to give you references or sponsorship in funds or in kind. Many students are asked back to work after they graduate, in the much more rewarding role of junior designer.

> '_I had the most wonderful time on my placement. I was really nervous when I first started and didn't dare speak to the designers, but everyone was so friendly that I soon got into it. The best part was helping out at the collections and seeing it all come together and knowing which bits I'd had a hand in. Now I know my way around Paris, too. I feel really sophisticated._' Third-year student

Your college will usually ask you to write an evaluative report on the structure of the company, the nature of its products and the tasks that you were given. It is a good idea to keep a work diary and to ask your colleagues for information and material you can use in your report.

The document is confidential but you may be expected to show it to your employer, so take care in your phrasing. Your employer may also be asked to fill in a form or give a verbal account of your conduct in the workplace. You may be awarded an academic certificate or academic credit on completion of the job, which can be added to your CV. Future employers are more confident about taking on employees who have some experience in the industry, and you increase your chances of finding work with this endorsement. The internship is a wonderful low-risk opportunity to find out what you are (or are not) best suited for within the industry. You may discover that you need additional qualifications and training for the job you aspire to, and might consider doing a postgraduate course.

If you finish your collection in good time, you can improve on your presentation with a photo shoot.

If you visit stands during Graduate Fashion Week you can see what colleges have to offer.

Post-graduate study and research

After you have completed a first fashion degree you may wish to continue your studies in another country or examine your subject more deeply. Or you may want to specialize in an area such as marketing, sportswear or computer-aided design, or in another aspect of fashion design that is not commonly offered in depth at Bachelor of Arts level. A wide range of options is available. Before making an application, contact the university or college to discover what the benchmarks are. At a higher-degree level you will be expected to take a more pro-active approach to your learning programme. It will be assumed that you have basic fashion skills to an established level, and little time will be allowed for catching up with other students. You may be expected to write a plan for your studies before you apply for a place. If possible, go to the degree shows of courses that interest you and visit institutions on their open days to ask questions. Research degrees in the arts, and especially the fashion field, are less common than in sciences and humanities, but many universities offer social and cultural studies, and have business and textile technology departments that may consider fashion-research proposals. Many colleges and universities offer part-time study modes.

Careers in fashion
After graduation

Every June an enormous number of fashion-degree graduates are available for work. The first few weeks after graduation can seem like a holiday and it is difficult to resist the temptation to relax. A large number of potential employers visit the degree shows and advertise and interview at this time. If you have received some interest, promptly follow up any leads. If not, don't become despondent and, most importantly, stay focused. The creative-design world thrives on networking and contacts, and many of the top jobs are never advertised. Word may go out to some select agencies, but many appointments are made by recommendations, sometimes from college tutors, or through previous contacts or by poaching or headhunting staff from competitors. The fashion industry is notorious for its lack of secure positions and many people enjoy the variety this brings.

While you are actively seeking work, organize your time and activities and consider enhancing your skills and experience with part-time work or study. For merchandisers and for production and promotional jobs fluency in Microsoft Word, Excel and PowerPoint are considered essential. These transferable skills can be learnt in many fields besides fashion. Experience gained on placement (internship) or in sales assistance will be an advantage when you are looking for employment and should be mentioned at interviews. Keep abreast of industry news, stay in touch with events and visit trade exhibitions. It is often worthwhile accepting a first 'foot in the door' job that may lead to a better position. You are more likely to hear about, or be offered, other work if you are already employed.

Employment prospects

Government statistics in the United Kingdom, Europe and the United States show that the number of vacancies in the fashion and textile industries are shrinking and forecasts are that the situation will continue. Wage work and salaried employment in the apparel industry is expected to decline by sixty-nine per cent through to 2012. The loss of jobs is concentrated mainly at the lesser skilled, full-time employment end of the manufacturing market because of offshore production. However, it is predicted that there will be a continuing demand for higher technical skills centred on pre-production in design, information technology (IT) and advanced computer-aided design and manufacturing technologies, and traditional handcraft skills associated with high-quality clothing. Growth areas include product development (design and technology), cutting and planning, computer-aided production, hand-tailoring, management and logistics. The need for textile and fashion designers should remain strong, and possibly increase, because the demand for fashionable clothing is substantial and expanding in the casual menswear, sportswear and childrenswear sectors, in plus-sizes and in clothing for the over-forty age group. Nevertheless, competition for design jobs is keen. Although a large number of jobs within the fashion industry do not require a degree, a minimum of two years certificated higher education is standard. And although some of the most famous designers and entrepreneurs, including Vivienne Westwood, Ralph Lauren, Helmut Lang and Michael Kors, did not have formal training, today a degree is an authoritative indicator of ability and commitment.

Real working conditions

Employment practices are shifting and recent graduates should expect difficulty in finding a position or are likely to be offered short-term entry-level contracts or asked to work on a part-time or freelance basis for little remuneration. Skills Training in information technology and production machinery processes is often available through local education or careers centres in the form of part-time or weekly classes, or can be gained while on the job. Empirical studies in both the United Kingdom and the United States show that four out of ten designers are self-employed. Surveys show that mature graduates face an even greater challenge in establishing themselves, and are more likely to be self-employed. It takes time to network and build up contacts and a reputation. It is important to maintain relationships with friends and colleagues as many jobs are obtained by word of mouth. Self-employment is fragmented and carries the ongoing burden of finding assignments, and the responsibility for record keeping and tax returns.

The Princeton Review of Careers states that the chances of becoming an internationally famous fashion designer are 160,000 to one. Only about one per cent of design graduates actually work as designers; seventy per cent take up satisfying work in other aspects of the industry, notably production, retail and administration. There are a wide number of opportunities that offer scope for creativity and knowledge. Realism and self-evaluation will help you to come closer to personal fulfilment. Nearly fifty per cent of graduates leave the fashion sector within five years because they are disappointed with their progress. Approximately fifteen per cent of students go on to do a postgraduate degree or a teacher-training course. There is no guarantee of funding for postgraduate studies, and the cost of financing a further period of training should be a carefully considered aspect of your career plan. For those who prevail and become senior designers, managers and retailers, remuneration rises steeply and the job satisfaction is rewarding. Beyond ten years of employment, there is some evidence of 'burnout' and stress as a result of shouldering the responsibility for success and maintaining fresh input. Design professionals often change tack to use transferable skills in business or merchandising. It is therefore essential to take a realistic and proactive approach to planning your future career and to be aware of the ladders of opportunity.

The fashion industry is the largest employer of women, many of whom earn low wages. Approximately seventy-five per cent of retail employees are women. Retail and production wages are generally calculated on an hourly or piecework basis. In higher positions a weekly or monthly wage is offered. The female share of employment is expected to increase by around four times as much as the increase in male employment over the decade through to 2012. The pay gap between men and women has shrunk to its smallest margin since modern records began – the average salary for women in the UK topped £20,000 for the first time in 2003. The average starting salary is approximately £12,000 in the UK ($13,500 in the US) and after five years the average salary rises to a mean of £24,000 in the UK ($35,000 in the US). Senior appointments bring considerably higher salaries – estimated at between $50,000 and $110,00 in the US. Many designers and managers also enjoy incentive systems and profit-sharing arrangements.

Employment conditions and working hours vary widely. Regular nine-to-five days are still commonplace, but larger businesses may expect shift work, and many retailers now open all weekend. In Europe most of the fashion and clothing sector is made up of small businesses; in the US the major employers are larger conglomerates and factories. You may be required to join a union. In design and managerial positions, job descriptions can be vague and a flexible approach is expected. The average number of hours worked by designers is fifty-five a week, which is substantially longer than the forty-eight hours stipulated in the European Union directive on working hours. Ask for written clarification if you are unsure of the hours, or of the duties you will be expected to perform. Employers are legally expected to provide a contract that explains hours, holiday and sickness entitlements and other features of a remuneration package. While environmental conditions are usually pleasant and congenial, there are often pressures of production deadlines and pre-show or seasonal demands for overtime work. Health and safety regulations ensure that factories and studios are normally safe and clean, but machinery can be noisy and sewing and computer-aided design can entail sitting in the same position for much of the day. Retail workers stand for long hours. As well as the qualifications and personal qualities appropriate to your chosen job, you may be expected to bring other less evident attributes. For example, punctuality, discretion, loyalty, connections in the industry, interpersonal and social skills or an air of authority, a good memory for names and details and smart self-presentation. In small businesses and sales jobs a clean driving licence is often required. Designing, production management and fabric sourcing involve time spent out of the office and foreign travel. Foreign language skills are beneficial and likely to only increase in value to employers. Sales representatives and textile designers are expected to liaise with overseas agents and customers, and may frequently carry heavy sample loads to trade shows and on visits. Any employer will seek cheerful enthusiasm and flexibility.

There are a great many unrealistic perceptions about the glamour of working in fashion. The final shows set the adrenalin flowing and hopes are high, but you should be prepared for disappointment. Only a lucky few are plucked from their college degree exhibitions and set on a glittering path. When you do find employment, you may have to start at the bottom, work hard and make slow progress to reach your goal. Thinking through where you want to work and why you are pursuing a career in fashion will help you decide wisely how to approach the stages of the ladder. It is often better to accept a lower-paid job with a well-respected company that offers training and wider opportunities than a narrow but highly paid short-term position. Entry-level jobs may not satisfy your desire to design, but they will teach you basic background skills and responsibility, and will look good on your CV when you apply for a higher-level job or set up a business at a later date. First jobs can be critical, and the value of a good start and a good reference when you move on cannot be overestimated.

There are, however, a wide number of career opportunities besides that of designer that offer scope for your creativity, skill and knowledge. Some are technical jobs, others involve statistics and logistics, and some have a high social aspect, involving liaison with press and public. It is a varied field. There is full-time, part-time and a great deal of freelance and consultancy work. There are too many levels of career and variations on a theme within fashion to list them all, but there is a broad guide below to the areas of employment you might consider, and an additional list on page 210.

Womenswear

Only the very talented can expect to start their career as designers of womeswear. It is more likely that you will start as a design assistant, work hard and make slow progress to reach your goal.

If you are employed by a middle-market company you will be expected to communicate your ideas and vision with sketches and design specifications in discussions with both technical and marketing staff, to given deadlines. You will be trusted to have an understanding and respect for the house style, brand and design budget of the company and to translate the taste and budget level of the target market into creative, desirable and profitable fashion products created in large quantities. Aspects of this will be learnt through given tasks such as cataloguing fabrics and trimmings, checking archives and familiarizing yourself with patterns, costings and ranges, and should be regarded as necessarily informative. Flexibility, responsibility and team-member qualities will be looked for before you are offered promotion. You will be required to keep up to date with current trends through analytical shopping, reading magazines and awareness of market influences – much of which will have to be done in your own time. Initial low earnings may necessitate another part-time job.

Daily tasks will include seeing agents and selecting fabrics and trimmings, creating mood boards, working with pattern-cutters and sample machinists on sample ranges, and making design decisions and alterations in fit and finish using elements of flat-pattern, draping and tailored-garment construction. As you move up the ladder you will be expected to supervise design-room staff, co-operate with salesroom staff, troubleshoot details in making and fabric problems, meet important clients and attend trade shows to place orders. You may be given responsibility for a subsection of design or a line, where it will be your responsibility to establish or maintain the silhouette, colours and 'look' of the range and to produce a mix of items that co-ordinate with or complement other lines. Balancing a range to excite the consumer with both classic and new items, fabrics or colours will be your task. You will be expected to be well organized and aware of logistic and production requirements. In large companies there may be a hierarchy of staff with whom you will be expected to interact, and you may have your designs edited or unattributed until you reach the position of head designer. The names of successful middle-market designers are often kept confidential by management in order to minimize headhunting.

Not all fashion companies have staff designers, and there is a growing demand for freelancers. Some freelancers work from home, but many companies expect them to work for short periods with the existing team. Establishing a good reputation takes time, reliable design skills, flexibility and hard work. Freelance designers may work for very short and intense periods with companies. While this can be exciting, it is also stressful and there is a lack of helpful feedback that allows you to gauge the response, uptake or financial success of your designs. Hiring a freelance designer enables a company to try him or her out before taking the risk of offering a permanent job. It is essential to get a written agreement and establish daily rates, based on the industry norms and workload expectations. Negotiating and networking skills are essential. However unpleasant the work, it is always worthwhile being polite and professional. The network is wide and recommendations or cautions are often by word of mouth and can have long-term repercussions. Freelancers should have business cards and stationery printed, both for professional self-promotion and to keep their accounts in order.

Exceptional talent or press coverage may see a designer rise to haute-couture status. Here the demands may be different and pressured by the need to serve individual celebrity clients for very visible public-occasion wear. Discretion, tact and flattery are skills that are needed, together with the ability to balance work with social events. The desire for creative independence leads many designers to establish their own signature label or brand. The womenswear market is saturated and such a decision would need to be well researched and resourced. A number of business and government agencies can help with advice and a financial checklist for starting a viable company. The independent ready-to-wear designer has more freedom to make design decisions, and select cloth and colour without consulting an executive panel. However, this carries a high level of risk and accounts for the demise of many start-up companies where a lack of experience in aspects other than design can lead to failure. If a brand is professionally managed, and there is a market demand, the rewards and satisfaction can be extraordinary.

Menswear

Trends in menswear move more slowly than in womenswear. Designing menswear requires an acute eye for subtle and incremental change because change often occurs in the details rather than the silhouette or colour. Thus, there are proportionately more jobs in management, manufacture and sales than in design.

The business suit and working uniform remain a staple of the clothing industry; menswear is more clearly split between formal or working attire and casualwear than womenswear. Since the skills and approach required are very different, menswear designers are wise to specialize. A large number of tailors and smaller companies died out with the increase in automation and the growth in mass-produced wear, which favoured larger firms. However, after thirty years in free fall the diminishing employment opportunities in the menswear industry have halted and the sector is experiencing a revival, especially in clothing for the fifteen-to-thirty-five age group. Men are now much more interested in their appearance both at work and play, and are spending more on clothing, than in the past. Diversity and choice are important aspects of demand and mid-market, middle-sized companies are gaining in strength. Low-cost stylish suits that can be replaced rather than valeted are now the norm.

Tailored styles are based on a tradition of measurements and practices (see Chapter V) and labour-intensive making-up. The suit and coat market offers work ranging from made-to-measure tailoring skills to mass-produced styles laser-cut using CAD/CAM equipment. Designers in this sector need an understanding of standards and quality, technical methodologies in British and European assembly, and an appreciation of the subtle differences in cut and styling that can distinguish a brand in the classic market and satisfy the confidence of the client.

The burgeoning casualwear and spin-off sports-style market demands a fast-fashion approach similar to that in the womenswear market but with less sharp delineation between seasons and years. Sports and the trend for fitness have an important impact on the market. Because tastes in style and fashion can change quickly, designers need to be aware of current trends, open to new influences, and quick to react. The ability to design logos and T-shirt imagery is an important part of this trade, and skills in information technology and the ability to draw accurate specifications and patterns is increasingly demanded of the graduates. As a response to earlier trading conditions, menswear companies often have fewer personnel than womenswear ones, and problem-solving skills and the ability to work independently and under pressure are important traits. People in this field need self-discipline to start projects on their own, to budget their time and to meet deadlines and production schedules. Casualwear garments are very likely to be made offshore and the need to communicate over long distances at odd hours, and the willingness to travel to meet suppliers and troubleshoot production, is part of the job description today. Good business sense and sales ability are also important, especially for designers who freelance or run their own businesses.

Knitwear

The opportunities for design within knitwear are broader and more diverse than often thought. Knitwear represents a very significant proportion of the fashion market, not only in T-shirts and sweaters but also in stretch-fabric fashions, sportswear, activewear, hosiery and 'intimate' apparel. Knitted garments are popular across womenswear, menswear and childrenswear, and with all demographic groups, because of their inherent qualities such as comfort, fit and softness, and performance factors like warmth and coolness through sweat absorbency, durability and easy laundering. The trend towards casualwear that is suitable for business travel has overtaken the career suit and is increasing the demand for knitwear in all sectors. Knitwear design runs the gamut from inspirational top-level labels such as Missoni and the eveningwear of Julien McDonald, to classic brands like Sonia Rykiel. Many design houses, particularly the better Italian labels, consider their knitwear lines to be the foundation of their collections.

The tasks and career ladder of knitwear designers are similar to those outlined in womenswear. Employment is generally more stable in knitwear than in cut-and-sew womenswear as the lead times for products are longer and require greater continuity of communication. Knitwear design may require the flexibility to create styles for a diverse market rather than a monobrand 'look'. A knitwear designer does not need to know how to hand-knit (although there are times when hand-knit looks are in fashion) as most knitwear is produced by highly complex machinery. Detailing is subtle and requires training in, and knowledge of, the capabilities of industrial machines. It also requires designers to be familiar with the nomenclature of fibres, stitches and techniques and their specifications, and to have the ability to communicate these. An appreciation of texture and trends in colour and style is essential.

There are two approaches to knitwear design and production: the fully automated and the labour intensive. The technology of knitting machinery has evolved to the point where entire garments can be produced without the labour costs of sewing and finishing. This makes knitwear more profitable per garment unit than most other forms of fashion, and manufacturing and retail costs have dropped accordingly. Conversely, hand-operated knitting machines allow for great flexibility of design and their use provides employment opportunities for a large number of people at a very low capital investment. Countries such as China and Bangladesh have made dramatic purchases in this area in recent years. Knitwear designers are likely to design electronically and to modem design specifications and data to distant manufacturers, who send samples for approval by return. A high level of CAD proficiency is therefore desirable; there is a strong demand for knitwear designers at all levels of the market, in design and drafting, and programming computer-aided machines. There are growing opportunities for experts in hosiery and seamless knitted underwear produced on high-tech cylindrical machines.

Manufacturing and production management

Fashion-manufacturing companies (see Chapter II) require fashion-oriented and fashion-trained individuals to steer their production, market their wares and liaise between their customers and the manufacturing process. Fashion designers with technical knowledge of fabric printing, weaving or knitting expertise are well placed to work closely with the manufacturing industry. Fabric companies and fibre and knitwear manufacturers frequently employ fashion designers and stylists to organize and co-ordinate their ranges, and to stage showroom and trade exhibitions to promote their merchandise. Fashion manufacturers who make garments for 'own label' stores and chains also require personable and well-presented sales staff, who can often earn more than buyers or designers. Many designers find their first jobs within manufacturing – as assistant pattern-cutters, production assistants or sample machinists. These positions are reasonably well-paid, highly instructive and satisfying ways of entering the industry.

Buying and retail

The fashion buyer may be the owner or employee of a single boutique or a member of a very large store team. Stores and chains subdivide their merchandise categories, so buyers specialize in a single field or market sector of product, such as ladies' knitwear or eveningwear. There are two main ways of operating: centralized and departmental buying.

Centralized buying allows chains to move stock from shop to shop; large quantities can also mean negotiable price reductions. Departmental buying is more local. Buyers are usually accountable to a fashion director, who will indicate the overall buying policy but usually allow the buyer to make decisions as to the content of an order. To join a professional store buying team as an assistant buyer you will need to have included marketing skills in your fashion training. Considerable shop-floor experience will be essential before you reach the glamorous and well-paid pinnacle of departmental retail as the job requires you to perform a skilful balancing act between a creative instinct for customers' desires and good commercial practice.

A buyer needs to keep abreast of what is actually selling and what is appearing in magazines, and must be able to predict customer demand six months to a year ahead. Many designers actively court the attentions of buyers by inviting them to parties and giving them preferential seating at shows. The buyer is in a position to give tactful feedback to the designer about how to improve a range as well as how to promote his or her work. A buyer is expected to make between two and eighteen marketing trips a year, and much of his or her time will also be spent viewing collections in showrooms or having meetings with salespeople. A buyer needs to convey a sense of maturity and must look professional and businesslike; creative vision, a head for figures and diplomacy in handling juniors and managerial staff and designers are all desirable attributes.

Merchandising

This vague term is sometimes applied to the buying and mixing of stock. More correctly, however, it denotes the job of financial arrangement that lies behind the buyer's tasks. A merchandiser will authorize mark-downs and discounts for multiple purchases or move them to another branch. Merchandisers are experts at shop layout and the distribution of goods, and work in close collaboration with buyers. Because the title is also used rather loosely for a sales assistant with responsibility for the arrangement of stock on the shop floor or windows, when applying for a position in merchandising it is important to ask for a clear job description. Good organizational abilities, a talent for numbers and skill with spreadsheets are needed for this post.

Fashion public relations

Fashion companies are often too busy to promote their designs themselves so they use the services of a public relations (PR) company to publicize them. The PR company's job is to generate buzz about a collection, and it is responsible for making connections with magazines, TV, newspapers and radio stations. Getting the right mix of people to attend the shows – fashion editors, buyers and stars – can make the difference between a newsworthy event and a fashion flop.

To work in PR you need literacy and journalistic skills; you must be articulate and able to provide the press with off-the-cuff sound bites or advise designers as to how to handle publicity should something untoward or dramatic occur. Personality is

Below Many colleges and courses create catalogues or yearbooks which are useful for attracting contacts.

Bottom Press and celebrities mix with the help of the fashion PR. Here, Plum Sykes of UK *Vogue* poses with actress Minnie Driver.

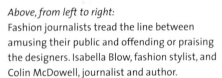

Above, from left to right:
Fashion journalists tread the line between amusing their public and offending or praising the designers. Isabella Blow, fashion stylist, and Colin McDowell, journalist and author.

The fashion stylist works closely with the model, make-up artist and photographer in developing or directing the mood and the look of the shoot through posture, accessories and arrangement of the clothing.

Fashion photography is a competitive and time-pressured job.

important. PRs are 'people persons' – at ease in social situations and good at smoothing the friction between diverse individuals. Understanding the hierarchies of seating arrangements at shows, schmoozing and partying, being chatty and upfront are key skills in this job. Being well connected and well dressed can help, too. A significant proportion of the work takes place at evening events, and a considerable amount of travelling is often required. Fluency in more than one language is an asset.

Fashion journalism

A mention – or mentions – in the media is a most effective way for a designer to become known, and fashion journalists can consequently wield a great deal of power. Writers such as Colin McDowell for the British *Sunday Times*, Suzy Menkes for the *International Herald Tribune* and American *Vogue* editor Anna Wintour hold some of the most respected positions in the fashion industry. It is the job of the fashion journalist to attend the shows and exhibitions, and to analyse and comment on the trends and news for public consumption. Journalists are much courted by the fashion companies, who shower them with goods and give them front-row seats in the hope that reviews will be favourable.

Their duty is to interpret designs and the broad changes in fashion, not only as they seem to their own well-practised eyes but with a view to the readers and advertisers who support their newspaper or magazine. They are under pressure from deadlines, and must come up with hot stories and angles on shows that hundreds of other fashion journalists have seen. Between the fashion-show seasons they may be expected to contribute to weekly planning meetings, and come up with stories and ideas to keep the public's interest.

Fashion journalism has expanded in recent years to include scriptwriting and presentation on websites and television programmes with magazine formats and style content. Today, desktop-publishing (DTP) and word-processing skills are essential and journalists are expected to file copy electronically.

Fashion stylist

A fashion stylist works closely with fashion magazines and photographers. A stylist is not a designer but an interpreter of fashion who puts together the looks for a photographic shoot – either interpreting what the editor has ordered or off his or her own bat. Sometimes people are surprised that the best stylists are not among the youngest operators. Taste and style are timeless languages and, like costume designers, stylists call on a vast, absorbed knowledge of clothing ideas that 'work'. Moreover, in a time-pressured industry, efficiency and experience are worthwhile attributes that grow with you.

Stylists often have a creative relationship with a particular editor or photographer that establishes a personal rapport. Others work with designers to help them crystallize the look for their fashion shows. For many years, Amanda Grieve was the stylist for John Galliano, and Katy England styles for Alexander McQueen. Magazines often use in-house stylists to give a continuity of approach to their regular pages. The stylist can have great impact on the way we dress and our bearing, but the job is one of the least visible or acknowledged in the fashion media. Stylists are not usually college-trained; they learn through a long and poorly paid apprenticeship, working with magazines and catalogues or assisting photographers.

Fashion photography

Fashion photography is a specialized branch of the magazine and graphics industry. For those with exceptional talent, it can be a lucrative and glamorous life. It is a very fast-paced and pressured job, and work must be turned out to publishing requirements and deadlines. Most photographers are freelance and self-employed. They often have agents who take enquiries and show their work to potential clients. There is considerable initial outlay on equipment, studio and travel, which may not be recouped until a much later date. Photographers are generally commissioned and will discuss with the fashion editor what is required of them. Only when they have become significantly well known can they produce and market editorial shots that they have initiated.

Being a fashion photographer is an arduous and sometimes quite lonely occupation. There is more time spent in the darkroom developing and printing than is popularly imagined, but there are also opportunities for travel to exotic locations in the company of beautiful people, all expenses paid. Photographers often work with a small team of assistants, stylists and make-up artists who work together to realize a fashion look. Catwalk photographers specialize in covering the shows and have to be ruthless about maintaining their rank in the hierarchy and getting the right shots back to base. Catalogue and newspaper photographers work on assignments. To become a fashion photographer you need technical camera skills; but more important is a creative eye, an understanding of lighting and fashion, and the ability to live with a near-constant adrenalin rush.

Prediction and forecasting

Prediction companies, or bureaus, offer a forecasting and reporting service to the fashion industry. They research the trends that might feed into it and put together bias-free information reports that they sell to the larger companies. They work approximately eighteen months to two years ahead. The larger consultancies employ a team of in-house designers to illustrate current fashions, analyse details and draw up variations on a theme. The standards of work and quality of information is high and

Additional Jobs in Fashion and Textiles

Academic research
Administrative support
Agent
Archivist
Bookkeeping, accounting and stockkeeping
Business management
CAD/CAM technician
Clothing technologist
Colourist
Costume designer
Dressmaker
Digital prototyper
Distribution manager
Dressmaker
Editor
Editorial assistant
Fabric buyer
Financial and clerical office support
Fit model
Forecaster

Graphic designer for clothing and branding
Higher education – teaching
House model
Industrial machinery maintenance
Industrial machinery operators
Internet designer for clothing and websites
Internet site maintenance
Journalist
Knitwear designer
Knitwear programmer
Logistics manager
Media editor
Museum conservator or curator
Negotiator
Pattern-cutter
Pattern-maker / marker-maker
Personal stylist
Personnel and human resources
Photography
Presser
Production assistant

Production manager
Public relations
Quality controller
Retail assistant
Retail buyer
Retail manager
Sales and related clerical positions
Sales representative
Sample machinist
Sewing machinist
Show and exhibition organizer
Specification illustrator
Supervisor
Tailor
Textile designer
  (woven, printed and knitted fabrics)
Textile technologist
Transportation
Visual merchandiser
Warehousing and order fulfilment

putting together the reports is expensive. Clients expect a lot of versatility and up-to-date information.

Account executives in prediction companies work closely with clients and travel to the trade fairs and fashion centres that are of interest to them. They are involved with commissioning artwork and photography from creatives, and write reports and statistical analyses. If you enjoy travel and the social scene, you might start on this career ladder by offering your services as a trendspotter.

Fashion illustration

Good commercial illustrators need to have a clear understanding of how clothing and the body work intimately together, but they may not necessarily be the most effective designers of fashion. Fashion illustrators frequently come from other design disciplines and are more interested in composition, artistic expression and capturing mood than in hands-on design. Like graphic designers and book illustrators, they tend to be freelancers – some have agents to promote them, find commissions, negotiate fees and co-ordinate jobs. In the industry some companies use illustrators to visualize the sort of silhouette and product they would like their suppliers to produce for their merchandise selectors. Trend and prediction companies use illustrators to present the themes and details of a forthcoming season. There is a small amount of magazine editorial work, but the media's preference is for photography. However, the tradition of runway show sketching is still maintained by some newspapers. Fashions in illustration come and go, often influenced by prevailing trends in graphic design. It is necessary to be aware of which styles or media are appropriate to a particular type of clothing and the market, and to be versatile. If you have a style that is original, edgy and eye-catching you could develop it into an art and a career. It helps to have a good grasp of technical graphic-reproduction processes: printing, brochure layouts, fonts and how to lay out text, etc. Adobe Photoshop and Illustrator skills are also an advantage. There is a strong demand for CAD skills in technical spec illustration and a growing demand for three-dimensional visualizing work. Being an artist or illustrator is more solitary than being a designer, which is about teamwork. You have to be self-disciplined, dedicated and practise every day. The more you draw the better and faster you will be, but it becomes harder to maintain a certain level of quality, and to avoid being slick or lazy. You must maintain a portfolio of fresh work, and perhaps even have a website to display successful commissions and give contact details.

Writing a CV or résumé

Whatever your chosen career path, getting your CV (curriculum vitae) and portfolio right from the start will give you a strong advantage. Because of the nature of the academic year, thousands of new graduates arrive on the job market at the same time, so you need to have an edge. A CV is a summary of your skills, accomplishments and education, designed to capture a potential employer's interest and secure an interview. It should be no more than two pages long. A short covering letter explaining why you are applying should also be included. Below are a few guidelines to bear in mind while compiling your CV.

Write your CV on a computer. It can be easily edited or updated, and looks smart.

Don't be tempted to use fancy typefaces. Keep it clear, concise and legible.

Use only the name that you are actually known by on your CV.

Present educational and employment information in reverse chronological order.

Don't list all your academic qualifications and grades, only the relevant ones.

List any honours, awards and exhibitions. Never lie about qualifications or experience; you will be found out.

List skills such as languages and computer training, and whether or not you hold a driving licence.

Don't give names and telephone numbers of references. You can put 'references available on request' at the bottom of the page.

Leave out photos and personal data such as marital status, health, religion, ethnicity and commonplace recreational activities.

List any positions of responsibility. Don't state how much you have earned on previous jobs or your salary requirements.

Have someone proofread your CV for typos and other errors.

Always make sure that you approach the right person in a company.

Always tailor your CV and portfolio to the job for which you are applying.

If you can, include a letter of recommendation or reference from a tutor or previous employer.

A single page of illustration or a postcard-style business card can be eye-catching if it is relevant to the position.

Follow up your CV with a telephone call about two weeks later, to see whether it is under consideration and if you can make an appointment for an interview.

Only a talented and dedicated few will make it to the ranks of designers with their own labels. Matthew Williamson takes a bow with Helena Christensen.

The interview – some dos and don'ts

Do some homework on the company so that you have a reasonable idea of its history, product line and market.

Make sure you know exactly where to go, and arrive in plenty of time so that you are not hot and flustered. You are likely to be nervous, so collect your thoughts quietly and run over the key things you would like to say or ask your interviewer about the company or job.

How you dress will make an impression, but don't overdo it. Wearing one of your own creations is appropriate, providing it is not out of place. Do not smoke or chew gum or make jokes. Try not to fiddle with your hair or fidget. Good posture and good body language will demonstrate confidence.

Be honest about your skills and back up your strengths with examples from your portfolio. Some companies will be prepared to give you training in specialist areas, so do not pretend you can do things you cannot.

A friendly, flexible and persevering demeanour can work wonders. There is a fine line between confidence and arrogance. Look on any job as an opportunity to learn and develop new skills and talents. Smile and make eye contact.

Ask about aspects of the job that you do not understand or which have not been mentioned, such as working hours and the number of people to whom you would report. Ask how the job could develop in the future. It is not wise to appear too eager to discuss wages; pick your moment. Don't, however, accept the job without knowing the financial package.

Don't appear either too cool or too desperate. Even if you have other job offers, do not talk about these at length. The company will want to hear that you are primarily interested in it.

Do not leave your portfolio behind to be looked at later by someone who is absent. Always make another appointment. Not all companies are honest.

If you are not successful on this occasion, don't be disheartened. An ability to bounce back and believe in yourself and the skills you have worked hard to achieve will be recognized sooner or later.

Whether graduating from your fashion course is marked by a fanfare of shows, exhibitions and ceremonies or the arrival of your certificate by post, it will be a moment of great personal pride. The acknowledgement of a rite of passage that has taken years of hard work, but has also brought you valuable creative and practical skills, friendships and fun indicates that you are ready to embark upon the first steps of a career that will be engrossing, rewarding and ever changing. Good luck!

Further reading and additional resources

The Hobsons Directory, Hobson's Publishing, 2004
    – an annual guide to UK graduate career opportunities
Dick Bolles. *What Color is Your Parachute?*, Berkeley: Ten Speed Press, 2004
Richard M Jones. *The Apparel Industry*, Oxford: Blackwell Science, 2003
Ulla Vad Lane-Rowley. *Using Design Protection in the Fashion and Textile Industry*,
    London and Chichester: Wiley, 1997
Astrid Katcharyan. *Getting Jobs in Fashion Design*, London: Cassell, 1988
Anne Matthews. *Vogue Guide to a Career in Fashion*, London: Chatto & Windus, 1989
M Sones. *Getting into Fashion: A Career Guide*, New York: Ballatine, 1984
Noel Chapman and Carole Chester. *Careers in Fashion*, London: Kogan Page, 1999

Graduate Fashion Week www.gfw.org.uk
New Designers Graduate Show www.newdesigners.com
The largest graduate design event in the UK presents emerging design talent
    from 4,000 design graduates from over 180 colleges
New Designers www.newdesigners.com
A showcase for exciting new work from across all the major design disciplines
Fashion Forum www.fashionforum.co.uk/flash/aboutus.htm
A directory and magazine for the apparel and textile industry,
    including company profiles and recruitment listings
The Portobello Business Center www.pbc.co.uk
Specialists in fashion start-ups
Skillfast www.skillfast-uk.org
UK nationwide organization for training in fashion skills
Fashion Capital www.fashioncapital.co.uk
London-Development-Agency – supported fashion initiatives for young designers

Organizations
The Association of Graduate Careers Advisory Service (AGCAS) publishes biyearly reports and
information booklets geared for graduates. They are available from:
AGCAS Administration Office
Millennium House
30 Junction Road
Sheffield S11 8XB
Tel 0114 251 5750
Fax 0114 251 5751
or through their website: www.agcas.org.uk

Advice for recent graduates
www.prospects.ac.uk
www.lffonline.com
www.wgsn-edu.com

Employment agencies
www.denza.co.uk
www.jobsinfashion.com
www.fashion-jobs.com
www.fashion.net
www.journalism.co.uk
www.cheeringup.com
www.project-solvers.com

Glossary

Apparel Clothing, this term is more commonly used in the US.

Assessment The formal evaluation and giving of marks for your design work.

Atelier French word for the designer's studio. Parisian Ateliers are designated flou (for dressmaking) or tailleur (for tailoring suits and coats).

Avant-garde A fashion or concept that is ahead of its time.

Baseline The lowest price or cost at which a manufacturer is prepared to provide goods.

Bespoke Individual made-to-measure tailoring for men's suits.

Blocks A set of basic individual or standard-sized pattern templates from which designs can be developed. Blocks are known as slopers in the US.

Bottom weights The heavier weight fabrics used for skirts and trousers.

Boutique French word for an independent, usually small shop with unique stock and atmosphere.

Brainstorming Open discussion amongst colleagues to bring up new ideas and concepts.

Brand A name or trademark used to identify a product and denote quality, value or a particular ethos.

Bridge fashion An American term for clothing placed between designer fashion and high street style.

Buyer The person responsible for planning, buying and selling merchandise.

Buying office The department responsible for buying within a store or an independent body who arrange to buy for chains and boutiques especially from overseas suppliers.

Cabbage The term given to unused fabric or garments made from over supply of fabric for manufacturing.

CAD/CAM Computer-aided design and computer-aided manufacturing.

Capsule collection A small range of related styles with a special purpose or impact.

Ceiling The highest price that a garment or product can be priced at.

Chain stores A group of stores, usually high street locations, which are centrally owned, operated and merchandised to sell under the same logo with a distinctive and recognizable product.

Classic A term for a style that remains constantly popular and changes very little in detail, e.g. men's shirts, the cardigan, jeans.

Cognoscenti Italian word for 'those in the know' ie. fashion aware.

Collection The term used for a group of better quality fashion clothes with related features or for a specific season. 'The Collections' is a colloquial way of indicating the Paris fashion shows.

Colour palette/gamme A limited selection of seasonal colours offered in a fashion or fabric range.

Colourway The name for the limited range of colours that may be offered in a style or collection and also for the choice of colours available in a printed textile.

Concession A leased use of department store space to sell another company's goods.

Conglomerate A financial parent organization that owns a number of companies which may not be related in terms of product or target market.

Consumer The end user or buyer of the product.

Conversationals Printed fabrics with unusual illustrated themes, such as Hawaiian shirts, animals, etc.

Converter A manufacturer who makes raw fibre into fabric or converts greige goods into printed fabric.

Coordinates Fabrics or items of clothing that relate in colouring or style and which can be worn together.

Costing The base price of the garment, determined by the materials, trimmings, labour and transportation.

Costing sheets A list detailing the time and cost of materials and processes used in making a garment.

Cost-plus pricing A method of pricing based on the cost of a item with the addition of a predetermined percentage mark-up.

Couturier French word for fashion designer.

Critique/Crit Discussion and evaluation of work, often held as a group session at the end of a project or assignment.

Croquis A line drawing made by the designer to illustrate a garment or a painted out design for a printed fabric.

Cruise A period immediately after the winter holidays when 'cruise' or resort wear is sold in the US.

CV (Curriculum Vitae) A chronological personal summary detailing educational and employment achievements and attributes. (Also known as a résumé).

Deconstruction A style of designing which originated with Belgian designers whereby garments were left rough and unfinished or revealing construction details.

Degree show The exhibition of work which is displayed and assessed to ascertain a student's degree classification.

Demi-couture High-end fashion, often the diffusion range of a couturier.

Demi-measure Similar to made-to-measure, but fewer adjustments are made to a standard pattern; waistbands, cuffs and pants may be shortened by an in-store machinist.

Demographics A marketing term for determining the distribution of statistics relating to a market segment, e.g. age, gender, income level, lifestyle and housing.

Design developments Drawings that progress through desirable or successful elements within a design theme.

Diffusion line A secondary, usually lower-priced garment line that allows consumers on a budget to buy into the designer look.

Discounting Marking-down or offering a percentage discount on the price of an item, line or brand as a sales strategy.

Dissertation A piece of academic writing, usually between 3000 and 7000 words, on a subject supporting your chosen fashion study. (Also known as a thesis.)

Distance learning Assignments and practical work done off campus, usually via the Internet.

Docket The paperwork for the manufacturers order for clothing.

E-commerce Trading via the Internet, usually with a website order page.

Elective A choice of study subject programme.

EPOS Electronic point-of-sale is the term used when the till is linked to a computer network, often with barcode scanners.

E-tailoring Sending measurements via the Internet to a tailor for made-to-measure garments.

Exclusivity An arrangement made between the retailer and wholesaler granting the exclusive right to sell a line in a neighbourhood.

External examiner An expert invited by the degree examination board to verify the marking procedure.

E-zines Internet magazine formats and news exchanges.

Fabrication The manufacturing detail and content of a material used for fashion.

Fad A very short-lived fashion.

Fascia The company logo, as shown on a shop front or display material.

Fashion cycle The calendar by which a company will plan, design, make and market its ranges.

Final collection The last college collection before graduation.

Findings A term for the trimmings or notions that are included on a style, e.g. buttons and lace.

Fit model A mannequin or live model that is the company standard for sizing samples.

Flats Diagrammatic drawings.

Focus group A marketing group who are asked their opinions in order to fine tune or get feedback on a product or market sector.

Franchise A type of business ownership: a manufacturer, wholesaler or service company sells a smaller firm or individual the right to conduct business under their brand for a start-up fee and a return of a proportion of the profits.

Fusible fabrics Heat sensitive fabrics which bond with other materials to strengthen them.

Geometrics Printed fabrics with lines, spots, squares and similar non-organic designs.

Glossies The high quality magazines.

Greige goods (pronounced grey) Fabric in its basic unfinished state, e.g. unbleached calico

Hand/handle The feel of a fabric.

Handwriting, signature Your personal designing style, design features or way of drawing.

Haute couture French term for the highest quality of dressmaking. A designer or company cannot call themselves 'haute couture' unless they have passed the stringent criteria of the Chambre Syndical of the Fédération Française de la Couture.

Interlining A fabric which is placed between the garment fabric and lining as a strengthening or padding material.

Internship, placement A period of study, usually between three weeks and nine months, spent within a business.

JIT Just in time, a way of manufacturing quickly in response to consumer demand.

Kimball A system for tagging clothing with tickets.

Knock-off A copy of a high price or desirable garment made with inferior fabric and trimmings and sold at a lower price.

Lab-dips Colour tests on swatches of fabric or yarn.

Label The tag which identifies the designer or manufacturer and the origin, fibre contents and wash care of the product. Sometimes used synonymously with logo.

Landmark Used in the sense of a point on the body, usually associated with a joint or prominent bone, from which measurements are taken.

Lay plan Also known as a marker, this is the template for cutting the pattern from the fabric to ensure as little waste as possible.

Layout pad A sketchbook with thin sheets of paper which can be traced through.

Lead time The length of time it takes from submitting a garment order to the manufacturer before it can be delivered to the store.

Licensing The authorization by contract for the use of a name, logo or product type to be used by another manufacturing company in exchange for royalty payments.

Light fast/colour fast The degree of permanence of a dye colour to light or washing.

Line A term used to denote styles related in theme and detail. In the USA it is synonymous with the European use of the word 'collection'.

Line-for-line copy An exact copy of a style, sometimes licensed but more often illegal.

Line-up A preview of toiles or finished garments on models to determine the balance and range and order in a collection.

Logo A brand name or symbol used to identify a product or designer.

Loss-leader A style sold at less than the usual mark-up in order to attract buyers to other designs.

Made-to-measure Clothing made to fit the individual customer by taking a series of personal (bespoke) measurements and cutting the suit or outfit accordingly.

Mark-up The difference between the cost price and the selling price including taxes.

Mass-customization The custom production of basic shoes or garments for individual customers, given a choice of parameters, such as fabric, colour, trim, logo.

Module A unit of teaching that can vary in length but has a specific learning outcome.

Mood board A presentation board which gives the overall concept and direction of a design collection.

Multifibre Arrangement (MFA) An international agreement among importing and exporting nations to prevent import surges and regulate trade.

Off-price Bargain goods sold at lower than the original wholesale price.

Off-schedule A fashion show that is not on the official show organizer's list.

Off-shore production Manufacturing abroad.

Off-the-peg Standard sized, store bought, ready-to-wear menswear.

Outworker An individual who makes up garments for a factory or designer from their home.

Over-dyeing, cross-dyeing Fabrics may require more than one application of dye to colour different fibre types and give depth to a material.

Palette A range or gamut of colours used in a collection.

Pattern-drafting, pattern-cutting, pattern-making The drawing out of a flat pattern from measurements or through the use of block templates.

Piecework The method of making a garment by handing it down a line of machinists who each carry out a different function.

Portfolio A large portable container for flat artwork and press cuttings that should give a potential client a comprehensive view of the designer's capabilities.

Première Vision Also known as PV. French for 'first look' and the name of the major fabric trade fair held twice a year in Paris.

Prêt-à-porter French for ready-to-wear, a term used for better quality and designer separates, also the name of a major fashion exhibition.

Price point Different ranges of price indicate quality and market level, e.g. budget, designer, luxury.

Private label Companies often use their spare manufacturing capacity to make garments for stores and other companies who will put their own label in the garments.

Proportion The relationship and balance of one aspect of a design with another, a principle of fashion design.

Psychological pricing A pricing strategy related to the consumer's sense of budget that uses cut-off points usually related to banknote denominations to encourage the appearance of a bargain, e.g. £19.95 or $49.99.

QR (Quick response) Very fast manufacturing in reaction to market demand.

Quotas The international trade in fabrics is limited by governments with a quota system to prevent their markets being flooded with cheap goods.

Rag-trade A slang term for the fashion industry, usually implying the lower end of the market.

Ready-to-wear Also known as off-the peg, prêt-à-porter, clothing separates.

Résumé A chronological personal summary detailing educational and employment achievements and attributes. (Also known as a CV – Curriculum Vitae).

Retail The selling of goods from a business to an individual consumer.

Roughs First stage drawings for designs, usually quickly made in pencil and without extraneous detail.

Sales channel profit Different approaches to selling the same goods will have differential costs and profits.

Salon/showroom A place or office where salespersons show a collection or merchandise to potential buyers.

Sample A first or test garment (also known as a toile) made from calico or inferior fabric.

Sample cut A short length of fabric used to make up a sample garment.

Sealing sample The garment that serves as the approved standard to which others must be made.

Seminar A lecture with a discussion component.

Separates Individual items of clothing.

Short run A small manufacturing order for clothes.

Silhouette The overall shape of a garment or of a collection reduced to a basic geometric or alphanumeric description, e.g. boxy, A-line, figure-8.

Somatype The classification system for the different types of body form and musculature.

Source book, look book Forecast reports available within the industry.

Sourcing The search for materials, trimmings and manufacturing at the best prices and delivery.

Specification sheet (also known as specs) A design drawing with measurements and manufacturing details such as stitching and trimmings used in manufacturing.

Staple The length of a basic fibre such as wool or cashmere, these are spun together to make a continuous thread.

Stories Design themes comprising fabric, colour or style associations used within a collection.

Storyboard Also known as a theme board, a presentation of the concept for a collection with the breakdown of styles and co-ordinates detailed.

Stylist A fashion expert who prepares fashion items for photographs or presentations.

Supply chain The sequence of manufacturers and processors that a garment will travel through from raw material to store.

Syllabus The detailed learning objectives of the teaching plan.

Tear sheets Also known as swipes, these are pictures lifted from magazines, etc. which are used as initial inspiration or corroboration for a concept, not to copy.

Thesis A piece of academic writing, usually between 3000 and 7000 words, on a subject supporting your chosen fashion study. (Also known as a dissertation.)

Trademark A logo or brand that has been protected or copyrighted by registration.

Transitional The period in between seasons when the weather is uncertain and styles overlap due to the demands of the public and the need for fresh merchandise.

Trimming A term used both for the decorative detail on a garment and for the process of finishing and cutting (cleaning) loose threads.

Trunk show Salesmen take garment samples on a tour of cities and arrange store viewings.

Tutorial A discussion with teaching staff to discuss progress.

2 for 1 Two items for the price of one.

UPC Universal product codes, standard codes on price tags which allow data to be read electronically at stocktaking or point of sale.

USP Unique selling point. That which differentiates a designer or company style.

Vendor Supplier or person who sells goods.

Vertical company A company that makes its products from the raw material to the finished item under single ownership.

Virtual catwalk Computer-aided visualization of a fashion show using digitally generated figures and clothing.

Visual diary A sketchbook worked over the period of a project to indicate developing ideas.

Warp/weft The warp threads of a woven fabric are those that comprise the lengthwise grain. The weft threads are placed in by shuttle at 90 degrees to the warp and run from selvedge to selvedge giving the fabric its width.

Wholesale The selling of goods from business to business, usually in bulk quantity and with terms and conditions which may include discounts and credit.

Yoke A piece of fabric used to support a fuller or gathered length, e.g. across the shoulders of a shirt or from the hipline of a skirt.

Zeitgeist A German word for 'spirit of the times' often used in conjunction with fashion as clothing reflects the era of its creation.

Useful addresses

UK

The British Fashion Council (BFC)
5 Portland Place
London W1N 3AA
Tel 020 7636 7788
Fax 020 7636 7515
The BFC supports British fashion designers and manufacturers, especially with export enterprises. It encourages new talent through annual awards to students, for example the 'Innovative Pattern Cutting Award' and for Graduate Fashion Week presentations.

CAPITB Trust
5 Portland Place
London W1N 3AA
Tel 020 7636 3173
Fax 020 7636 3174
Email capitbtrust@capitbtrust.org.uk
The National Training Organisation for the British Apparel and Leather Goods Manufacturing Industry which publishes a directory: The Graduate Post to help manufacturers to find student graduates.

The Register of Apparel and Textile Designers
5 Portland Place
London W1N 3AA
Tel 020 7637 5577

The British Knitting and Clothing Export Council (BKCEC)
5 Portland Place
London W1N 3AA
Tel 020 7637 5577

Fashion Awareness Direct (FAD)
10a Wellesley Terrace
London N1 7NA
Tel/Fax 0870 751 4449
Email info@fad.org.uk
An organization committed to helping young designers succeed in their careers by bringing students and professionals together at introductory events.

The Prince's Youth Business Trust (PYBT)
18 Park Square East
London NW1 4LH
Tel 020 7543 1234
Fax 020 7543 1200
www.princes-trust.org.uk

The Prince's Trust gives business advice and professional support and awards funding for young and unemployed people planning to set up a potentially successful new idea in business.

Shell LiveWire
Hawthorn House
Forth Banks
Newcastle upon Tyne NE1 3SG
Tel 0191 261 5584
Fax 0191 261 1910
www.shell-livewire.org
Competitive awards scheme, advice and training on business start-ups for young people.

Portobello Business Centre
2 Acklam Road
London W10 5QZ
Tel 020 7460 5050
www.pbc.co.uk
The Portobello Business Centre offers an advisory service and DTI training classes in fashion management to those wishing to set up a fashion business in West London.

The Crafts Council
44a Pentonville Road
London N1 9BY
Tel 020 7278 7700
Fax 020 7837 6891
craftscouncil.org.uk
Besides having an excellent contemporary gallery and crafts bookshop at this address the Crafts Council offers many services, such as a reference library, advice and development grants and publishes a magazine to promote crafts.

The Department of Trade and Industry (DTI) (Clothing, Textiles and Footwear Unit)
1 Victoria Street
London SW1H 0ET
Tel 020 7215 5000
www.dti.gov.uk
A Government Department that advises UK businesses on legal issues; also a fount of information concerning export regulations.

OneLondon (formerly London Enterprise Agency)
28 Park Street
London SE1 9EQ
Tel 020 7403 0300
Fax 020 7248 8877
www.gle.co.uk/onelondon
A consortium of companies and the Corporation of London dedicated to developing small businesses, education projects and giving financial advice.

The Business Technology Support Centre
London College of Fashion
100 Curtain Road
London EC2A 3AE
Tel 020 7514 7526

The Nottinghamshire and Derbyshire Clothing and Textile Association Ltd (A Division of East Midlands Textiles Association – EMTEX)
Ashfield Business Centre
The Idlewells
Sutton in Ashfield
Nottinghamshire NG17 1BP
Tel 01623 440612
Fax 01623 442102
enquiries@emtex.org.uk
A support centre for Midlands business and start-up help.

Cotton Council International
Empire House, 5th Floor
175 Piccadilly
London W1J 9EN
Tel 020 7355 1313
Fax 020 7355 1919
Email cci-london@cotton.org

USA

Fashion Information
The Fashion Center Kiosk
39th and 7th Avenue
New York
Tel 212 398 7943
Fax 212 398 7945
Email info@fashioncenter.com

Council for American Fashion
1710 Broadway, 5th Floor
New York, NY 10019

New York Fashion Council
153 East 87th Street
New York, NY 10128

United States Small Business Administration
26 Federal Plaza, Suite 3100
New York, NY 10278
Tel 212 264 4354
Fax 212 264 4963

National Art Education Association
1916 Association Drive
Reston
VA 20191-1590
Tel 703 860 8000
Fax 703 860 2960

Fabric and resources

Two major directories are used to resource fabrics, trimmings and supplies:
Fashiondex
The TIP Resource Guide

Fashion trade publications

Womens Wear Daily (WWD)
W
Tobe Report
Fashion Reporter
California Apparel News
Daily News Record (DNR)

See also shops and suppliers

Fabric libraries, information and colour services

American Wool Council
50 Rockefeller Plaza
New York, NY 10020
Tel 212 245 6710

The Wool Bureau (Woolmark)
330 Madison Avenue
New York, NY 10017
Tel 212 986 6222

The Cottonworks (fabric library)
Cotton Inc.
488 Madison Avenue
New York, NY 10022-5702
Tel 212 413 8300
Fax 212 413 8377

DuPont Global Headquarters
DuPont Building
1007 Market Street
Wilmington DE 19898
Email info@dupont.com
www.dupont.com

Mademoiselle (fabric library)
350 Madison Avenue
New York, NY 10017

Vogue (fabric library)
350 Madison Avenue
New York, NY 10017

Knitted Textile Association
386 Park Ave. South, Suite 901
New York, NY 10016
Tel 212 689 3807
Fax 212 889 6160
Email info@kta-usa.org

Fashion Services of America
411 East 50th Street
New York, NY 10022-8001
Tel 212 755 4433

The Color Association of the US (CAUS)
315 West 39th Street, Studio 507
New York, NY 10018
Tel 212 947 7774
Fax 212 594 6987
Email caus@colorassociation.com
www.colorassociation.com

Pantone Color Institute
590 Commerce Boulevard
Carlstadt, NJ 07072-3098
Tel 201 935 5500
Fax 201 935 3338
www.pantone.com

Money in the Bank (forecasting)
121 Madison Avenue
New York, NY 10016
Tel 212 683 7418

Popular fabric types

Acetate Lustrous synthetic fibre that is usually woven in fine and compact fabrics to simulate silk and linings.

Bird's Eye A fabric woven with a pattern of small diamonds.

Brocade A luxury Jacquard patterned woven fabric used for evening wear.

Calico Medium weight natural undyed cotton used for prototyping garments. It is also offered as the substrate for traditional Indian and American prints.

Cambric Better quality light to medium weight cotton fabric used for shirts and blouses.

Cashmere The combings of the undercoat hair of mountain goats, which creates a very fine, warm, and luxurious fabric for coatings and knitwear.

Chambray A class of yarn-dyed, plain-weave fabrics with a coloured warp and white filling giving a denim-like 'shot' effect.

Chenille Soft, fuzzy yarns stand out around a velvety cord on this fabric, whose name comes from the French word for 'caterpillar.'

Chiffon A very light, fine woven fabric used for scarves and evening dresses.

Chintz A plain or floral printed and glazed cotton furnishing fabric, sometimes fashionable for skirts and summer dresses.

Corduroy A ribbed or 'waled' woven fabric. Supple, comfortable and durable, used for trousers and jackets.

Crêpe Used to describe all kinds of fabrics – wool, cotton, silk, rayon, synthetics and blends – that have a crinkly, crimped or grained surface. From the French word crêper, which means 'to crimp' or 'to frizz'.

Crêpe de chine A fine, lightweight silk or polyester crêpe.

Crochet Loose, open knit made by looping thread with a hooked needle. Used for light, summer sweaters. Crochet effects can now be made by machines.

Denim A white warp and indigo blue weft and twill weave is the characteristic of this hardwearing cotton fabric, originally from Nîmes in France.

Devoré This is the French word for 'eaten' and describes luxury fabrics where some of the surface has been either acid etched or burnt away decoratively.

Embroidery Fancy needlework or trimming consisting of coloured yarn, embroidery floss, soft cotton, silk or metallic thread. Although hand embroidery is still a widely practised craft, most commercially produced embroidered clothes are made by machine.

Engineered print Also called a placed print because it is integrated into a specific area of the design. Border prints are often engineered into place.

Faille A dressy, flat-ribbed fabric with a light lustre that drapes and tailors well. The ribs are flatter and less pronounced than in grosgrain. Traditionally used for women's dresses, suits and coats.

Flannel A durable woollen woven fabric, usually in grey, suitable for trouser suits and the under-collars of coats

French terry A circular knit fabric with a looped pile back and smooth face.

Gabardine Durable, tightly woven fabric made in a twill weave with distinct diagonal ribs and given a clean finish. Made of cotton, wool or rayon, gabardine wears extremely well. Commonly used for sportswear, suits, uniforms and raincoats.

Georgette A sheer, lightweight plain-weave fabric with a fine crêpe surface. Sometimes silk, sometimes synthetic. Also called crêpe georgette or georgette crêpe.

Hopsack A loosely woven coarse fabric of cotton or wool used in clothing. Hop growers originally used the fabric for bags.

Interlock A type of cut and sew knit fabric that is characterized by the interconnecting of the knit stitches.

Jersey A generic term for a plain knit fabric without a distinct rib. Originally made of wool, jersey fabric was first manufactured on the island of Jersey.

Lawn Very fine weight cotton, usually printed with delicate florals.

Lycra® DuPont's registered trademark for its brand of elastomer.

Marl or Mouliné Two single yarns of different colours twisted together. You see this mottled effect most often in sweaters.

Matte jersey A dull, flat knit fabric made of fine crêpe yarns used for slinky evening wear.

Microfibre Generic term for any synthetic fibre finer than silk. Fabrics made with microfibres are soft, lightweight, breathable and durable.

Moleskin A heavy quality brushed cotton, used for trousers and jackets in dark colours.

Peau-de-pêche (peach skin) Like moleskin but lighter and softer, often in microfibre weaves.

Pinpoint oxford Lightweight, soft, cotton-like fabric with a small 2x1 basket (rib) weave repeats. High quality. Very smooth surface; used for shirts.

Piqué A knitted cotton fabric with a waffle, or diamond-shaped, pattern. French piqué knits became an international favourite when René Lacoste, a 1920s French tennis champion, designed the polo shirt.

Pointelle Very feminine, delicate-looking rib knit fabric made patterns of eyelets.

Poplin A durable, plain weave fabric similar to broadcloth but with a heavier rib and heavier weight. Made of silk, cotton, synthetic fibres, wool or blends.

Ripstop A fabric woven with a double thread at regular intervals so that small tears do not spread.

Sateen A semi-lustrous surface distinguishes this smooth, durable fabric in a satin weave. Sateen is usually made of cotton.

Satin A glossy and slippery fabric often made in silk, viscose or acetate, used for formal wear, wedding dresses and linings.

Schiffli A type of embroidery characterized by vine-like floral pattern on sheer/mesh-like fabrics, named after the type of machine it is produced on (Schiffli machine).

Seersucker A popular warm-weather cotton fabric with permanent woven crinkled stripes.

Shantung Medium weight, plain weave, silk-like fabric with pronounced slub filling yarns (slub means yarns are uneven or nubby). Used for dresses.

Taffeta A crisp, rustling, lustrous evening fabric, often woven with plaids or shot warp and weft effect.

Terry A fabric with loop pile on one or both sides.

Toile Light/medium weight, plain weave, fine, cotton-type fabric.

Tweed Winter weight Scottish woollen fabric with colour weave effects and patterns.

Twill A fabric that shows a distinct diagonal wale on the face (e.g., denim, gabardine, tricotine). Used for bottom weights and coats.

Velour Soft plush fabric with a close, dense pile.

Velvet A short, closely woven cut pile fabric with a rich, soft texture.

Venetian A luxurious sateen woven wool used for suitings and coats.

Viscose A manufactured fibre made of regenerated cellulose. It is soft, absorbent and drapes well, it is made up in many knitted and woven forms and weights both matte and shiny. It does not stand up well to vigorous washing.

Voile A lightweight, sheer fabric with a crisp, wiry hand.

Vyella™ A proprietary fabric of cotton and wool, can be colour woven or printed and used for medium weight winter wear and school uniforms.

Wincyette A brushed cotton fabric used for pyjamas and childrenswear.

Worsted Durable wool fabric used for men's suitings.

Fashion schools

This is not a comprehensive list but represents some of the leading schools.

UK

Central Saint Martins College of Art and Design
School of Fashion and Textiles
107 Charing Cross Road
London WC2H 0DU
www.csm.arts.ac.uk

Royal College of Art
School of Fashion and Textiles
Kensington Gore
London SW7 2EU
(postgraduate studies only)
www.rca.ac.uk

Middlesex University
School of Arts
Cat Hill
Barnet
Hertfordshire EN4 8HT
www.mdx.ac.uk

Kingston University
Faculty of Art, Design and Music
Knights Park
Kingston upon Thames
Surrey KT1 2QJ
www.kingston.ac.uk

London College of Fashion
20 John Princes Street
London W1G 0BJ
www.fashion.arts.ac.uk

University of Brighton
School of Architecture and Design
Grand Parade
Brighton
East Sussex BN2 2U
www.brighton.ac.uk

Manchester Metropolitan University
Faculty of Art and Design
Ormond Building
Lower Ormond Street
Manchester M15 6BX
www.mmu.ac.uk

France

ESMOD
There are 17 ESMOD fashion schools
in nine countries. The head office is at:
16 Boulevard Montmartre
F-75009 Paris
www.esmod.com

Studio Berçot
29 rue des Petites Ecuries
F-75010 Paris
www.studio-bercot.com

Ecole Duperré
11 rue Dupetit-Thouars
75003 Paris
www.essa-duperre.scola.ac-paris.fr

Germany

ESMOD
Fraunhoferstr. 23h
80469 München

Italy

Marangoni
Via M. Gonzaga 6
20123 Milano

Polimoda
Villa Strozzi
Via Pisana 77
501443 Florence

Academia di Costume e Moda
Via della Rondinella 2
00186 Roma

Belgium

Flanders Fashion Institute
Mode Natie
Nationale Straat
Drukkerijstraat
Antwerpen

La Cambre
Ecole Supérieure des Arts Visuels
21 Abbaye de la Cambre
1000 Brussels

USA

The Fashion Institute of Technology (FIT)
7th Avenue at 27th Street
New York, NY 10001

Parsons School of Design
66 5th Avenue
New York, NY 10011
www.parsons.edu

Pratt Institute
200 Willoughby Avenue
Brooklyn, NY 11205

Japan

Kobe Design University
8-1-1 Gakuennishi-machi
Nishiku
Kobe 651-2196
Japan

Museums and costume galleries

A number of museums offer reduced rates to students or free admission on certain days.

Victoria and Albert Museum (V&A)
Cromwell Road
South Kensington
London SW7 2RL
UK
www.vam.ac.uk

Museum of Costume
Assembly Rooms
Bennett Street
Bath BA1 2QH
UK
www.museumofcostume.co.uk

MoMu
Antwerp Fashion ModeMuseum –
Nationalestraat 28
B – 2000 Antwerpen
Belgium
Tel + 32 (0)3 470 27 70
Fax + 32 (0)3 470 27 71
Email info@momu.be

Musée des Arts de la Mode
Palais du Louvre
107 rue de Rivoli
75001 Paris
France
www.ucad.fr

Musée de la Mode et du Costume
10 Avenue Pierre 1er de Serbie
75016 Paris
France

Centro Internazionale Arti e del Costume
Palazzo Grassi
S. Samuele 3231
20124 Venice
Italy

Kostumforschungs Institut
Kemnatenstrasse 50
8 Munich 19
Germany

Lipperheidesche Kostümbibliothek
Kunstbibliothek
Staatliche Museen zu Berlin
Matthaikirchplatz 6
10785 Berlin
Germany

Costume Institute
Metropolitan Museum of Art
1000 5th Avenue at 82nd Street
New York
NY 10028-0198
USA
www.metmuseum.org

Museum at the Fashion Institute of Technology
7th Avenue at 27th Street
New York
NY 10001-5992
USA
museuminfo@fitnyc.edu

Brooklyn Museum
200 Eastern Parkway
Brooklyn
NY 11238
USA
www.brooklynmuseum.org

Costume Gallery
Los Angeles County Museum of Art
5905 Wilshire Boulevard
Los Angeles
CA 90036
USA
www.lacma.org

Kobe Fashion Museum
Rokko Island
Kobe
Japan
www.fashionmuseum.or.jp

Galeria del Costume,
Firenze,
Italy
Located in a wing of the Palazzo Pitti

Museum Salvatore Ferragamo
Palazzo Spini Feroni
Via Tornabuoni 2
Florence 50123
Italy
Tel 055 3360456
Fax 055 3360475

Le musée des Tissus et des Arts Décoratifs
34 rue de la Charité
F-69002 Lyon
France
Tel +33 (4)78 3842 00.
Fax +33 (4)72 4025 12.
www.musee-des-tissus.com

Websites

www.costumes.org

La Couturière Parisienne
www.marquise.de

Musée (links to musems worldwide)
www.musee-online.org

What is fashion
www.pbs.org/newshour/infocus/fashion/whatisfashion.html

www.fashion-era.com
by Pauline Weston Thomas and Guy Thomas

Film and literature

Novels

Lauren Weisberger, *The Devil Wears Prada*. Written by a former assistant to *Vogue* editor Anna Wintour.

Caroline Hwang, *In Full Bloom*. The story of a young Korean-American woman in the magazine world.

Laura Jacobs, *Women About Town*. Former *Vanity Fair* editor describes the social-climbing exploits of two New Yorkers in the design and media industries.

Plum Sykes, *Bergdorf Blondes*. A *Vogue* stylist, barely disguised, behind the scenes at a glossy magazine.

Isaac Mizrahi, *The Adventures of Sandee the Supermodel*. A comic book.

Films

Funny Face, directed by Stanley Donen (1957). Audrey Hepburn wears Hubert de Givenchy.

Rebel Without A Cause, directed by Nicholas Ray (1955). James Dean as the archetypal teenager.

The Wild One, directed by László Benedek (1953). Marlon Brando in motorbike leathers.

Beat Girl, directed by Edmond T. Gréville (1960). As a Saint Martins Fashion student who spends more time in Soho dives than in the studio.

Prêt-à-Porter, directed by Robert Altman (1994). The surreal spirit of the Paris fashion circus, featuring Jean-Paul Gaultier and Christian Lacroix shows.

Unzipped, directed by Douglas Keeve (1995). Isaac Mizrahi is the subject of this highly acclaimed documentary about the industry.

Belle de Jour, directed by Luis Buñuel (1967). Catherine Deneuve wears Yves Saint Laurent.

Performance, directed by Donald Cammell and Nicolas Roeg (1970). Mick Jagger and Anita Pallenberg in clothes by Ossie Clark.

Annie Hall, directed by Woody Allen (1977). The Annie Hall look by American fashion designer Ralph Lauren.

Model, directed by Frederick Wiseman (1980). The world of New York fashion.

Qui etes vous Polly Magoo, directed by William Klein (1996). Strange send-up of the fashion circus by a photographer.

The Conformist, directed by Bernardo Bertolucci (1970). Elegant portrayal of the tensions in fascist Italy in the 1930s.

Barbarella, directed by Roger Vadim (1967). Jane Fonda in kitsch, futuristic Paco Rabanne.

Blade Runner, directed by Ridley Scott (1982). Integration of science fiction and modern Los Angeles.

The Fifth Element, directed by Luc Besson (1997). Starring model Mila Jojovich and Jean-Paul Gaultier costumes.

Shops and suppliers

UK

Name	Supply	Address
Alma Leather	leather	12–14 Greatorex Street, London E1
		Tel 020 7375 0343
Barnet & Lawson	ribbons, lace, fringes, cords, elastics, feathers	16 Little Portland Street, London W1N
		Tel 020 7636 8591
Borovick	glitzy evening fabrics	16 Berwick Street, London WC1V
		Tel 020 7437 2180
Celestial Buttons	unusual buttons and haberdashery	162 Archway Road, London N6 5BB
		Tel 020 8341 2788
The Cloth House	fabric, broad range	130 Royal College Street, London NW1
		Tel 020 7485 6247
The Cloth Shop	fabric, designers' unused fabric samples bought	14 Berwick Street, London WC1V 3RF
		Tel 020 7287 2881
Ells & Farrier	beads, sequins and crystals	20 Beak Street, London W1R 3HA
		Tel 01494 715606
		Fax 01494 718510
Eastman Staples Ltd	student and studio equipment for pattern-cutting and making	Lockwood Road, Huddersfield HD1 3QW
		Tel 01484 888888
George Weil and Sons Ltd	fabrics, dyes, printing equipment, books	18 Hanson Street, London W1P 7DB
The Handweavers	studio yarns, fibres, dyes, books	29 Haroldstone Road, London E17 7AN
		Tel 020 8521 2281
London Graphic Centre	portfolios, designers' materials, student discounts	16–18 Shelton Street, London WC2E 9JJ
		Tel 020 7240 0095
MacCulloch & Wallis Ltd	fabrics, trimmings and haberdashery	25 Dering Street, London W1R 0BH
		Tel 020 7409 0725
Morplan Fashion	stationers and cutting-room equipment	56 Great Titchfield Street, London W1P 8DX
		Tel 020 7636 1887 Freefone 0800 435 333
Pongees Wholesale	plain silks	28–30 Hoxton Square, London N1
		Tel 020 7739 9130
R.D. Franks Ltd	fashion books and magazines, tools, dress stands	Kent House, Market Place, London W1W 8HY
		Tel 020 7636 1244
Rai Trimmings	tailoring supplies	9/12 St Anne's Court, London W1
		Tel 020 7437 2696
Rose Fittings (James & Alden)	buckles, eyelets, metal fittings	398 City Road, London EC1
Soho Silks & By the Yard	quality fabrics and fancy silks	24 Berwick Street, London WC1V 3RF
		Tel 020 7434 3305
Whaleys (Bradford) Ltd	plain, natural and greige cloth	Mail order
		Tel 01274 576718
William Gee	linings, haberdashery, trims	520 Kingsland Road, London E8
		Tel 020 7254 2451

USA

Name	Supply	Address
Active Trimming	shoulder pads and trims	250 W. 39th Street, New York, NY 10018
		Tel 212 921 7114
Adel Rootstein USA Inc.	display mannequins	205 W. 19th Street, New York, NY 10011-4012
		Tel 212 645 2020
Alpha Trims	trimmings	6 East 32nd Street, New York NY 10016
		Tel 212 889 9765
Apple Trim Sewing	notions and trims	260 W. 36th Street, New York, NY 10018-7560
Art Station Ltd	art and design materials	144 West 27th Street, New York, NY 10001
		Tel 212 807 8000
Brewer-Cantelmo	custom portfolios	350 Seventh Avenue, New York, NY 10001
		Tel 212 244 4600

Button Works	buttons and trims	242 W. 36th Street, New York, NY 10018
		Tel 212 330 8912
Duplex Buttons and Beads	small findings and trims	575 8th Avenue, New York, NY 10018-3011
Fashion Design Bookshop	books and fashion tools	234 W. 27th Street, New York, NY 10001
		Tel 212 633 9646
Le Lame Inc.	stretch and party fabrics	250 W. 39th Street, New York, NY 10018
	and elasticated trims	Tel 212 921 9770
M & J Trimming Co.	trimmings	1008 6th Avenue, New York, NY 10018
Pearl Paint	artists' supplies	308 Canal Street, New York, NY 10013
		Tel 800 221 6845
Sam Flax	artists' materials	425 Park Avenue, New York, NY 10021
		Tel 800 628 9512
Service Notions	trimmings and display suppliers	256 W. 38th Street, New York, NY 10018
		Tel 800 508 7353
Superior Model Form Co.	dress stands, also repairs	306 West 38th Street New York, NY 10018
		Tel 212 947 3633
Swarovski Crystal Company	crystals and components	29 W. 57th Street, 8th Floor, New York, NY 10019
		Tel 212 935 4200
The Pellon Company	interfacings and appliqués	119 W. 40th Street, New York, NY 10018
Vogue Fashion Pleating	custom pleating	264 W. 37th Street, New York, NY 10018
		Tel 212 921 8666
Zipper Stop	zippers and threads	27 Allen Street, New York, NY 10002
		Tel 212 226 3964
Mood Fabrics		250 W. 39th Street, 10th Floor, New York, NY 10018-1500
Paron Fabrics Inc.		206 W. 40th Street, New York, NY
Long Island Fabrics		406 Broadway, New York, NY 10013-3519
		Tel 212 925 4488
Britex Fabrics		146 Geary Street, San Francisco, CA 94108
		Tel 415 392 2910
Far Out Fabrics		1556 Hight Street, San Francisco, CA 94117
		Tel 415 621 1287
Satin Moon		32 Clement Street, San Francisco, CA 94118
		Tel 415 668 1623

Paris

Name	Supply	Address
Marché St Pierre	four-storey fabric shop. Every imaginable type of fabric from standard cottons to luxury embroideries	2 rue Charles Nodier Montmartre, Paris, 75018 Tel 01 46 06 56 34
Bouchara	old-fashioned home and fabrics store	corner of boulevard Haussman and rue Lafayette
Reine	end of line fabrics	Montmartre, Rue Charles Nodier, Paris
Moline Tissus	household fabrics and laces	1 Place Saint-Pierre, Paris, 75018 Metro: Anvers Tel 01 46 06 14 66
Marché Carreau du temple	traditional roofed market – excellent fabric and clothing bargains	rue Perrée
La Samaritaine	department store with both modern and traditional fabric	floor 75, rue de Rivoli, 75001 Paris Metro: Pont Neuf
Le Rouvray	patchwork and craft suppliers	3 rue de la Bucherie, 75005 Paris Tel 01 43 25 00 45
Dominique Kieffer		8 rue Hérold, 75001 Paris
Pierre Frey		22 rue Royale, 75008 Paris

Pattern-drafting and sewing terms

A

Allowance
extra fabric added to 1) a seam line
2) a garment for ease of movement
3) for pleats and gathers

Appliqué
decorative patch of fabric sewn onto another

Arm scye
the area on a bodice pattern that describes the underarm

Asymmetrical
uneven or unequal sides of a garment

Awl
sharp pointed tool for making holes in patterns or leather

B

Bag-out
a method of making up whereby the lining and main fabric are machined
wrong-sides together and then turned inside-out

Balance
1) the correct hang of a garment with straight, even side seams
2) pleasing proportion in the design

Balance marks
guide marks in the pattern to centralize the balance of fabric

Basic block
the master pattern from which others are drafted

Basting
temporary stitching, also called tacking, to hold fabric together for fittings
and before machining

Bias
the diagonal line at 45° to the straight and crosswise grain of fabric

Bias binding
tape cut 'on the bias'. This tape has pressed folded edges, it has more give than
flat woven tape and is ideal for curved hem and seam binding

Blocking
1) flat pressing of knitwear
2) steaming of hat shapes

Bodice
the upper body of a garment (without sleeves)

Boning
once whale bone, now metal or covered plastic stiffener for corsetry

Breakline
the line against which a lapel folds back on the front of a jacket

Breakpoint
the point at which the lapel turns back at the chest

Button
common fastening: two-hole, four-hole, fisheye, shank, covered

Buttonhole
Buttonhole edges can be finished by hand, bound, corded, in-seam,
or made on special machinery such as the Reiss keyhole machine

Button line
buttons are measured by a standard line (or ligne) sizing: 18, 22, 26, 30, 36, 45, 60

C

Casing
a channel of parallel stitching made for an elastic or drawstring

Chalk
waxy tailor's chalk is puffed or drawn onto fabric to mark positions for
the guidance of machinists. The chalk is easily removed with steam

Chevron
the decorative joining of striped fabric at angles to form v lines

Clip
to cut into corners or the curves of a seam allowance to reduce bulk or allow
the fabric to lie flat when pressed open

Collar stand
the undercollar, before the 'fall' or foldback of a collar, often reinforced
and buttoned on a shirt

Contoured
following the body lines

Crossgrain
the direction of the fabric from selvedge to selvedge

D

Dart
a stitched-down fold, tapering at one or both ends, to allow fabric
to follow the shape of the body

Décolleté
a very low cut neckline

Die cutting
metal templates used in a press to cut large quantities of garments

Double-breasted
a wide front lapel wrap-over that usually has two rows of buttons,
evenly spaced from the centre line

Drape	1) the way a fabric falls
	2) to gather or form pleats in a garment
Dress stand	a body form of the torso, usually with a stand on which it can be rotated to help the dressmaker work on a garment

E

Ease	similar to allowance – extra fabric to allow for loose fit or comfort
Embroidery	decorative stitching, either by hand or machinery
Empire line	dress with a short bodice, usually with a seam or drawstring under the bust
Eyelet	small hole in fabric to allow a drawstring, finished by a metal ring or stitches

F

Facing	a way of neatening a raw edge by sewing a matching shaped piece of fabric to it, sandwiching the raw edge between and turning it
Fastenings	the many ways of keeping garments closed: buttons, zips, hooks and eyes, Velcro, toggles, etc.
Feeler	a sample piece of fabric offered by salesmen to help the designer make a choice of material or colourways
Fitting	adjusting a garment on a model or client
Flare	extra width at the lower edge of a garment to give it attractive swing
Flexicurve	flexible edge tool for drawing neat curves
Fly	buttoned or zipped trouser opening
Fly front	concealed buttoned or zippered opening, often in coats
Fray	the cut edges of woven fabrics will unravel and 'fray' in many fabrics and must be stitched or bound to prevent the garment deteriorating
French curve	pattern-cutting tool with a 'golden-mean' curve to aid the drafting of tight and open curves
Frog	looped braid stitched to garment for decoration or button fastening
Fusing	the application of heat or chemicals to attach adhesive interfacings to fabric

G

Gathers	fabric drawn up for ease or fullness on a double line of stitches
Gimp	heavy duty thread used in buttonhole reinforcement and embroidery
Godet	a triangular fabric inset into hems for flare
Gore	a shaped panel of fabric, often adding flare at one end
Gorge	the point where the collar is attached to the lapel forming the Notch (either double-breasted or single-breasted)
Grading	sizing a pattern up or down the standard measurement fitting
Grain	the direction of the fabric warp (lengthwise grain), weft (crosswise grain). Garments are said to be 'off-grain' if they have not been cut following the straight grain
Grosgrain	a broad, stiff ribbon used for waistbanding and hat trimmings
Grown on	pockets, hems or facings cut in one with the main pattern piece
Gusset	a triangular or boat-shaped piece of fabric inset into another piece for added shape or ease of movement at crotch or underarm

H

Haberdashery	a term for trimmings
Handstitch	there are many stitches sewn by hand, rather than machine, which are either useful or decorative to the dressmaker or tailor: tacking, herringbone, overcasting, buttonholing, stabstitching, etc.
Hanger appeal	a trade term for garments which are pleasing without having to be seen on the body, as in the case of some draped or stretch garments
Hem	the finishing of a fabric edge by folding it under
Hemline	the line, or body position at which the hem is turned

I

inset	a piece of fabric or trimming used decoratively in a seam
Interfacing	also **interlining**. Fabric used for strengthening or shaping a garment and stitched or fused between the shell fabric, facings or linings

J

Jetted pocket	a pocket made with bound edge strips, usually in suits, also known as a welt pocket

L

Lacing	two edges with eyelets and ties that can be adjusted to vary fit
Laminate	to coat or glue or heat-bond two fabrics together
Lapel	the top front edge of a blouse or jacket folded back from the neck
Lay	the amount of fabric and the 'lay plan' that a garment will take to make
Lay plan	the plan for the pattern pieces to be cut according to the width or type of material
Layering	cutting away of fabrics in a seam at varied widths to reduce bulk
Lining	the material, usually light and smooth, which covers the inside workings of a garment and protects the body from abrasion
Links	two buttons held together by a shank of thread or metal chain as a fastening

M

Machine stitches	the flat-lock sewing machine makes a straight stitch; there are many special machines to overlock, merrow, zig-zag, blind-stitch, etc.
Marker	the layer of paper on which the lay plan is drawn before batch cutting
Match	to bring together 1) colours of fabrics and trimmings 2) stripes, checks and prints in a garment 3) pairs of notches and construction guides
Mitre	to make a neat corner by means of a diagonal seam
Modelling	another term for draping and designing three-dimensionally on the body or dress stand
Mounting	stitching or fusing interlinings to the main fabric
Muslin	a cotton gauze fabric used for 'toiles' or garment trials

N

Nap	a pile fabric reflects light according to the direction of fibres. On napped fabrics the garment pieces must be layed in one direction only
Needle	needles are measured in metric (70–110) and Singer (11–18) sizes. There are different points for various tasks: sharp, ball-point, twin, leather point, also handstitching needles: glovers, beading, milliners
Needleboard	velvet and corduroy are pressed on a board set with fine needles to prevent flattening the pile
Notches	marks cut into the seam allowances of patterns to indicate sewing positions and match balance points
Notions	haberdashery and trimmings

O

Off/on-grain	fabric which has been finished badly and twisted or a garment which hangs badly due to the pattern being pieced at the wrong angle
One-way	many printed fabrics can also only be cut in one direction. Nap fabrics are 'one-way' designs
Overlock	a machine used to oversew raw edges to prevent fraying, also known as serging and merrowing

P

Pad-out	to build up parts of a garment with fabric or wadding to make it fuller
Paper	there are many types of paper and card useful to the fashion designer. The most commonly used are: brown kraft, plain drafting, spot and cross, oak tag, manila card and graph paper
Pattern-hook	commercial patterns are usually stored by hanging rather than folding
Peplum	a flared lower edge of a jacket, usually attached at the waistline
Petersham	heavy ribbon used to finish and reinforce a waist on skirts and trousers
Picot	a decorative, serrated edge finishing stitch on knitwear and lingerie
Pile	the woven, looped or cut fibres which stand up to form a texture as in velvet, towelling, fur fabric
Pinking	cutting fabric or seam allowances with serrated shears to prevent fray
Pins	dressmakers use fine steel, non-rust pins, T-pins and glass head pins
Piping	fabric or braid run into a seam to bind or decorate the edge
Pivot point	1) turning point when machine stitching inserts and godets 2) using the apex of the dart to relocate the dart in pattern-drafting
Placket	a piece of fabric which binds an opening, often with buttons
Plaids	fabric woven with coloured warp and weft threads to create checks
Pleats	pleats can be made by regular manipulation of fabric into a yoke or band or by industrial permanent steaming process. There are many types, e.g. box, flat, kick, inverted, knife, sunray, mushroom, crystal
Presser-foot	sewing machine attachment which holds down the fabric while sewing
Pressing	the use of steam and pressure to remove or create creases
Princess line	a slim dress or bodice shape using only vertical seam lines
Production pattern	a pattern that has been corrected of errors, marked with all particulars and made in card for use in manufacturing

Q

Quilting	sewing two fabrics together with a soft filling for warmth and decoration

R

Rever, revere	the turned back front edge of a fabric at the neck or cuff
Roll line	the line along which a collar or lapel folds back
Rouleau	a narrow strip of fabric turned through to make rounded straps or loops
Ruching, rusching	fine gathering, often made with fine elastic in the sewing bobbin

S

Scissors	the dressmaker or tailor requires a number of specialist scissors for cutting materials: paper shears, fabric shears, electric shears, dressmaking scissors, embroidery scissors, trimmers and thread snips
Seam ripper	a useful tool for undoing seams quickly and opening buttonholes
Self fabric	to use the same fabric as the main body of the garment as a trim
Selvedge, selvage	the finished lengthwise woven edge that binds the width of a fabric
Serge	1) A term for overlocking raw edges 2) a wool fabric
Shank	the fibre or metal loop that attaches a button to the fabric
Shears	long-bladed variety of scissors for heavy duty cutting seams. The stitching together of fabric at the edges.
Shoulder pads	either pre-formed foam or material, shaped and placed in a garment to reinforce and form the shoulder shape
Slash	1) to cut into fabrics 2) to cut and spread a paper pattern to alter it
Sleeve head	top of sleeve at shoulder, also known as the crown
Smocking	careful gathering of fabric with decorative stitches

Suppression	the moving of flat fabric into darts, gathers, folds or seams over the contours of the body to make shape
Swatch	a small, sample piece of fabric also known as a **feeler**
Symmetrical	design of evenly balanced halves

T

Tacking	temporary stitches, also known as **basting**
Tailor's tacks	sewing with long thread loops through both halves of a garment. The threads are snipped and used as guides for darts or balance points
Tape	to reinforce a seam which may otherwise stretch with woven tape
Tape measure	an essential dressmaking tool, non-stretch, flexible measure
Toile	calico or muslin trial garment to test pattern and fit
Top-pressing	the final pressing of a suit or garment
Top-stitching	visible and both functional and decorative machine stitching around the edge or on the outside of a garment
Tracing-wheel	transferring marks from paper to pattern or card or vice versa using a pinwheel
True bias	the 45° diagonal of woven fabric where the cloth is most pliable
Trueing-up	correcting patterns for badly drawn lines, smoothing curves and matching seam lengths
Tuck	a decorative fold
Turn-up	an added cuff at the trouser hem

U

| Under-pressing | opening seams and pressing garment parts during assembly gives a better finish to a garment than top pressing only |
| Under-stitching | a method of stitching down facings and collars to prevent them from rolling out |

V

| Vent | a split or lapped pleat added to give ease of movement |

W

Waistbanding	the strip of material which finishes off the waist edge, also a commercially available product for men's trousers
Webbing	a heavy, narrow ribbon with a twill weave, used for strapping
Welt	1) a strip of fabric binding a pocket edge 2) the ribbed edge on knitwear
Wing seam	a curved seam line which travels over the shoulder blade or breast
Working drawing	a design drawing which shows the construction lines of the garment and is often given to the machinist as a guide
Wrap	the overlap of the front edge of a jacket or 'wrapover' skirt

Y

| Yoke | a shoulder piece on a shirt or jacket or a broad waistband onto which other fabric is gathered |

Z

| Zig zag | stitch used to bind or finish edges decoratively or where the seam must be allowed to stretch safely |
| Zippers | fastener of which there are a large number of types and applications |

Further reading

Bina Abling. *Fashion Rendering with Color*, New York: Prentice Hall, 2001

Teri Agins. *The End of Fashion*, New York: William Morrow, 1999

Anne Allen and Julian Seaman. *Fashion Drawing: The Basic Principles*, London: Batsford, 1996

Sandy Black. *Knitwear in Fashion*, London: Thames & Hudson, 2002

J Bohdanovicz and L Clamp. *Fashion Marketing*, Oxford: Blackwell Science, 1995

Dick Bolles. *What Color is Your Parachute?*, Berkeley: Ten Speed Press, 2004

Laird Borelli. *Fashion Illustration Now*, London: Thames & Hudson, 2000

Laird Borelli. *Stylishly Drawn*, New York: Harry N. Abrams, 2000

Janet Boyes. *Essential Fashion Design: Illustration Theme Boards, Body coverings, Projects, Portfolios*, London: Batsford, 1997

SE Braddock and M O'Mahony. *Techno Textiles: Revolutionary Fabrics for Fashion and Design*,
    London: Thames & Hudson, 1998

EL Brannon. *Fashion Forecasting*, New York: Fairchild, 2002

Margaret Bruce and Rachel Cooper. *Fashion Marketing and Design Management*,
    London: International Thomson Business Press, 1997

Harold Carr and Barbara Latham. *The Technology of Clothing Manufacture*, Oxford: Blackwell, 2001

Gerald Celente. *Trend Tracking*, New York: Warner Books, 1991

Noel Chapman and Carole Chester. *Careers in Fashion*, London: Kogan Page, 1999

Chlöe Colchester. *The New Textiles: Trends and Traditions*, New York: WW Norton, 1997

Nicholas Coleridge. *The Fashion Conspiracy*, London: Heinemann, 1988

Gerry Cooklin. *Bias Cutting for Women's Outerwear*, Oxford: Blackwell, 1994

Connie Amaden-Crawford. *Guide to Fashion Sewing*, New York: Fairchild, 2000

Leslie De Chernatony. *Creating Powerful Brands in Consumer, Service and Industrial Markets*,
    Burlington: Elsevier, 1998

Robert Doyle. *Waisted Efforts: An Illustrated Guide to Corsetry Making*, Stratford: Sartorial Press, 1997

Caroline Evans. *Fashion at the Edge*, New Haven: Yale University Press, 2003

John Feltwell. *The Story of Silk*, New York: St. Martins, 1991

J C Flugel. *The Psychology of Clothes*, Guilford: International Universities Press, 1966

G Stephens Frings. *Fashion – From Concept to Consumer*, Upper Saddle River: Prentice Hall, 2002

Carolyn Genders. *Sources of Inspiration*, London: A&C Black, 2002

Debbie Ann Gioello and Beverly Berke Fairchild. *Fashion Production Terms*, New York: Fairchild, 1979

Malcolm Gladwell. *The Tipping Point*, New York: Little, Brown, 2001

Susannah Handley. *Nylon: The Manmade Fashion Revolution*, London: Bloomsbury, 1999

Dick Hebdige. *Subculture: The Meaning of Style*, London: Methuen, 1973

Thomas Hine. *I Want That! How We All Became Shoppers*, London: HarperCollins, 2002

The Hobsons Directory, Hobson's Publishing, 2004

Anne Hollander. *Sex and Suits: The Evolution of Modern Dress*, New York: Kodansha, 1995

Yajima Isao. *Fashion Illustration in Europe*, Tokyo: Graphic-Sha, 1988

Richard M Jones. *The Apparel Industry*, Blackwell Science, 2003

Astrid Katcharyan. *Getting Jobs in Fashion Design*, Cassell, 1988

Injoo Kim and Mykyung Uti. *Apparel Making in Fashion Design*, New York: Fairchild, 2002

Naomi Klein. *No Logo*, New York: Harper Collins, 2000

Ernestine Kopp. *New Fashion Areas for Design*, New York: Fairchild, 1972

Kojiro Kumagai. *Fashion Illustration: Expressing Textures*, Graphic-Sha, Tokyo, 1988

Ulla Vad Lane-Rowley. *Using Design Protection in the Fashion and Textile Industry*, London and Chichester: Wiley, 1997

James Laver. *Modesty in Dress*, Boston: Houghton Mifflin, 1969

Oei Loan and Cecile de Kegel. *The Elements of Design*, London: Thames & Hudson, 2002

Alison Lurie. *The Language of Clothes*, London: Hamlyn, 1983

Alice Mackrell. *An Illustrated History of Fashion: 500 Years of Fashion Illustration*,
    New York: Costume and Fashion Press, 1997

Ezio Manzini. *The Material of Invention*, Cambridge: MIT Press, 1989

Anne Matthews. *Vogue Guide to a Career in Fashion*, London: Chatto & Windus, 1989

Catherine McDermott. *Made in Britain: Tradition and Style in Contemporary British Fashion*,
    London: Mitchell Beazley, 2002

Colin McDowell. *The Designer Scam*, London: Random House, 1994

Colin McDowell. *Dressed to Kill: Sex, Power and Clothes*, London: Hutchinson, 1992

Fashion design

Angela McRobbie. *British Fashion Design: Rag Trade or Image Industry?*, London: Routledge, 1998

Angela McRobbie. *Zootsuits & Secondhand Dresses: An Anthology of Music and Fashion*,
Basingstoke: Macmillan, 1989

Sian-Kate Mooney. *Making Latex Clothes*, London: Batsford, 2004

Karen Morris. *Sewing Lingerie That Fits*, Newton: Taunton Press, 2001

Carol Mueller and Eleanor Smiley. *Marketing Today's Fashion*, Upper Saddle River: Prentice Hall, 1994

Deborah Newton. *Designing Knitwear*, Newtown: The Taunton Press, 1992

Ted Polhemus and Lynn Procter. *Fashion and Anti-Fashion: An Anthropology of Clothing and Adornment*,
London: Thames & Hudson, 1978

Ted Polhemus. *Streetstyle: From Sidewalk To Catwalk*, London: Thames & Hudson, 1994

Ted Polhemus. *Style Surfing: What To Wear In The 3rd Millennium*, London: Thames & Hudson, 1996

Faith Popcorn. *Clicking*, London: HarperCollins, 1996

Edmund Roberts and Gary Onishenko. *Fundamentals of Men's Fashion Design: A Guide to Casual Clothes*,
New York: Fairchild, 1985

Mary Schoeser. *International Textile Design*, London: Laurence King, 1995

Julian Seaman. *Professional Fashion Illustration*, London: Batsford, 1995

Hugh Sebag-Montefiore. *Kings on the Catwalk*, London: Chapmans, 1992

Claire Shaeffer. *Sewing for the Apparel Industry*, Upper Saddle River: Prentice Hall, 2001

RL Shep and Gail Gariou. *Shirts and Men's Haberdashery (1840s–1920s)*, Fort Bragg: RL Shep, 1998

Martin M Shoben and Janet P Ward. *Pattern Cutting and Making Up – The Professional Approach*,
Burlington: Elsevier, 1991

M Sones. *Getting into Fashion: A Career Guide*, New York: Ballatine, 1984

Penny Sparke. *As Long as it's Pink – The Sexual Politics of Taste*, London: HarperCollins, 1995

David J Spencer. *Knitting Technology*, Cambridge: Woodhead, 2001

Steven Stipelman. *Illustrating Fashion: Concept to Creation*, New York: Fairchild, 1996

Elaine Stone. *The Dynamics of Fashion*, New York: Fairchild, 1999

Joyce Storey. *Manual of Textile Printing*, London: Thames & Hudson, 1977

Linda Tain. *Portfolio Presentation for Fashion Designers*, New York: Fairchild, 1998

Sharon Lee Tate. *The Complete Book of Fashion Illustration*, New Jersey: Prentice Hall, 1996

Francoise Tellier-Loumagne. *Mailles – les mouvements du fil*, Paris: Minerva, 2003

Paco Underhill. *Why We Buy: The Science of Shopping*, London: Orion, 1999

Peter Vogt. *Career Opportunities in the Fashion Industry*, New York: Checkmark, 2002

Hannelore Von Eberle. *Clothing Technology: From Fibre to Fashion*, Haan-Gruiten: Verlag Europa-Lehrmittel, 2000

Petrula Vrontikis. *Inspiration=Ideas: Creativity Sourcebook*, Rockport, Mass: Rockport, 2002

Peter York. *Style Wars*, London: Sidgwick & Jackson, 1980

Index

Numbers in *italics* refer to captions

Picture sources and credits

Adrienne Alaimo 97 (bottom)
Peter Anderson 28, 34
Gaia Brandt Rasmussen 172
Nicholas Burt 95 (left)
Yan Cheung 118 (bottom), 131
Lynette Cook 103, 108
Yvonne Deacon 20–3, 79, 84–7, 90, 91 (top),
    92, 106–7, 142
David Edelstein 157, 159 (left inset)
Courtesy of East Central Studios
    121 (image 6 courtesy of Reiko Sudo,
    photo by John Forsdyke/Oxford Microscopy
    Consultancy) 129, 135
Courtesy of Eastman Staples Ltd 141
Kyoko Fukui 93 (left)
Tim Griffiths 7, 166 (top), 207 (bottom),
    208 (left and right), 211
Ian Hessenberg 147 (except upper left)
Courtesy of Hulton Getty Archive
    19 (Sasha), 31 (Adam Rountree),
    37 (Nina Leen/Time Life), 40 (Wesley/
    Keystone), 74, 78 (John Chillingworth/
    Picture Post), 81 (Jo Hale), 93 (top right, RDA)
Esther Johnson cover, frontispiece, 88–9, 152–3
Sue Jenkyn Jones 12, 19, 64, 66, 67, 68, 82, 117,
    127 (top), 155, 174, 191, 195
Hannah Jordan 154 (top right)
Courtesy of Learning Resources,
    London College of Fashion Study Collection,
    University of the Arts 161 (top), 170
Chi Lau 93 (bottom), 96
Jieun Lee 83
Garth Lewis and Ferdy Carabott (Chromafile)
    114–5
Nazanin Matin 199
Courtesy of Alexander McQueen,
    photo by Gainsbury and Whiting
Savannah Miller 178 (Tomek Sierek)
Courtesy of Miralab, University of Geneva 97
Courtesy of Carol Morgan 208 (centre)
Niall McInerney 6, 7, 10, 11, 13, 80 (lower left,
    centre, right), 81 (lower), 100, 102, 104, 105, 113,
    116, 117, 123, 127 (lower three), 132 (upper left
    and right), 145 (bottom), 147 (top left),
    161 (right), 162 (lower left, right), 163 (top),
    164 (bottom), 166 (top), 168 (bottom), 169 (top),
    171, 173, 175, 176, 184, 190, 193, 213
Ilaria Perra 102, 106–7, 144–6
Courtesy of Popperfoto 24–7, 38, 43
Courtesy of Adel Rootstein 80 (top)
Claire Robertson 186 (lower right), 196–7
Teerabul Songvich 145 (upper six images),
    154 (left), 177 (bottom)
Jonna Sykes 58, 59
Riccardo Tisci 177 (centre), 179
Mark Tynan Courtesy of Charlie Allen 161 (left)
Courtesy of Department of Textiles UMIST
    121 (1–5 Trevor Jones), 123 (bottom), 124
Malin Vester 14
Andrew Watson 186 (lower left), 187
Christopher Wilson (diagrams) 51, 52, 73, 128
Ada Wong 95 (right)
Naoko Yokoyama 91 (bottom)

Fashion design and illustration credits

Carola Euler 7
Matthew Williamson 10
Jieun Lee 11
Kentaro Tamai 13
Malin Vester 14
Dean Gardiner, Anthony Kwok, Keiran Tolman 80
Stella McCartney 81
Jieun Lee 83
Anthony Kwok, Naoko Yokoyama, Tristan Webber
113
Kyoko Fukui, Chi Lau 93
Lynette Cook 94
Nick Burt and Rose Armstrong, Ada Wong 95
Chi Lau 96
Adrienne Alaimo 97 (bottom)
Philippa Reiss 98
Lucy Baker, Connie Groh, Christine Bertelsen,
Tariq Ali, Jason Lim, Arkadius 100
Nak Hyun Kim, Marie Langlois, Susanne Lieb,
Oliver Steinhaus, Andrew Groves 101
Claire O'Connor, Diane Mainstone, Laure Riviere,
Karen Bagge 104
Kimino Honma, Dean Statis, Danny Margolin
105
Jeremy Au Yong, Naoko Yokoyama, Tristan
Webber 113
Gerard Wilson 116
Michael Sikinakis, Fumie Majekodunmi, Jenna
Highman 117
Anne-Loiuse Roswald 123
Yurika Ohara, Noora Niinikoski, Luke Goidadin
125
Charlotte Palmer, Mark Durno, Claudine Abou-
Sawan 127
Aimée McWilliams 130
Kenichi, Jasper Gurrida 132
Teerabul Songvich 145
Top second image – emulation of Alexander
McQueen design by Lucy Griffiths, top row third
image – emulation of Pierre Cardin design by
Anthony Wilkins, bottom row first and second
images – emulations of Shelley Fox design by
Kathleen Thompson, bottom row third image –
emulation of Vivienne Westwood design by
Loran Whiffin 147
Carlos Marcant Filo 150 (right)
Teerabul Songwich 154
Charlie Allen, Rose Armstrong 161
Ingeborg Hunskaar, Manuel Vadillo-Benitez 162
Charlie Watkins 163
Miguel Freitas 166
Rebecca Owens 167
Adam Richardson 168
Munchmart Namenjipol 169
Niall Sloan, Aimee McWilliams, Katie Pugh 171
Gaia Brandt Rasmussen 172
Rory Meyler, Mariama Tushimeriwe 173
Daniel Barry 175
Peter Cash, Hussein Chalayan 176
Riccardo Tisci 177
Savannah Miller 178
Riccardo Tisci 179
Kevin Morley 180

Claire Robertson 181
Arkadius, Jason Masterson-Copley, Danielle Rees,
Joe Casely-Hayford, Mercedes Gallego Ruiz, Sam
Willis, Signe Rose, Richard Lo, Katia Machenko
184
Sandra Westin 186
Augustus Griffith 190
Claire Robertson 196–7
Nazanin Matin 199
Katie Pugh 213

Acknowledgements

With heartfelt thanks to the students, and fellow
staff, past and present, who have inspired the
writing of this guide through their design work,
comments and contributions. In particular,
thanks to Jane Rapley and Dani Salvadori of
Central Saint Martins College of Art and Design
for their support and guidance. Special mention
must be made of Jo Lightfoot and my editor, Gina
Bell, at Laurence King without whose patience
and coaxing this edition would not be in your
hands. And to Christopher Wilson who found
room for, and improved on much of the content
with his painstaking manoevering and vision.

To all those whom I consulted and who gave
generously of their time and experience,
especially colleagues at the University of the
Arts, London and the fashion school at Central
Saint Martins: Willie Walters, Howard Tanguy,
Christopher New, Nathalie Gibson, Toni Tester,
Caroline Evans, Lee Widdows, Carol Morgan,
Garth Lewis, Leni Bjerg, Jacob Hillel, Christine
Koussetari, Steven Bateman and Katherine Baird.

To numerous companies and individuals in the
fashion Industry who are supportive to
education, many of whom invited me behind the
scenes: Shelley Fox, Joe Casely-Hayford, Suzanne
Clements, Anne-Louise Roswald, Tim Williams,
Crombie Ltd, Sandy McLennan and Hilary Scarlett
at East Central Studios, Alison Lloyd, Catherine
Lover, Adel Rootstein, Eastman Staples Ltd and
the British Fashion Council. To Timothy M. Gunn,
Associate Dean at Parsons School of Design, New
York and the Gladys Marcus Library at the
Fashion Institute of Technology, New York.

To the photographers and illustrators who
have contributed so generously: Esther Johnson,
Niall McInerney, Tim Griffiths, Yvonne Deacon,
Ilaria Perra and Lynette Cook. And to those too
numerous to list who supported me with
technical help, arrangements and picture
research.

Dedication

To my dearest family and friends who had the
tolerance and wisdom to know when and how to
leave me in my lair or tempt me out with tea and
tango.